The SEARCH for The BELOVED

JOURNEYS IN MYTHOLOGY AND SACRED PSYCHOLOGY

JEAN HOUSTON, Ph.D.

Jeremy P. Tarcher/Putnam
a member of Penguin Putnam Inc.
New York

For
Elisabeth Zinck Rothenberger
and
Robin Van Doren

Jeremy P. Tarcher/Putnam
a member of Penguin Putnam Inc.
200 Madison Avenue
New York, NY 10016
http://www.putnam.com

Library of Congress Cataloging-in-Publication Data

Houston, Jean.
The search for the beloved.

Bibliography.
Includes index.
1. Consciousness—Problems, exercises, etc.
2. Mind and body—Problems, exercises, etc.
3. Imagery (Psychology) I. Title II. Title
Sacred psychology.
BF311.H655 1987 153 87-6495
ISBN 0-87477-871-9

Interior design by Deborah Daly
Cover design by Stefan Gutermuth
Front cover photograph by Susie Cushner/Graphistock

Printed in the United States of America
10 9 8 7 6 5 4 3 2 1

This book is printed on acid-free paper. ∞

Contents

Acknowledgments

This book is dedicated to two women who, for many years, have been part of the work described here. They understand it at levels and in ways that I do not, and their efforts in helping bring this book into existence have been extraordinary. Elisabeth Zinck Rothenberger transcribed and organized thousands of pages of my lectures and processes, and worked intensively with me over several summers to develop the initial draft of the manuscript. Robin Van Doren, whose brilliance is matched only by her persistence, provided an editorial effort as mythic as any of the stories contained here. Without the inspiration, industry, and ingenuity of these two colleagues, this book would not be at all.

I also owe an enormous debt of gratitude to the keen skills and sensitive eye of Caroline Whiting, the in-house editor, and to my publisher, Jeremy Tarcher, who invested so much time and personal interest in the birthing of this work.

Introduction to the Second Edition

It is September of 1992. I find myself accompanied by some new friends, including several Maori elders, to the northernmost point of New Zealand, or Aeorotora, as the Maoris refer to their beautiful land of the floating white cloud. We are standing on the ridge at the end of the island, looking below us at the place where three seas, the China Sea, the Tasmanian Sea, and the Pacific Ocean, meet and come together in roiling fractal waves. Each of the three seas brings its own wind, so one is buffeted by strong airs from all sides. Something uncanny is here. There is Presence here. Could it be that the waves also bring with them the spirits of other lands? These seas, which in one way or another have touched upon all seas and every shore, are they bringing global news of Nature's plans and human folly? The winds are growing stronger. The waves crash upon each other in some giant argument, or is it a mating, an exchange of essences? Is this the place where the planetary DNA gets coded anew? "It could be," my host, John, shouts over the roaring of the winds. "But it is also the place where all Maoris go when they have died to lift off to the Other World." He points to a small spit of land near which the meeting of the three seas is the most intense, a boiling vortex that seems a plausible place from which to leave the planet. My host is a most knowledgeable man, himself a receiver of the waves of human speculation from many lands. He is a holder and practitioner of the traditional Maori wisdom and culture, he has a physicist's knowledge of the new science, he is a metaphysical and speculative thinker of the first order, and he is also a storekeeper. I have found in my meetings with the Maoris that they, perhaps more than any other indigenous culture I have ever worked with, have made considerable strides toward restoring the Essence of their culture even after more than a hundred and seventy years of colonial rule. In spite of experiencing the problems that afflict all indigenous peoples, they are relearning their language, getting their land and fishing rights back, rebuilding their communities, developing their ancient arts and sciences, and generally moving as a culture toward the realization of their own innate greatness. Also, many among them—like John—have acquired, appreciated, and even improved upon the knowledge of other cultures. John has just astounded me with a brilliant theoretical riff showing how Maori metaphysics anticipates and goes beyond quantum physics. I ask him at the top of my voice to tell me how it is that the Maoris have recovered so much of their genius. "It is because of places like this," he bellows, "where the spirits of many peoples and many lands can meet and refresh themselves. And it is here as well as in our great meeting houses, our Marais, that we remember who we are and . . ." His voice takes on new power, equal to the winds. "And call our spirits home!"

The premise of this book is that we must call our spirits home, lest we forsake our origins, and lose hope, meaning, health, and the ability to serve and participate in the greatest change that history has ever known. We are living in the parenthesis, at the end of one era and not quite at the beginning of a new one. We are in liminal history, on a planetary vision quest, seeking and searching with few clues in sight. Everything is in dissolution, a state of traveling from no-longer-thereness to not-yet-hereness. It is not unlike the Arthurian saga of Percival, who crosses a bridge of glass to get to an unknown shore only to hear the bridge crash behind him as he goes forward. And yet, when whole systems and cultures and ways of being are in transition, the future is suddenly opened, depths of culture and persona can be probed, and realms of creative potential become available. We all are being asked, both singularly and collectively, to cross a bridge and to meet halfway a rising reality, a sacred reality. Thus the need for training in journeys into the Sacred. Thus too, the need for a sacred psychology, one that speaks to the fullness and dimensionality of our condition, and gives us ways and means to explore these realms.

Some of the ways I offer here were inspired by my own journeys and work with indigenous people—Maoris, Australian Aborigines, Native Americans—as well as the exemplars of classic spiritual traditions. Other ways grew out of my more than three decades of research into the nature and application of latent human capacities. Through use of myth and story, mental and physical exercises, a reconsideration of the nature of wounding, the search for essence, and the journeys of the soul, I try to give the reader a feeling for the fact that his existence is nested in a Nature that exceeds while it comprehends his human nature. These findings suggest very strongly that our evolutionary potential lies in the vast geographies of our inner world. Mystics, visionaries, and high creative folk have always known this. In my Father-Mother's house there are many mansions. In fact there is an entire metaphysical city there! We are treasure troves of realities, and up until very recently we have allowed ourselves to access these troves only under the auspices of formal religions, which told us how far we could go—not too far. Because, quite simply, once we start, the world turns a corner, and we are in the unimagined universe. The news from the universe suggests that what we think of as ego or identity is but a frail raft floating on the vast ocean of Consciousness. Think of times of being in love, or the rapture of dissolution into Nature, or states of deep communion, or creative breakthrough, and you realize how much of our vital existence resides in another state of being. In *The Search for the Beloved* I try to give you access points to the realms where the Higher Self resides.

A particular focus of this book is on the yearning for the Divine Beloved, since it is this yearning that is often the start for most spiritual journeys. It is the wound of the heart, this yearning for what is felt to be lost, that brings us finally to the full power of our potential being. In suffering, in wounding, at a deeper level than we are even aware of, we journey to the Sacred, the sphere of redemption. We may lose connection to our former selves—and yet what we will discover by the journey's end is a deeper sense of ourselves, a new homeland that is a land within, a merging of spirit and body, and the creation of new life.

The great desire for the Beloved of the Soul, while always present, moves to the foreground when civilizations undergo whole-system transitions. Today we are undergoing a profound transition, moving from a cosmopolitan to a planetary culture. Our cultures, beliefs, and practices intertwine. We are experiencing a revolution in relationships between men and women. We are revising our notions of community, of other cultures, of our relationship to Nature. Critical to this is the emergence of a new natural philosophy based on love as the creative force of evolution. This lure of becoming finds renewed expression in the rising archetype of the Beloved of the Soul. Quite simply, we are attempting to figure out how to work together as copartners, not only in our relationships and jobs and communities but with the planet and the cosmos at large. And in so doing, we must recognize that in each other there is the Divine Being for whom we have searched. The passion that drives our lives drives the life of the entire planet. Like cells of a single body, we are inextricably intertwined. We are sought by the Beloved as we seek the Beloved, so that our spirits may at last come home.

—Jean Houston
Pomona, New York
December 1996

How to Read This Book

This book is intended to serve as a guidebook to several of the realms of sacred psychology, particularly the search for the Beloved of the soul. In a field so vast and rooted in so many traditions, there is no way that a single book can encompass the variety and richness of the subject. Suffice it to say that in nearly all traditions, sacred psychology assumes that the deepest yearning in every human soul is to return to its spiritual source, there to experience communion and even union with the Beloved. This relationship is then expressed in the deepened and renewed forms of your daily life. The emphasis on this union and transformation is what distinguishes sacred psychology from other depth psychologies. Thus the methods of sacred psychology involve processes that enhance the connection between the historical self and the ultimate reality. These processes have the effect of regeneration, so that you come gradually to have an extended body, an amplified mind, a compassionate heart, an active soul, and a new life of high service. Through sacred psychology, you become a citizen in a universe larger than your aspiration and more complex than all your dreams.

The themes from sacred psychology that I include here—the Sacred Wound, the Mythic Journey of Transformation, the Discovery of the Larger Story, and Union with the Beloved of the Soul—are those that I have found to be most evocative in my seminars and training programs in human capacities development and sacred psychology throughout the world. I hope they may stimulate your soul with the shock of recognition and call you to a deeper journey.

I have attempted to order this book in a way that encourages you to experience sacred psychology as a developmental path. But life lived on many levels exceeds and evades logic, so if my order is not yours, browse through the book to the section that most appeals to you and begin there.

The book is divided into four parts, reflecting the way I teach this material. Part One provides the ancient and modern settings for sacred psychology, and suggests the premises from which the practice of sacred psychology flows. Part Two offers basic exercises that are designed to attune mind and body for the work of sacred psychology. Part Three inquires into several of the basic themes and mythic structures from which this work springs, and provides experiential processes relevant to these themes.

Finally, in Part Four you are invited to participate (preferably with a group) in the actual living journey of transformation drawn from two great scenarios of the journey of the soul. In re-creating and harvesting these old stories, you are challenged to discover within yourself the new story that is emerging.

The glossary, the list of suggested musical compositions, and the selected bibliography will enhance your understanding and experience of sacred psychology.

While this book stands alone as an introduction to sacred psychology, it may be used in conjunction with my earlier works in extending human capacities: *Mind Games* and *Listening to the Body* (both with Robert Masters), and *The Possible Human.* Of these, *The Possible Human* will be the most helpful. Another earlier book, *Life Force: The Psycho-Historical Recovery of the Self,* represents my first written foray into the realm of sacred psychology, although I had not yet identified it in this way. In that book, I suggest that the growth of the human psyche parallels the stages of historical cultural development, and I present a program of group evocation and ritual for exploring and deepening journey through life. My own journey has taken me further into this field, with the result that I am publishing a series of books on individual myths of transformation that are similar in form and content to the journeys in Part Four.

Sacred psychology has evolved over thousands of years as an oral tradition. The rhythm and rhetoric of oratory are of its essence. It exists in a context that is difficult to express adequately on the cool isolation of the printed page. The language may sometimes seem extravagant; in fact, it may be extravagant. Thus you are urged to hear as you read, to translate words on a page to a dynamic and lived reality. Before actually reading the book, you may want to relax fully, put on some especially evocative music, and let your consciousness move away from the patterns, insistences, and resistances of your daily routine.

In writing this book, I am talking with you, the reader. Thus I speak to "you" with the hope that you will talk back to me, writing in the margins commentaries, questions, insights. Our journey is a mutual one.

Sacred psychology always unfolds as a shared journey, from Socrates conversing with the young men of Athens, to Jesus and his disciples, to Buddha and the Sangha, to the knights in the twelfth century in quest of the Grail, to modern pilgrims on a journey through southern India to visit the temples of Shiva. Always there was and is and shall be much laughter, many tears, deep confidences, the sharing of pain, of memories, of new roads seen and taken together, the exaltation of discovery, the celebration of "coming home."

I hope that you will continue this tradition by seeking out and inviting co-journeyers to join you on the path through the many landscapes and inscapes of sacred psychology.

Prologue

The Madman.—Have you ever heard of the madman who on a bright morning lighted a lantern and ran to the marketplace calling out unceasingly: "I seek God! I seek God!"—As there were many people standing about who did not believe in God, he caused a great deal of amusement. Why! is he lost? said one. Has he strayed away like a child? said another. Or does he keep himself hidden? Is he afraid of us? Has he taken a sea voyage? Has he emigrated?—the people cried out laughingly, all in a hubbub. The insane man jumped into their midst and transfixed them with his glances. "Where is God gone?" he called out. "I mean to tell you! *We have killed him*—you and I! We are all his murderers! But how have we done it? How were we able to drink up the sea? Who gave us the sponge to wipe away the whole horizon? What did we do when we loosened this earth from its sun? Whither does it now move? Whither do we move? Away from all suns? Do we not dash on unceasingly? Backwards, sideways, forwards, in all directions? Is there still an above and below? Do we not stray, as through infinite nothingness? Does not empty space breathe upon us? Has it not become colder? Does not night come on continually, darker and darker? Shall we not have to light lanterns in the morning? Do we not hear the noise of the grave-diggers who are burying God? Do we not smell the divine putrefaction?—for even Gods putrefy! God is dead! God remains dead! And we have killed him! How shall we console ourselves, the most murderous of all murderers? The holiest and the mightiest that the world has hitherto possessed, has bled to death under our knife,—who will wipe the blood from us? With what water could we cleanse ourselves? What lustrums, what sacred games shall we have to devise? Is not the magnitude of this deed too great for us? Shall we not ourselves have to become Gods, merely to seem worthy of it? There never was a greater event,—and an account of it, all who are born after us belong to a higher history than any history hitherto!"—Here the madman was silent and looked again at his hearers; they were also silent and looked at him in surprise. At last he threw his lantern on the ground, so

> that it broke in pieces and was extinguished. "I come too early," he then said, "I am not yet at the right time. This prodigious event is still on its way, and is travelling,—it has not yet reached men's ears. Lightning and thunder need time, the light of the stars needs time, deeds need time, even after they are done, to be seen and heard. This deed is as yet further from them than the furthest star,—*and yet they have done it!*"[1]

The planet has turned around the sun more than 100 times since Nietzsche wrote those words. In that journey it has seen exactly what Nietzsche predicted would occur after the death of God—a profuse sequence of "breakdowns, destructions, annihilations, revolutions . . . a spreading darkness and a total eclipse, the like of which has never before occurred on this earth."[2] Economists and social philosophers might say that these casualties of progress and industrialization are due purely to socioeconomic factors. Some of us would say otherwise.

Consider that in the twentieth century the Chinese lost, almost overnight, the gods and spiritual forces that had sustained them for five thousand years. In a few short years, the Russians—among the most religious people in Europe—lost a religion of rich aesthetic heritage and spiritual complexity. If Marx had not appeared, it would have been necessary to invent him to provide the numinous dialectic of Holy Nature and Sainted Economics that replaced the niches stripped of Russian orthodox icons and saints.

We do not need to go so far afield. The growing abuse of alcohol and cocaine, the rash of teenage suicides, the great increase in fundamentalism on all levels, the pursuit of passionless pleasures, and the accumulation of matter that doesn't matter, all attest to the desperate loss of meaning in the lives of so many. The Madman speaks down the years, "God is dead, and we have killed Him."

In the distance, just over the horizon, there is a growing murmur, difficult to hear or see at first. Put your ear to the ground and listen.

It is the voice of the gathering of a new group of Mad Folk. They have gone to their edges and fallen off the horizon.

> We live in an old chaos of the sun,
> Or old dependency of day and night,
> Of island solitude, unsponsored, free,
> Of that wide water inescapable.
>
> —Wallace Stevens, "Sunday Morning"

The period of loss, of waiting, could not end until life had been lived without the old supports and dependencies. They had to collapse so that the Mad Folk could experience the Dark Night of the Soul.

This was the time of gestation—a time to wander unsponsored, free—bumping into Things in the Dark, learning, learning from all the hurts. The News of the Day beset them like a series of outrageous Zen koans, shattering illusions, erasing expectations. So the Mad Folk were brought to the illumination of "beginner's mind."

The inescapable wide waters of the spiritual depths returned, and with them the new sun, and with it, the new responsibility to earth, to community, to self, to each other, to God.

Invited to join in co-creation, the Mad People are coming over the horizon singing, "Come let us play God. Let us learn God games that we may prepare ourselves for our destiny."

Yet the old dependencies still draw breath, still seek to betray the Mad Ones with their caviling: "But who are you that you should dare so great a step?"

And the Mad Folk answer:

"We are solar beings, the latest formations of the metabolism of the galaxy.

"Galactic patterns and energies are coded in everything we are, and we are *sui generis* galactic beings.

"We are cloned from sun spots, and remember at some primordial level our union in the light and the great heaving fireworks of separation.

"Then, too, we are of the sea.

"The rhythms of waves and oceans continue to beat on the shore of our skin, our hearts, our pulse points—the million waves that come up on our million different shorelines.

"The frail craft of ego rides upon these waves and thinks itself ocean.

"Briny is our brain, and our blood flows with creatures indistinguishable from those found at the bottom of the sea.

"But like all creatures we are divided within and among ourselves.

"The immune response which kept us from feasting on ourselves also kept us bifurcated, membraned subsets of compartmentalized life, insulated, isolated, privatized, and famished.

"And yet we remember, if only as a dream, Sun Self, Sea Self, Unitive Being, the Beloved of the soul. And we cry to dream again."

Now the Mad Folk are clambering back from Who Knows Where with the news that it is time for the rebirth of the spirit. However unlikely it may seem, we are to be the midwives of God. The Apocalypse is over where it happened—in the inner city of our hearts.

PART ONE
Perspectives

Overleaf: A patient dreams of being healed by the God Asclepios and his daughter, Hygeia. Stone votive relief, Hellenic Era, ca. 400 B.C., National Archaeological Museum, Athens.

1

THE ANCIENT ASCLEPIAN

Arise Asclepios! Lord of man and healer, gentle-minded child of Apollo and noble Coronis. Dispersing sleep from your eyes, heed the words of your worshippers who, rejoicing greatly, propitiate your prime power, health. Gentle-minded Asclepios, arise and be pleased to give ear to your hymn. You whom we invoke with a cry: "Hail!"

—FROM AN ANCIENT HYMN TO ASCLEPIOS

It is the year 403 B.C., and you are an Athenian in need of a healing of mind and body. You and your family have just come through a half century unlike any ever known in memory. In your lifetime you have seen the soul of man touch the sky as you witnessed the height and glory of the Athenian empire, the establishment of democracy, the centralization of the Delian League in Athens, a long period of relative peace, the *Oresteia* of Aeschylus, the comedies of Aristophanes, the poetry of Pindar, the sculpture of Myron, the philosophy of Anaxagoras, the call to "know thyself" of a stonemason-philosopher called Socrates, the building of the Parthenon, the *Antigone* of Sophocles, Phidias's statue of the Athena Parthenos, part of the Thirty Year Peace, the *Medea* of Euripides, the medicine of Hippocrates, the *History* of Herodotus, the war accounts of Thucydides, and the production of *Oedipus Rex.*

But you have also seen this Golden Age collapse in the horrors of the long twenty-five-year war which has pitted the Peloponnesian cities of Greece against each other. Never have so many cities been taken and laid desolate, never has there been so much exile and bloodshed. You have lived through the grim misery of a plague, unexpected and inexplicable, which has killed more than half the citizens of Athens. You have looked for your friends among the unburied dead that lay heaped in the temples.

You have heard the wailing of widows and the cry of newly orphaned children. You have seen the perversion of all value as words that once meant noble behavior have taken on the meaning of stupid and foolish ways, while the most despicable and amoral actions have been exalted as virtues. You have witnessed in disgust as ranters and ravers have won the day and besmirched the old Periclean ideals. Nature herself has mirrored the moral catastrophe and produced an unparalleled number of earthquakes and eclipses, famines and droughts.

Where are the gods, you wonder? Where is the Athenian vision of a world understood by human intelligence and controlled by divine purpose? Everywhere you look the old ideals have been degraded, the old order has broken down, the world has been rendered absurd. Still you remember the glory that was and will not die and are haunted by the lines of Euripides, "So I have a secret hope of someone, a god, who is wise and plans. . . ."

You remember such a god, Asclepios, the god of *Nootherapeia*, of mind-healing, whose practices are said to purify and reweave one into a new harmony of body, mind, and spirit. And so, one day, you decide to make the journey to the Asclepian at Epidaurus to turn a corner on your reality, to see your life and life itself in a new way, to be rewoven to new form.

The day you enter the great healing center you are struck by the words carved on the magnificent marble arch which forms the entrance to the ancient sanctuary:

> Pure must be he who enters the fragrant temple;
> Purity means to think nothing but holy thoughts.[1]

You wonder how you will be able to sustain such thought given the weariness of your spirit. But others have tried to do so, and you will try also.

After settling into one of the guest houses, you walk down the streets of Epidaurus where you see marble temples blazing with color, beautiful paintings of the lives of gods and heroes, and sculptures whose haunting harmonies speak of the godded human and the humanized god—dedicated to the Asclepian by the great artists of the day, Praxiteles, Phidias, Polygnotus. Your eyes quickened and your senses stimulated, you sight the sacred street processions going by—stately files of priests hymning Apollo; drumming, dancing ecstatics devoted to the cult of Dionysius waving ivy-covered wands; chanting worshippers of Aphrodite bearing an ancient wooden icon of the Goddess. This prompts you to enter the temples of the gods—the Olympian gods and the lesser gods as well—where you pray and invoke their powers.

Back on the street your attention is drawn to the oratory of gray-bearded philosophers arguing and discoursing to anyone who will listen on the nature of goodness, beauty, and truth.

Moving on, you then enter the magnificent circular marble theatre of Epidaurus with its acoustical perfection, where you watch the masked and booted actors and chorus playing the soul-charging, terrifying, awful dramas of hubris, guilt, tragedy, and transformation. This day they are performing the *Oresteia* of Aeschylus, the tragic trilogy of murder, revenge, and madness that haunts the descendants of Atreus.

As you witness the unfaithful Clytemnestra preparing the murder of her long-absent husband, Agamemnon, you think to yourself, "I thought I had problems. They can't compare with those of the House of Atreus!" As you watch the action, you enter totally into the story, and with the people around you holding on to you and to one another, you shake with dread and delicious shuddering thrills. Then, when the action gets too intense, when the tragedy overwhelms you with its sorrow, the thousands of you erupt together with one choral voice wailing "Aaaiiiiii" in a symphony of pity and terror.

The high tragic drama is followed by wild and woolly satyr plays—ribald, rascally comedies often featuring men dressed in goatskins bopping each other over the heads with six-foot phalluses—and this elevates your spirits. This is followed by a high comedy of Aristophanes satirizing the fashionable fools and political foibles of the day, and you laugh yourself into another state altogether.

Leaving the theatre you seek a place to enjoy a massage or an herbal bath, and then later that night you go to the "House of the Comedians," where rowdy jokes, sight gags, and barbed satires fool your expectations, unlatch your reason, and generally give you the benefits of the world's oldest therapeutic tool—the healing power of humor.

Still laughing, you visit a physician who gives you both spiritual and medical guidance before you turn in at the guest house, your sleep enhanced by incense of pine and the quiet chanting of prayers. You are not the same person who began the day. Your thoughts as you drift into sleep, if not yet "pure," are at least relaxed and content.[2]

In the days that follow, you avail yourself of the many opportunities that the Asclepian offers, imbuing yourself with the ideal of physical grace as you view beautiful bodies competing in the stadium. You exercise in the gymnasium to acquire some of this grace and stamina, listen to harmonious sounds at the concerts, have sessions with the physicians—the mind healers as well as the body healers—laugh with the comedians, argue with the philosophers, and quake in pity and terror with Medea, with Antigone, and with Oedipus the King.

Then one day you are given a bath in the sea by the priests, who also burn incense to purify mind and body. Offering sacrifice, you are permitted to enter the beautiful temple of Asclepios himself where you view the gold-and-ivory statue of the god in the distance. To the sound of powerful music and chanting, you approach the statue asking for a vision of meaning, a relieving of the sorrow which has consumed you. Priests accompany you, relating the legends of the cult and pointing out the remarkable cures by the god recorded on the marble steles and tablets which line the walls. Among them you read the following:

> A lad who was mute had gone through the customary rites and was standing by his father when the attendant asked if he would promise to offer the proper sacrifices to the god within a year if he gained the object of his coming. The boy suddenly exclaimed "I promise," repeating the word at the bidding of his astonished father, and he was cured from that time.
>
> A women from Athens called Ambrosia was blind in one eye. She came as a suppliant to the god. As she walked about in the temple, she laughed at some of the cures as incredible and impossible, that the lame and the blind should be healed by merely having a dream. In her sleep she had a vision. It seemed to her that the god stood by her and said that he would cure her, but that in payment he would ask her to dedicate to the Temple a silver pig as a memorial of her foolishness. After saying this, he cut the diseased eyeball and poured in some drug. When day came, she walked out of the Abaton completely sound.[3]

Now you almost believe; certainly your enthusiasm is growing. You are anxious to reach the statue whose outstretched hand seems to beckon you to healing and the resolution of misery. You step forward and soon hear a dry slithering sound, and squinting your eyes in the incense-wreathed twilight, you make out the coiling shapes of many snakes who circle the statue of the god. You feed these sacred snakes with honey cakes to divert their attention and to divert your own fears as well. Now an ally of the snake world, the world of the healing energies of earth, you reach the statue and touch the god's fingers with an outstretched hand. You then bring your head in contact with the ivory hand, and then your heart, and then your lips. A peace that is almost certainty, that is almost communion, fills your body and succors your spirit as you touch and are touched by the god.

That evening, dressed in white, you join with other patients and suppliants and go to the Abaton, the place of dreaming the healing dream, and there you are assigned a pallet. Placing an offering on one of the small altars, you go to your couch. An old man on the pallet next to you groans in pain as he settles himself down for the night, muttering about the stiffness in his bones. The priest collects the offerings and then invokes the god, chanting:

> O Son of Apollo, O Asclepios! Who in times past have stilled the waves of sorrow for many people, lighting a lamp of safety for those who travel by sea and land, be pleased in your great compassion to accept this prayer which in sleep and vision you have inspired according to your loving kindness to all people. Preserve me from sickness and imbue my body with such a measure of health which may suffice it for the obeying of the spirit.

After the prayer, you are told to be very silent and be frightened at nothing that might occur during the night. As the priests and priestesses leave, the lamps are extinguished, and you hear the words chanted,

> Sleep now, dream now, and dream the dream of the healing god who will come in the night. Sleep now, dream now. . . .

Sometime in the middle of the night you seem to be aware of a little dog licking your face with great tenderness and a snake flicking its tongue in your ears. Are you awake? Are you asleep? You don't know. Priests and priestesses—or is it Asclepios and his daughters Hygeia and Panacea?—pass among you carrying jars of ointments and medicines, putting remedies on the diseased parts and directing the attention of serpents and dogs to lick these parts. In the darkness you hear the priest speaking to a patient concerning his ailment and giving advice, but then you fall into a state that is at once part ecstasy, part waking dream. You cry with happiness. You listen and hear things so strange and so wonderful that there is no naming them. Your hair stands on end and your heart swells, and you seem to be filled with a vision of that which could set your life aright.

Your sleep deepens, your vision continuing into dream, and it seems that Asclepios himself stands before you, looking on you with great sweetness. With one hand the god opens your skull and takes something out and puts something back in. He then opens your heart and does the same.

Panoramas of great beauty unfold where the good is to be seen everywhere and a sea-tide of light washes through the hills of Athens, purifying wherever it touches. You hear the words, "Where chaos was, there cosmos shall be. Go and bring light into your world."

The following morning you are awakened by the stomping and laughing of the old arthritic man who has slept on the pallet next to you. He is marching around, flexing his fingers and knees with great enthusiasm, shouting, "Kaire, Asclepios! Evohe, Asclepios!" (Hail Asclepios! Rejoice,

Asclepios!), a shout that is echoed by others in the Abaton as they too celebrate the healing of the night. For certainly some are healed and others feel better in mind and body, and almost all have had a dream of significance for their lives. In the midst of all this congratulation and celebration and singing of paeans in praise of Asclepios, the priests verify the healings that have happened and listen closely to the dreams that have been dreamed. In the sharing of dreams, interpretation is offered, further treatment is prescribed. Those few who have had neither healing nor dreaming are told to continue to enjoy the many experiences which Epidaurus offers and then come back again to this place of sacred dreaming until they too receive the healing dream.[4]

After offering the traditional gift of a little silver pig and prayers of thanks to Asclepios, you leave Epidaurus to return to your home in Athens. Your steps are lighter, your stance taller than it had been when first you came. The world looks as fresh and new as it must have been on the first day of creation. You feel connected with all the beauty around you and with all that you have seen and known. As you pass through the gateway of the Asclepian you note again the inscription and reflect that your thoughts, if not yet pure, are joyous. The bee-loud glade sings around you, and you hum with it.

* * *

In taking this journey through the Asclepian at Epidaurus, you have experienced sacred psychology in one of its finest and fullest forms, for this ancient Asclepian was a complex of healing centers where art, mystery, and science met in ways that have yet to be matched in the modern world.

The life of the ancient Greek at Epidaurus was watched over by a gracious, totally benevolent, constantly caring, healing daimon—the god-man Asclepios. Legend has it that Asclepios was a Thessalonian born before the Trojan War. He was sent as a child to be instructed by the Centaur Chiron. More may have been involved in this than meets the modern eye; the depth training of the child prefigures the adult.

Mary Renault suggests that the Centaurs, denoted in art and myth as being half man and half horse, were actually Neanderthals who, as recent evidence implies,[5] did not die out entirely 25,000 years ago, but rather removed themselves to remote and hilly country where they were often seen riding shaggy ponies, their hairy bodies indistinguishable from their mounts'. Apparently these people retained the botanical knowledge and natural philosophy of a hundred thousand years or more which they passed on to selected students. According to legend, priests, princes, and physicians-to-be were sent regularly to the Centaurs for training. The favorite student was Asclepios, who showed such promise that the great Centaur physican Chiron trained him in the arts of healing.[6]

Continuous with the knowledge of the most ancient ones, filled with their reverence and knowledge of the natural order, Asclepios became the greatest healer of Greece, his vast knowledge matched only by the depth of his compassion. He could apparently heal almost any ill of mind or body, sometimes using herbs and medicines or surgical procedures, but more often than not healing through spiritual and psychological means, attuning his patients to their own capacity for health and wholeness.

Legend has it that he even succeeded in raising the dead—too many, it seemed, for the god of the Underworld, who complained to Zeus that he was losing his clients to Asclepios's resuscitations and that the order of the world was being seriously threatened. Zeus responded by striking down Asclepios with a thunderbolt, an act which had the effect of deifying rather than just destroying Asclepios.

The memory and love for Asclepios was such that people elevated him to divinity, remythologizing his life so that he was seen to have been a son of Apollo by a mortal woman Coronis. His spirit, conceived as an earth daimon with a double emblem of chthonic serpent and heavenly thunderbolt, continued his healing activities, sending forth from the depths many cures and healing prophecies, as well as wisdom, renewal, and transformation.

Asclepios became the most sought and celebrated god for healing, his cult spreading and often usurping the healing shrines of his "father" Apollo. His children, including Panacea and Hygeia, and their descendants become the Asclepidai, the priest-physicians of ancient Greece who carried a growing knowledge of medicine, psychiatry, and pharmacopia. Our modern oath of Hippocrates is of Asclepidian origin.

The healing centers of Asclepios covered the Greek, Egyptian, and later Roman world. The fullest flowering of these was found at Epidaurus. The rest of this book addresses the need for, and offers practices to help accomplish, a global Asclepian for our time.

2

THE GLOBAL ASCLEPIAN

Indeed man may now be defined as the latest expression of the cosmic-earth process, as that being in whom the cosmic-earth-human-process becomes conscious of itself.[1]

—THOMAS BERRY

The ancient Asclepian is the great Western model for transformation, offering an enormous richness and variety of experience to awaken both healing capacities and dormant potential. With its powerful evocation of so many levels of reality, it accomplished a kind of therapeia of person and polis. *Therapeia,* a word from which our English word *therapy* is derived, primarily refers to support and caring, but it may also imply "service to the gods" or "doing the work of the gods." Today we might refer to therapeia as "doing the work of the Whole." Over the past ten years, it has been my model in developing the practice and process of sacred psychology.

Our century is not unlike the fifth century B.C. in its prodigious invention and its moral blight, its vision of a new humanity and its immensity of mass destruction, its soaring hope and its proliferating despair. Technologically we possess the powers of a second Genesis and the psychological preparedness of a boy Faust. We are on the eve of a truly transformational therapeia, a global Asclepian, that demands a rigorous evocation and orchestration of the potentials of body, mind, and psyche, as well as those of art, science, and culture, if we would survive our time.

The citizens of Greece who made the pilgrimage to the sacred temples of Asclepios were offered an invitation to become what they could be, to gain a larger perspective on the self and the social order. As we have seen, this process involved a quickening of the total person through art, music, dance, drama, healing therapy, sacred practice, laughter, altered states of consciousness, and communion with archetypal realities. Once again such an invitation is needed. Evoking the making of new connections in brain, body, mind, and spirit, sacred psychology seeks, like the ancient Asclepian, to bring one's entire self to a higher order.

In essence, the principle behind both sacred psychology and the ancient Asclepian is similar to what Ilya Prigogine, the Nobel Prize-winning physicist, offers as a theory of how a higher order emerges from the fluctuations created through new information. Prigogine's theory has been summarized as follows:

> The more complex the structure, the more energy it must dissipate to maintain all that complexity. This flux of energy makes the system highly unstable, subject to internal fluctuations—and sudden change. If these fluctuations or perturbations reach a critical size, they are amplified by the system's many connections and can drive the system into a new state, even more ordered, coherent, and connected. The new state occurs as a sudden shift.[2]

As more information or more stimulation enters the system and then disperses internally, the system is driven to a whole new dynamic regime. However, this process can also be applied to human development, the evolution of cities, theologies, systems of knowledge, nations, and perhaps the planet itself. In the Asclepian mode, the growth of consciousness as well as the healing of the body-mind was encouraged by a rhythm of dynamic input through theatre, philosophy, athletics, and so forth, followed by experiences like the one described in the incubation of the sacred dream. Such experiences created a context for the body and mind to shift into a more complex, coherent state of being. This state organically effected healing by reconstituting the reality of body and mind into a higher order. Thus, too, the process of wholing was encouraged, for by taking in and integrating more ideas and experiences, both sacred and profane realities, the participant in the Asclepian became deeper, wiser, and more available for new inspiration and creativity.

The Asclepian reminds us that the individual who is in a situation that friends, family, and colleagues may define as "creative neurosis" or "on the brink" may also be viewed as a highly dynamic system available to more information than we normally allow through our many filters. At this vulnerable time, instead of retreating in panic before the multiple stimuli that are a part of modern existence, we can orchestrate this input and be carried to the next stage. William James prefigured Prigogine when he wrote:

> A mind is a system of ideas, each with the excitement it arouses, and with tendencies impulsive and inhibitive, which mutually check or reinforce one another. . . . But a new perception, a sudden emotional shock, or an occasion which lays bare the organic alteration, will make the whole fabric fall together; and then the center of gravity sinks into an attitude more stable; for the new ideas that reach the centre in the rearrangement seem now to be locked there, and the new structure remains permanent.[3]

Today one of the roles of sacred psychology is to provide the new perception that precipitates an organic shift within the psyche.

The model of the Asclepian, however, does much more than provide us with a barrage of stimuli, of techniques, of "too-muchness." On very deep levels it asks us to remember who we are—to know again our sourcing through the sacred. It provides an opening through which the emerging myth and archetypal energies may enter into time, renewing the individual and the larger context in which we live. It becomes increasingly apparent to me, after several decades of work with extending human capacities, that capacities evolve and change in response to the larger cultural and mythic patterns of which we are a part. We can only extend our capacities when we are conscious of these larger patterns and assume our role as their co-creator.

We are in a time of radically changing story, dying to one and waking up to another. We are in a time of great shaking up, of bridging and interaction with a veritable smorgasbord of realities. And it seems that all of the systems, psychologies, and symbologies that ever existed, à la Prigogine, are needed to stimulate and drive us to a whole new regime. This global Asclepian is, in turn, shaken further by a number of factors unique in human history that amplify the charge toward accelerating individual and cultural evolution.

What is happening, I believe, is way beyond what has been called "paradigm shift." It is whole-system transition, a shift in reality itself. Whereas paradigm shift could be compared to turning a kaleidoscope and watching the pieces assume a new pattern and relationship to each other, whole-system transition would call for the addition of entirely new pieces into the whole. The world itself is changing on a deep ontological level; fundamental structures are no longer what they once were.

The change crosses all boundaries, and we are in the midst of living that change. Traditional epistemologies and scientific understandings pale before the present mystery. What seems called for is a metaphoric mode, one that has the breadth of many cultures as well as the depth of many histories, to create a context rich enough for understanding and participating in this whole-system transition. This metaphoric mode is what sacred psychology tries to be.

With this as background, let us look now at five unique factors that I think are critical to understanding the phenomenon that is taking place. Although these factors will be familiar to any intelligent observer of the world scene, their significance is changed and their importance deepened by viewing them in tandem with sacred psychology. These factors are:

1. Planetization.
2. The rise of the feminine.
3. The emergence of a new science and new scientists, accompanied by a miniaturization of technology.
4. The new understanding of the potential for extending both human capacities and the ecology of consciousness.
5. The emergence of a global spiritual sensibility.

The emergence of the new culture would almost inevitably have to involve each of these themes in some way, for they appear to be providing the coordinates upon which the new story and the deeper consciousness is being woven. These are the temples and the templates of the global Asclepian. Exploring, albeit briefly, these unique elements can give us insight into the forms and forces that are shaping our lives.

PLANETIZATION

Ever since the first man went to the moon and viewed this planet in all her beauty from afar, our souls have been charged with the symbol of this living, spinning entity.

On their return journey, the astronauts were free to contemplate the astonishing vision of our blue and green and silver planet as it hung in space. Edgar Mitchell reported that the crew turned on the stereo system and the capsule was flooded with the music of *Camelot.* As the title song evoked the image of a once and future kingdom, Mitchell felt an overwhelming connection with Mother Earth. He experienced simultaneously an "instant global consciousness" and a deep knowing that, having been born out of the womb of the earth in the moon voyage, the human being now returned as partner of the earth.

His sensibility was shared by millions who followed the journey through television, deeply and symbolically revisioning their relationship to this planet. The human/earth story had changed forever.

In a time of planetization we all become stewards of the living planet, whether or not we choose this stewardship consciously. We are no longer tribal, village, national, or even cosmopolitan people. We are planetary people, sharing in the responsibility of caring for a world that up to now has mostly cared for us. Innocence is sacrificed in our exponential growth of responsibility. What we do makes a profound difference.

As planetary citizens, we share in the ecology of cultures. We eat sushi and tacos, wear clothes from Taiwan and Guatemala, study Tibetan Buddhism and Peruvian shamanism, and drive Japanese cars manufactured in Southern California. Through our satellites we participate in events all over the globe as they are happening. Today political borders no longer offer security. The old political story was organized around stratified bureaucracies, empires, and nation-states. Communication between these tightly defined and defended borders was very limited. In an age of interdependence, the old territorial stories must give way to a story of a mutually shared and protected planet.

Scientists have suggested that the earth itself is a living organism of which we are an intimate part. If this hypothesis is true, then new kinds of responsibility, both secular and sacred, challenge us at the very edge of our being, asking us to partner this most crucial of turning points in human history. On the secular level, it would seem that in the Earth's living system we are the nervous system; that is, we are the individual neurons of the brain of the planet, with the consequent responsibility for organizing and orchestrating the functioning and well-being of the planetary body. This responsibility includes evolutionary governance and whole-system management. Living organism to living organism, we and earth are now co-trustees of those processes.

On the sacred level such a co-trusteeship implies that we are receivers of the spiritual and psychic life of the planet. Individuals and spiritual communities have always had this awareness and have communed with that piece of Mother Earth on which they lived and through which they received her messages. But never before has the vision widened to include awareness of and responsibility for the entire planetary "person." Conversely, never before has the earth herself had a plenitude of listeners available to her planetary song.

This stupendous shift is one of the main reasons, I believe, that so many people all over the world are so concerned with waking up to themselves, to the planet, and to the spiritual dimensions that are calling them. On the secular level, we know we are inadequate to the challenge. On the sacred level, however, the need for planetary communion and co-creation is activating capacities in ourselves that had to remain latent until we came to this place and time in history. Thus the rising spiritual intensity in our time is not merely an individual or cultural phenomenon; it is also a critical result of the spiritual quickening of the earth. This quickening could not have occurred without the prior phenomenon of planetization.

THE RISE OF THE FEMININE

> The patriarchy's time has run out. What new cultural pattern will secure for humanity a new lease on life on earth?[4]

We are standing attendant at a phenomenon that is too deep to be denied, too necessary to be negated. Fifty-two percent of the human race is about to join in as full partners in the business of human affairs. An exclusive preoccupation with child-bearing and -rearing has reached its completion as the earth quickly approaches her saturation point in human density.

If the earth is indeed a living organism and its nervous system is nearly in place, then women's roles must necessarily be greatly expanded in all fields of human endeavor, both to allay population growth and to make women available for the complex requirements of the emerging planetary culture. The "noosphere" of Teilhard de Chardin may be more real than mythic. The global mind-field may be closer than we think. And essential to its happening may be the rich mind style of woman, now ready to emerge after centuries of gestation in the womb of preparatory time. This emergence is perhaps the most important event of the last five thousand years, and its consequences may well have an immense, unimaginable effect on cultural evolution. The emergence of the genius of female sensibility and potential is as critical to the issue of human survival as it is confusing to the traditional styles and standards of most cultures.

There is no turning back from the fact that women are now joining men in full partnership in the domain of the human agenda. As this partnership develops, not only will men be released from the old polarities of gender that force them into limited and limiting roles, but qualities of intelligence will be added to the human mind-pool that will render most previous problem solving obsolete. Linear, sequential solutions will yield to the knowing that comes from seeing things in whole gestalts, in constellations, rather than in discrete facts. The appreciation of *process* will be celebrated along with the seeking of end goals.

Cultures in which the feminine archetype is powerful emphasize being rather than doing, deepening rather than producing and achieving. Such cultures are nonheroic; they tend to make things work, cohere, grow. If, for a hundred thousand years, you've been stirring the soup with one hand and holding the baby with the other, kicking off the woolly mastodon with one foot and rocking a cradle with the other, watching out for the return of the hunters with one eye and determining with the other on which cave wall you will paint a magical bison, then you are going to develop a very complex consciousness. This is a consciousness that is extraordinarily well adapted to orchestrating the multiple variables of the modern world.

Philosophically, in the reality structure of the feminine archetype, Great Nature is just as important within as it is without. The principle of the *unus mundus*, the unified reality stream, is operative here; the realm of inwardness has as much ontological status as the external world has. The feminine principle expresses itself as an unfolding of levels of existence, not as the conquest of facts.

In the supreme dialectic between logos and eros, the feminine reveals a movement toward eros. Logos, the principle of ordering and mastery, is essential to the creation and sustenance of civilization.*

But eros is of a different order; it is concened with the interrelationship of psyche and nature. Under the principle of eros we become not systematic but systemic, orchestrating our lives to mesh creatively with the finely balanced systems of nature. We become aware of ourselves as organism-environment, engaged in fields of life—from the subtle awareness of the psychic weave between ourselves and others to the networking of ourselves with the larger social organism.

Today it is essential to avoid the domination of one principle over the other. If eros is rising, it is as a necessary corrective to the tyranny of logos. Dominated by logos, eros becomes stalemated in obsessive sexuality and desire. Conversely, dominated by eros, logos is stalemated in dogmatic, habituated patterns of social order and ritual. The creation of a new reality, in both its social and personal forms, must manifest a new blending and rich interplay of eros and logos. Then eros can become a deepening, unifying principle, granting us resonance with larger fields of life, leading us to become planetary persons, and bringing true global and psychic interdependence. Logos can then grow in kind and become a more sensitive regulating principle, subtly guiding the interchange of psyche and social order toward the flowering of a world civilization that preserves human difference, partners the planet, and engenders the soul.

Many of us in research and clinical psychology have recently witnessed in our research subjects and clients a remarkable activation of images of female principles, archetypes, and goddesses. The recent proliferation of books, articles, and conferences on the "rise of the goddess" is a phenomenon that has great implications for culture and consciousness. The women's movement may be the outward manifestation of what is happening on depth levels in essential, mythic, and archetypal space-

*As it is used here, *logos* is more of a social principle denoting ordering and mastery. This is in contrast to *Logos* as used theologically to denote the energy, coding, and incarnation of the creative spirit of God.

time. Whether the movement has evolved because the crisis of the external world is calling for the rise of the goddess to restore the balance of nature, or because the release of women into full partnership demands a similar release of its archetypal principle, or even because, in the cosmic cycle of things, the time of the goddess has come round, we cannot say. But all the evidence indicates that the feminine archetype is returning.

Denied and suppressed for thousands of years, the goddess archetype returns at a time when the breakdown of the old story leaves us desperate for love, for security, for protection, for meaning. It leaves us yearning for a nurturing and cultivation of our whole being, that we might be adequate stewards of the planetary culture.

THE EMERGENCE OF A NEW SCIENCE

It is fascinating to live in a time in which many of the implications of the new science are coming to be embodied in a new technology. As I travel 35,000 feet in the air, I look down and note that almost everywhere the smokestacks are coming down and the dish antennae are going up. This is a wonderfully visual statement of the movement in our time from industrialization to high technology, from mechanistic systems to a miniaturization that echoes the poet's seeing of infinity in a grain of sand. Microchips bring electronic communion, and the instantaneous play of information is systemically linking the networks of all human cultural and economic processes.

Miniaturization also has tremendous implications for person and culture, for if machines are small and no longer blighting the landscape and the inscape, then you can again listen to the messages of the wind, read the great plans of Being inscribed in the bark of trees, feel the rhythms of awakening in your fingertips, and dance them with others—who are also being released from the industrial nightmare and are now truly free to wake up. Already, miniaturization is carrying us into a high shift from hardware to information, from capital-intensive economies to communal forms of regional production, and from consumer values to contemplative and creative values.

The source of this shift is fundamental and will be revolutionary in its effects on human experience. The science that we all knew as objective, linear, and quantified is radically diminishing in its claims. A new science has emerged, along with a new scientist. With the premises of higher physics being consonant with the knowledge of deeper mysticism, a new rapprochement is occurring between science and the sacred.

For example, the English botanist Rupert Sheldrake has introduced a radically innovative hypothesis of formative causation concerning how things function in the universe. This theory suggests that the form, development, and behavior of everything from atom to organism to human and social patterns to the universe itself are not so much determined by unchanging scientific laws as by invisible, self-organizing units that Sheldrake calls "morphogenetic fields."

These fields, acting across space and time, serve as blueprints for establishing new structures, forms, and behaviors. They contain the memory of past organized systems and account for the way that organisms can "tune in" to the morphogenetic fields of their species and be influenced by the cumulative effect of previous similar organisms. Changes and innovations are thus added to the species "memory," and future organisms can draw upon it. Therefore, once a substance or an individual or even a society learns a new behavior, the causative, morphogenetic field of that entity is changed, and the next substance or individual or society learns the new behavior more easily and quickly.

Sheldrake's hypothesis has extraordinary implications for the nature of learning, the development of change, and evolution. It also raises the possibility that memory is not just stored in the brain but receives some of its codings from the morphogenetic field in which the past experiences of the human race are contained.

The implications of this hypothesis for sacred psychology are even more far-reaching, for if these fields are as universal as claimed, we may have found evidence for the nature of inspiration, for tapping into patterns and possibilities, and even for tuning into an archetypal level of morphogenetic resonance. This archetypal level contains the great symbolic and mythic patterns that charge the human spirit with meaning and direction. Sheldrake's theory would also support the belief that prayerful, meditative, and mystical experiences are those states of grace in which the mind-body system attunes to the primary field of Being and, for a time, has the accumulated knowledge of the patterns stored in the mind of God. Although such experiences have been known for millennia, an explanation that Westerners can appreciate is only now becoming available as a result of the speculation of the new scientists.

Presently we are living at a time of extraordinary spiritual insight into both the micro-phase and the macro-phase of the phenomenal world. Such insight demands a concomitant expansion of our ways of inner or subjective knowing.

THE EXTENSION OF HUMAN CAPACITIES

In this planetary age we are challenged, as never before, to achieve a new humanity and a new way of nurturing the species to achieve its genius in harmony with nature and one another. New explorations and current advances in brain, mind, and body research are increasingly allowing us to view and probe the vast and subtle range of human capacities and learn how to use these capacities more productively and more humanely. The inventory of human resources has increased exponentially as a result of cross-cultural and anthropological studies. How Africans walk and move and think, how the Chinese teach and study and paint, how Eskimos see complete models of inner imagery, how Balinese develop such fine eye-to-hand motor coordination, how a tribe along the Amazon raises happy and unneurotic children—these are learnings no longer limited to place and culture; they are available to the whole family of humankind.

Again, investigations into styles of learning around the planet give us a perspective on human latency simultaneously thrilling and disturbing. It is thrilling to glimpse the extent of human potential, and disturbing to discover that so little of it is utilized. So much of it has been educated out of people during childhood. There is no such thing as a stupid child; there are merely incredibly stupid and diminishing forms of education. Given the present findings concerning the immensity of human variation, we now have the task of discovering and implementing forms of education, evocation, and training that empower and elicit the tremendous potentials in these variations for thinking, feeling, sensing, learning, knowing—both within and among us. This is a necessity of the planetary culture.[5]

We also know, given the new understanding of mind-body dynamics, that most people's bodies can be psychophysically reeducated and a much better physical functioning achieved. As the body's capacities are extended, so are its capacities for awareness, movement, and sensing. Cognitive and feeling functions improve as the brain's motor cortex changes, altering the muscular system and affecting adjacent brain areas. Thus the activation of the motor cortex through mindful psychophysical work helps to disinhibit neighboring neural structures, even those that affect complex intellectual processes and creativity. Extending the capacities of the body, then, must go literally hand in mind with extension of mental and emotional abilities if one wants to accelerate and deepen human functioning. Similarly, people can be taught to "speak" more directly to their own brains, thereby entering into the conscious orchestration of mood, attitude, learning, and creativity. As we will see later in this book, it is possible, too, to order some of the earlier evolutionary structures of brain functioning so that the genius of millennia neither fights nor takes flight, but is available for conscious use in the more complex requirements of modern life.[6]

I have written, both by myself and with my husband, Robert Masters, six books on the subject of the exploration and application of dormant human capacities. We also teach many seminars and graduate courses, as well as offering a three-year human capacities training program in this field. This work provides much information and many practices for releasing the capacities of mind, body, and spirit. Yet in terms of the uniqueness of our time, it does not go far enough. In our pursuit of the nature and development of human capacities, it was fascinating to discover that the most precise and pragmatic methods covering the full range of human development were to be found within sacred traditions.

Throughout history, deeper answers to the questions of life have been offered in the various traditions of sacred psychology—and not just answers, but practical methods of training to grow the godseed. Be it the sophisticated psychophysical methods found in various forms of yoga, or the spiritual practice of oriental martial arts, or the training of mindfulness in Buddhism, or of the imagination in Islamic mysticism, or the activation of courage and creative power in the shamanic practices of the North-South axis of the world, the tradition of the development of the god in us is very rich and always contemporary. What I am offering here as sacred psychology is an expression of this perennial practice for our present mythic time, a practice that builds on past tradition by incorporating the latest findings of human capacities research into the experience of the transformative power that regards us as godseed.

THE EMERGENCE OF A GLOBAL SPIRITUAL SENSIBILITY

There is no question but that we are the gods that our ancestors told stories about. We fly from one part of the globe to another in a matter of hours; we instantly communicate over thousands of miles; we can commit mayhem in moments, move mountains in minutes, and every night we sit in front of our magic picture box and find out what all the other gods are up to. This "divine" activity is, of course, the workings of our new technology, which prosthetically extends our hands and eyes and nervous system and gives us capacities once regarded as mythic. We are magnified through space and time, our senses enlarged, our whims accelerated. But what has been amplified is an *earlier verson of ourselves*, just as the gods that we have become are very early editions of goddedness. What is the next edition?

We are at a time in human history and planetary development when we are becoming aware of the stupendous unconscious knowledge and skillful orchestration that is going on in ourselves as well as in the outer cosmos all the time. We are at a crossing point in human history, and before and after this point there is a chasm of unimaginable dimensions.

It is good scientific orthodoxy to assert that the world we see and experience in everyday life is simply a convenient mirage attuned to our very limited senses, an illusion conjured by our perceptions and our minds. Everything around us (including our own bodies, which appear so substantial) is ultimately nothing but ephemeral networks of particle-waves whirling around at tremendous speeds, colliding, rebounding, disintegrating in almost total emptiness. What we call matter is mostly emptiness, proportionately as void as intergalactic space, void of anything except occasional dust spots and scattered electrical charges. Any single one of the roughly 10^{27} atoms in the average human body has almost all its mass concentrated in a nucleus so small that if all the nuclei of all the atoms that make up the whole of humankind were packed together, their aggregate would be the size of a grain of rice.

When I was a young student at a theological seminary, I had the good fortune to attend a series of lectures given as a term course by the great German theologian Paul Tillich. Throughout the term Professor Tillich, who spoke with a pronounced accent, kept referring to a term that was obviously key to the understanding of his argument. The term was *wokwoom.*

We theological students spent many hours pondering the term, which we could find in no lexicon of words, either sacred or profane. Our intense and prolonged speculation led us to consider an epistemology of *wokwoom*, a hermeneutics of "wokwoom," and "wokwoom" as the ontological foundation of all being. By the end of the semester we had compiled a formidable philosophical theology around this term. Yet my fellow students longed for some final revelation and urged me to raise my hand and address the great man.

"Yes, Miss Houston," Tillich asked as I stood trembling amidst the several hundred older and wiser male graduate students.

I went blank, all the brilliant questions I had prepared disappeared from my mind, and I was left with a question of blithering naiveté.

"Professor Tillich, how do you spell *wokwoom*?"

"Yes, *wokwoom*," Tillich replied, and turning to the chalkboard he wrote:

VACUUM

We might suggest that since nature abhors a "wokwoom," and since most of nature appears to be a "wokwoom," we could postulate—as have both scientists and mystics—that what occupies this "wokwoom" is consciousness and psyche. What we call consciousness, then, might be the fundamental stuff of reality. Rather than seeing consciousness as a secondary epiphenomenon derived from a particular arrangement of particles and atoms, we might say instead that time and space, particles and atoms, are spun out of consciousness. We might then see high creative experience or experience of mystical insight as one of moving from particles to background—thus the mystic's experience of an unfathomable oceanic feeling of depth beyond depth.

Consider that enormously great man Thomas Aquinas and his equally great production of theological and philosophical studies. While celebrating mass in a church in Naples he had such an experience of unitive depth that he was left unable to write, talk, or even tell about his experience. When a good friend begged him to recount his experience, he replied, "Reginald, I cannot. For what I have seen makes all of my work seem mere chaff." Many have had this experience, some by virtue of grace, others by years of search and inner discipline, still others through some kind of trauma that lowered the particle resistance that keeps us so firmly entrenched in "the foreground." By delving into the background, one is able to bring the great intentional cosmic purposes and patterns back into the particularized foreground of space and time. What is true of the experience of individuals is also true of cultures and, by extension, of the planet. Unprecedented trauma and unequaled challenge have created the conditions for an opening in the foreground of existence and a rising of the background of consciousness and psyche, of high pattern, and deep purpose. Whether we want them to or not, the depths are rising out of the vacuum of divine no-thing-ness, which contains the seeds and codings of all that can ever be.

We have seen how the earth has grown through us a brain and nervous system, but now these systems need to grow a larger psyche to contain them and to learn how to use them. Thus the task of our time, evolutionary governance, is one of matching the increasing complexity of external reality with a corresponding increase in the depth and breadth of our psychic reality. Our biological equipment, especially our brain, is gifted, or cursed, with a prodigious loaded latency. It can be argued that we have scarcely needed our brain's capacity and range, except perhaps during the Ice Age for survival, and perhaps again today for survival and transformation. Meister Eckhart, the great medieval German mystic, spoke of our being planted with godseeds that can bring forth gods. Our loaded latency is now ready to be born, to be schooled, to be grown, to be used to co-create the world and ourselves, as well as to nurture the psychogenes of what we have called "gods."

3

WHAT IS SACRED PSYCHOLOGY?

True illumination, like all real and vital experience, consists rather in the breathing of a certain atmosphere, the living at certain levels of consciousness, than in the acquirement of specific information.[1]

—EVELYN UNDERHILL

In the cartography of human experience, sacred traditions have tended to map three major realms of experience. Doubtless there are many more realms, with levels upon levels inside each, but three stand out as significant: the realm of the historical and factual, the realm of the mythic and symbolic, and the realm of the unitive or source level of being. To suggest their nature, I have called them the realm of THIS IS ME, the realm of WE ARE, and the realm of I AM, respectively.

Each realm seems to have its own reality; that is to say, while each is reflected within you, each exists independently of you. You are not the only center of reality; you do not singularly create all you behold and experience, as some psychologies have suggested. The ancient metaphor of Indra's net and the modern formulations of quantum physics remind us that we are all woven together. The human challenge is to become full participants in and co-creators of the historical, the mythic, and the unitive realms.

The first and certainly most familiar realm, the THIS IS ME reality, refers to everyday, ordinary existence. It is bounded and limited by geographical space and calendrical time. When you operate in this realm, you are guided by habit patterns, cultural codings, and personal conditionings. Your reality is structured by the definitions of gender, physical characteristics, name, local identity, profession, family, and other relationships and affiliations, all of which terminate upon your death. THIS IS ME is filled with codes (zip codes and others) and categories and is guided by dictums, by "oughts" and "shoulds."

THIS IS ME is the mask we wear, the persona of our everyday existence. It reflects the categories of our curriculum vitae and of our biography. Thus THIS IS ME is Jean Houston, an American woman, born in a certain time and place to certain parents, educated at particular schools, very fond of dogs, teacher of sacred psychology, author of books on human capacities, and so on.

Some practitioners of medicine and psychology function as if THIS IS ME were the only level of existence available, asserting that healing can only take place within its limited confines. In so doing, they cut off their clients' access to deeper realms and render the transformational aspects of psychology impotent. Towards the end of his life, in *Civilization and Its Discontents,* Freud wrote about the frustrations of living within a highly cultivated, all-inclusive, THIS IS ME reality. Limited to the pathology of the particular, many people see the pearl only as the disease of the oyster.

The description above is not meant to diminish the THIS IS ME, but to point out its limitations when we do not perceive its relationship to the other two realms. Many of us never quite accept the THIS IS ME as a final statement of who we are, and so we perpetually yearn for the self from Someplace Else. Whenever the THIS IS ME is seen in and only for itself, it is a cul-de-sac, a world without poetry, without art, without music, without inspiration, without the sacred. Limited to the objective, definable, and measurable, we would be stuck in a brutish, gray existence.

Beyond the realm of the THIS IS ME is the realm of the WE ARE, the residence of symbols, guiding archetypes, and myths. Durative and nonhistorical, the WE ARE realm functions as the contact point for sacred time and sacred space, the container of that which never was and is always happening.

Because the WE ARE realm is so abundant, it is the place where the self joins its polyphrenic possibilities, including the gods and goddesses and their courts. In Sanskrit these celestial beings are referred to as *yidams,* the personified "rivers to the Ocean of Being." The gods—Athena, Asclepios, Sophia, Shiva, Quetzalcoatl, and thousands of others—are those forces that have been crystallized in human cultures and worshipped as personalized emanations of a greater unknowable and unnameable power. Sometimes they assume a humanized form, as did Jesus, Krishna, Buddha, and Zoroaster. We may feel a particularly loving resonance with such beings who have been elevated to godhood. We may identify with their numinous power as well as their storied humanity. By virtue of this identification, we are evoked to become much more fully what we can be in the depth and breadth of our existence.

Virtually every culture has tapped into the WE ARE realm to acquire the energies of the archetypal stories that illumine rites of renewal and social transformation. For example, since the WE ARE realm is the residence of creation myths and the energies of origins, many cultures have their priests, priestesses, and kings enact the creation myth at the time of the New Year. They play the parts of the gods who conquer the principles of chaos, restoring order and re-creating the world. In this way they bring the Great Time of Creation into the punctual circadian time of the THIS IS ME realm. Thus Nature is restored and the psyche of both community and individual are granted the healing energies of new life. How radically different this is from our own New Year's Eve celebrations!

The realm of the WE ARE is also the source of patterns of innovation and creativity that manifest in the world of THIS IS ME. This culture of the depths, sometimes referred to as the *mundus imaginalis,* the imaginal world, or in the Arabic mystical tradition as the *alam al-mithal,* is as real as everyday, objective life—perhaps even more real, since it is the place where the forms and creations of your existential life are conceived. It coincides with the realm Plato has called "the world of forms" from which our local forms emerge. And sometimes you have to go through the black hole of the universe of yourself to get there.

My studies of many creative thinkers and artists point directly to their capacity to delve into these depth levels of reality. We might say, for example, that Einstein drew his insight into the nature of relativity and the discovery of the quantum universe not only from the workings of his own capacious and well-trained mind, but also from the great creative archetypal realm of the WE ARE, which stores the principles that source the creation of new ideas and forms. Whenever you come up with creative insights and solutions to problems, you, too, are tapping into this realm.

The WE ARE realm penetrates the veil of the THIS IS ME through your dreams, through fantasy, through prayer and meditation, while you are jogging, showering, or doing the dishes; indeed, at any time when the THIS IS ME realm lets down its guard. You don't have to go looking for it; you only need to open the door when it knocks.

Beyond and within the other two realms is the realm of the I AM, that is, Being itself, pure potency, a realm of love and organicity, the very stuff of reality. It is the realm many of us know as God. I do not mean the gods, for they live in the WE ARE, but rather, God as the Unity of Being. This is the I AM in "I AM THAT I AM," spoken by God in self-definition in the Old Testament, not to be confused with the "I" of the human ego. And it is the explicit inclusion of this realm that differentiates sacred psychology from many of the depth psychologies. Sacred psychology assumes that the inherent yearning in every human soul is to experience union with this ultimate reality.

In the optimal experience of the consonance of the three levels, the I AM floods into the WE ARE, priming the archetypal realm with its power. Then, in more familiar form, these archetypal stories and storied beings of the soul give inspiration to the health and creative life of the THIS IS ME. In turn, the THIS IS ME realm, operating in its creative fullness, charges the realm of the WE ARE, renewing the I AM, the Source of Being itself. When it happens, such a consonance brings about the ultimate therapeia, the healing of the soul.

The term *psychology* implies the use of a structured process based on a conscious developmental program to release the psyche from the constraints and limitations that inhibit its fullest realization. A sacred psychology, however, assumes that one's fullest realization comes from the living experience of union with God, which is then expressed through the forms of daily life. The WE ARE realm serves as the mediating field for the practice of this developmental program.

The leap from the bounded, conditioned, lensed reality of THIS IS ME to the Unity of Being of the I AM is too great for most people. There are spiritual paths, of course, that do make this leap, such as the one found in Zen Buddhism. But, in order to go beyond the restraints of the THIS IS ME, many people need the archetypal amplification of the personal-particular when it is drawn into the personal-universal of the WE ARE. In the state of extension that results from identity with the themes, myths, and stories of the archetype, if not with the archetype itself, one gains the enhanced sensibilities to receive the numinous presence of the I AM.

In the light of our discussion about the three realms of experience, what can we say about the nature of sacred psychology? What does it do? What are its effects? How is one trained in sacred psychology?

Sacred psychology asks how the THIS IS ME realm can be placed in the service of the I AM realm. How do you place the local self in the service of the Higher Self, where the immanent God resides? How do you tap into the great concentration of high evocative energy necessary to both motivate and fulfill the deep evolutionary processes of life? How do you transcend your local lensing and access the depths? How in the world do you find the passion to extol the possible when you're feeling no passion yourself?

Sacred psychology shows you that you are richer, deeper, stronger, and more a mystery than you know. The work of sacred psychology is to school you in your own depths. Your energies, power, stamina, and moral force seem limited only because your personal and cultural expectations set limits. These multifaceted expectations are formed by your family, your profession, your biology, your schools, your churches, your social organizations, and your nation. They help you set up your routines and they govern your automatic response patterns. All of these existential cultures are helpful, indeed crucial, to your well-being; but when they are permitted exclusively to define your life, then entropy and exhaustion soon follow.

Sacred psychology creates another kind of culture, which states what our daily cultures do not: that the horizon of our limits is infinitely expandable, that more is possible, and that what is perceived to be extraordinary is, in the larger framework of reality, both necessary and ordinary. In sacred psychology you may be introduced to the foreign culture of your own depths, to the WE ARE and I AM realms, perhaps for the first time. Yet this culture may be foreign or alien to you only because you have not visited it. Or you may have been warned, as the margins of medieval maps cautioned, "Here There Bee Monsters!"

Sacred psychology attempts to help you engender and nurture a deep familiarity with the culture of your own depth realities, which in virtually all traditions is assumed to exist autonomously and apart from your everyday reality. Sacred psychology says that this WE ARE culture of the depths is substantively real, as real as your everyday objective life, perhaps even more real, since it is the place where the forms and creations of your existential life are sourced. Here the great creative principles yearn at the crossroads of the realities, waiting to enter into time. Without this WE ARE realm to which sacred psychology provides access, we would have neither poetry nor music, neither art nor science, neither architecture nor agriculture, nor much of anything at all.

Tapping into this world does not guarantee personal sanctity or success. The history of genius, creativity, and the turned-on mind is filled with examples of people who were pretty foolish in their personal lives, yet who could access a world of such numinous creative form that our culture is much richer because of them. Witness Mozart, a great silly in his own way, who said of his own stupendous creativity that he did not know from whence it came, but thanked God that it was at least Mozartish. Such a statement does not imply that skill is irrelevant to inspiration. Mozart was one of the most skilled musicians who ever lived, but what he tapped into was deeper and richer than even he knew.

All of you have skills; if you hone them through training and practice and *then* gain access to these ontological depths, your creativity can rise exponentially. If, in addition to this, you also do your human homework, then you become more than a creative, interesting person; you also become a moral force for good.

What sacred psychology does is help you build the bridges that connect your everyday life with your depth life. It provides you with practices that quite literally reorchestrate your brain, your body, your nervous system. It elicits the evolutionary, latent codings within your body/mind/soul that have waited for tens of thousands of years to be activated—until various aspects of complexity, joined to crisis, joined to challenge, joined to our present point in history, converged to jolt you out of your sloth into the willingness to allow that which has been gestating in you for these many millennia to be born.

We are the fetuses of the future. Sacred psychology helps us to redesign this fetus. As fetus in our mother's womb, we had no choice about our physical development. In our present embryogenesis, not only do we have choice, but indeed we are invited to join Great Nature in the re-creation and the regeneration of ourselves neurologically, psychophysically, mentally, and emotionally.

Many of you have felt called, challenged, provoked in ways that perhaps you did not some years ago. Have you noticed a subtle acceleration of that calling, accompanied by a nausea of disgust over being stuck in the same old patterns? It would appear that the level of disgust is not just local. It is almost a species-wide disgust, a rising of planetary, cross-cultural bile. What is rising in you is not just impatience with the unskilled behaviors of your local self. It is almost like the nausea of the whole human species saying, "Enough already. It's time to grow!"

We have reason to believe that a little baby feels tremendous nausea at the time of being born, with all the tossing and turning and spinning down the vortex of the birth canal. Nausea both accompanies and accomplishes birth. It may be that nausea accomplishes what happens in sacred psychology with its emphasis on second birth, and that this is why the ritualization of rebirth plays so key a role in sacred psychology.

THE TRAININGS OF SACRED PSYCHOLOGY

The trainings of sacred psychology reorganize your circuitry so that you are able to receive the subtle and powerful forms and forces of the deep psyche and the larger universe. This reorganization allows you to receive all kinds of new programs, as well as activate the universal and evolutionary programs and patterns with which you are coded. These trainings must, therefore, include the following, each of which provides for considerable psychophysical and neurological restructuring of the body and brain.

Exercises in mind-full-ness and awakeness. By training to be awake to every moment, you switch off "robot" and enter into more conscious orchestration. This training includes practices in multimodal patterning and thinking, and the experience of doing many things at once to break the pattern of robot. When you consciously experience an overload of ideas, information, and events, you break the pattern of tunnel thought, tunnel vision, and tunnel sensibility. You temporarily exhaust the cortex so as to suspend the barriers between different structures of the mind.

Practice in the self-orchestration of states of consciousness. There is no such thing as an altered state of consciousness. Consciousness is always altering; that is its nature. But there are aspects of consciousness that you get stuck in, and then you go into robot. It is possible for you to learn to orchestrate the different states of your consciousness almost like a symphonic conductor. Then you can get into different dimensions of learning, knowing, and perceiving. Obviously, in a hyperalert state, when you are able to focus with great clarity, you are able to see the world very differently from the way you do in a state of dullness. In a state of deep quiet and centering, you know things differently from the way you know them in ordinary consciousness. In meditative states, the dwelling "in the center of things" brings greater brain recruitment into play so that there is more of you available to receive the great patterns into the physical template of your being.

Experience with the selective use and orchestration of energies. In the work of sacred psychology you are involved with the amplification of physical energies—neurological, psychophysical, chemical/electrical—and the interchange of these with energies from the deep source levels of being. The selective use of these energies is crucial; if you don't know how to use them, you're like a baby driving a huge truck. The use of such energy must be joined with compassion, service, and the rigorous practice of daily life as spiritual exercise. Unless this grounding exists, the local personality can become foolishly inflated.

Preparation of the mind and body for the reception of depth charges. This is what is often referred to as preparation for "transcendent experience" so that it can be assimilated in a healthy manner. If you don't extend the circuitry, chances are you are going to be blown out, or even become a "bliss ninny."

It's very easy to fall into bliss; we are only a fraction of a psychic centimeter away from it all the time. But we may be so unconscious of bliss that when we finally fall into it, we enter a stupor. How do we learn to raise our bliss tolerance without becoming ninnies?

One of the reasons we are not possessed by the passion for the possible is that we do not have a sense of the naturalness of ecstasy. If you watch a flower, a fish, a puppy, a kitty, the sun, the moon, or the wind whipping around, you know the state of bliss as innate and natural to the order of being. One reason we love nature is that it causes us, however briefly, to release the cramping hold of our local self and to relax into that natural state. The amplifying of bliss tolerance acts as a tonic for the whole system; it gives us the vital charge to continue in the work of self-transformation. Otherwise life is reduced to putting one foot in front of the other, day after day after day. The grace of bliss is as natural as breathing, but because we've forgotten this, we act as if we have no breath. We need to recover the sense of being breathed into union, which provides the impetus for us to do what we need to in the world.

The healing and wholing of the self and others. In the gaining of greater wholeness, healing happens, restoring balance. Thus the extraordinary is experienced as ordinary. You become a channel, or, if you will, a way *through which* the forces of wisdom and the forces of healing can manifest.

The training and extension of the interior proprioceptors. An inner sensing system is developed: visual, auditory, olfactory, gustatory, tactile. The psychospiritual organs are educated and extended so that one is able to access with heightened inner senses the realms of creative forms. There are various mappings and chartings of these organs; the Eastern chakra system drawn as wheels of light surrounding major endocrine centers is an example, and there are many others.

A charged, cooperative collectivity of heart. Sacred psychology makes use of an attuned community so that great physical, emotional, mental, and spiritual resources are tapped and integrated. Having worked one-to-one with several thousand research subjects, and having worked also for many years with hundreds of large groups representing a collective of several hundred thousand people, I have concluded that you can often go deep faster in community than in a one-to-one situation. This conclusion does not negate the need for the journey of the alone to the Alone; and working with a therapist or counselor can be critical to one's development, as is the practice of deep personal work. But there is something about the psychological, intellectual, and experiential richness of an attuned community that amplifies the possibilities manyfold. (Consider, for example, that in a group of fifty people you might have something like 2400 years of collective life experience to draw upon.)

The harvesting and orchestration of your polyphrenic self. This means the gaining of access to your inner crew. If schizophrenia is the disease of the human condition, then polyphrenia, the orchestration and integration of our many selves, may be the health.

Western culture is one of the few cultures that demands a limited and singular self. The genius of the child is to become what he beholds—dog, kitten, tree, bug, cloud. The child seeks understanding by incarnating the world. So as a child you were permitted to enjoy many and manifold selves. At a certain point they were declared unreal or inappropriate, and your genius for identity was truncated. In some, this loss of psychoecology, of being permitted to have leaky margins with reality at large, can result years later in pathology. Because the yearning of the manifold self to complexify is kept in a pressure cooker, it can eventually explode and fracture. If we can only recognize and encourage the healthy development and orchestration of our various selves, we will avoid much incipient neurosis and pathology.

Thus in sacred psychology we try to evoke what has been suppressed, the full harvest of the crew of many selves, and to do this in a healthy way so as not to fragment the self, but rather to gain access to the skills and genius of your various personae. With the polyphrenic self you are never lonely! You've got all of you. There's always a party of selves going on. You can say with Emerson or with Margaret Mead (who was, in my experience of her, the all-time polyphrenic lady), "I am never less alone than when alone, or less at leisure than when at leisure."

Tapping into the entelechy of the self. Entelechy, as I use it, refers to the dynamic purposiveness of the patterns of possibility encoded in each of us. Thus, it is the entelechy of an acorn to be an oak, it is the entelechy of a baby to be an adult, and of you to be the God only knows who or what. What happens in sacred psychology is the tapping into the entelechy of the self, the level most directly related to the Divine Self. With some, the experience of tapping into the entelechy is very quiet; with some it can be explosive; with others it is a steady unfolding. However it occurs, it is a purposive and powerful unfolding and recognition of your own potential.

This Entelechy Self is also the supreme orchestrator and ground of all of one's other selves, and serves as the protector and provider of balance and mental health amid the complex and polyphrenic structure of one's inner life. It is the Root Self, the ground of one's being, and the seeded, coded essence in you which contains both the patterns and the possibilities of your life. It is the operant angel, or in modern terms, the operant agent of the process of your present life, and the ordinary ego of your godly or extended life. *Again, the entelechy is the ordinary ego of your godly life, and the operant angel of your present life.*

Why have apparently so few people found their entelechy? Perhaps because, until recently, they didn't need to. As long as the planet herself was growing a nervous system, very few people really needed to find more than a tribal or communal version of the entelechy. The rules have changed since the bomb went off and we discovered we could destroy the entire planet. They've changed since we touched down on the moon—leaving the womb of the mother and coming back as co-creators. The rules have changed, and it means that what had been reserved for mystics, crazies, wise ones, or very creative people, has now become true for many. Our time has brought the democratization of the entelechy. It is as though part of the fetal coding has been activated, not unlike what occurs in the movie *2001: A Space Odyssey.* At a certain point in evolution, the great rectangle was encountered, activating an acceleration of evolution—a powerful image that still moves in the mythic dimensions of many people. The entelechy that used to be for the few, yet is coded in all, now is available for the many. Its rise in our time is part of the complexification of the mind of the planet herself. As we become more and more person/planet, there is less and less distinction between the questions, "What do I want from the universe?" and "What does the universe want from me?" The entelechy provides the bridging between the two agendas.

The exploration and enactment of archetypal/mythic stories and patterns. By studying and dramatizing the great universal myths, as well as by tapping into the place of your own mythology, you can discover where your personal story joins a universal Story. At this point the personal-particular of your everyday life opens to the personal-universal world of myth and archetype. You find yourself involved in broader contexts and richer, wiser formulations, with more abundant cues and patterns on which to draw and from which to redirect your life. This aspect of sacred psychology is consonant with the work of archetypal psychology found in the Hillman school of Jungian psychology. As I have developed it, the myth is seen as providing critical clues to the process of evolutionary unfolding, as well as revealing the deeper meanings behind the apparent incoherencies and meaninglessness of your experience. How do you take your woundings, your betrayals, your "holes" and make yourself holy instead of battered? This process involves the dramatic remythologizing of yourself and your life, and the gaining of a very different perspective on the woundings and betrayals, the varied road of trials of your own history.

In sacred psychology the work always involves both/and, plus much much more. This, however, is done with the understanding that we now have access to knowledge and process that may illuminate some of the material of traditional sacred psychologies in ways that could not have happened before. Biophysics, quantum-field physics, the ability to probe both atomic and galactic structures, the understanding of ecological systems, as well as many new scientific paradigms, show us that the old Hermetic dictum, "As above, so below," is true. There is a curious parallelism between physical realities and metaphysical structures.

Furthermore, our growing access to Eastern psychological, psychospiritual, and psychophysical systems extends our range of the mapping of consciousness and gives us a great many more techniques and psychotechnologies to add to the natural province of sacred psychology. Our increased knowledge of primal shamanic traditions—African, native Australian, Eskimo, and North and South American—gives us a great deal of available wisdom in working with natural forces. We are fortunate to recognize the power and complexity of such global knowings, for they add much to the present harvest of the genius of the whole human race and its call to move forward. That we are reaping such a rich human harvest augurs well for the continuation of the human experiment. The density of knowing that exists in our time is calling to us in ways that it could not have done before. Gnosis, the sacred loaded knowledge, is ready to enter into time; we have all been invited to become citizens in a universe larger than our aspirations and richer and more complex than all our dreams. Since this knowledge is now finding some justification in terms of scientific explanation, it appeals to our left brain. The aesthetics of it appeal to our right brain. The global brain, with its message of grow or die, appeals to our sense of planetary partnership, and our spirits are dogged by the Hound of Heaven who barks, "Get on with it!" That is why we are at a unique point in human history.

TRANSFORMATIVE RESULTS OF SACRED PSYCHOLOGY

If you fully engage the work of sacred psychology, you can expect certain phenomena to start appearing in your life. You may discover that your life has taken on added dimensions, just as Cambridge anthropologist Thomas Lethbridge did when he became involved in parapsychological activities: "From living a normal life in a three-dimensional world, I seem to have fallen through into one where there are more dimensions. The three-dimensional world goes on as usual; one simply has to adjust one's thinking to the other." You have a sense of living in nested realities. You are at once an atom, a molecule, a cell, an organism, a body, a soul, a beloved within the mind of God.

Part of the work of sacred psychology is to reeducate the brain and nervous system for reception of this nested reality. As you do this work regularly, you may notice some curious physiological phenomena such as energy rushes or perhaps significant mood changes. Such occurrences often indicate a change in your brain and nervous system, the creation of new electrochemical connections, and more dendritic growth than usual. These changes provide the necessary increase in complexity in your biological equipment, permitting you clearer access to larger realities without going into overload and feeling blown out. Thus this work deconditions you from old habit structures of mind and body and reeducates and refines your biological structures.

As you engage the work of sacred psychology more deeply, your old structural associations may put up quite a battle and the "sunset effect" will set in. (The "sunset effect" refers to the often-observed phenomenon that when old traditions, politics, or institutions are about to fade out, they generally cut loose with a blazing rush of activity that belies their coming mortality.) And so, at critical times of self-transformation, the sunset effect of the old habits of your life will blaze on your horizon, blaring, "No! No! No!" Every damning conceit, every roaring doubt that you have ever had will rise to gargantuan proportions. When this happens, try to observe it with candor and whimsy, without judgment, saying, "By God, there is a resistance because I'm about to go over." Furthermore, when the sun of the old order goes down, it may not necessarily stay down. No one gets off that easily. This is why it is helpful to do the work of sacred psychology within an attuned group or community so that you have a place to be nourished during the time of parenthesis between the old and new suns.

Doing the work of sacred psychology will move you from lackluster passivity into conscious orchestration of your life. You stop living what Keats referred to as a posthumous existence. As you move out of passivity, the usual forms of fatigue, depression, and despair which attend life in limbo will not occur with the same frequency or intensity. Instead, you may begin to notice occasional flashing states of unusual intenseness and aliveness, which in turn begin to extend themselves in time as your nervous system gets used to them. For some of you, the beginning of these states may be attended by melting moods of sudden excitement, vitality, even ecstasy. These may often have a timeless quality, for you are, in fact, operating out of more levels of your being, most of which do not belong in timed zones of the brain, body, or behavior. The categories of your being will be strained by the tensions of eternity. Eternity will have flooded the gates of your local timing, and you will realize both viscerally and intellectually that you live on many levels, of which everyday consciousness is only one. You will probably discover that the reason you felt the world was absurd or incomplete was that you viewed it from only one level of consciousness.

As we have discussed, you may experience the emergence of the entelechy of yourself in the community of yourselves. And it is very much an autonomous personality, this Entelechy Self, this high being, who may even be felt as the Beloved of the soul. It may begin to be experienced as a full personality initially, in most cases apart from you, almost like a guide, a beloved, or an angelic helper. You will learn to recognize shifts in energy or feeling states, announcements of its presence, and as you do, you become more skilled in allowing the psychological and physiological correlates of the Entelechy Self to occur. These correlates—meditation states, subtle attunement states, communion states—will facilitate the arrival of the High Self.

Finally, from the deep and timeless culture of sacred psychology, some of you may find yourselves accessing memories from many different places in time. You will, in effect, seem to tap into the aggregate of sacred psychology and the mind field of this aggregate, now virtually an archetype, a loaded presence. Archetypal sacred psychology seems to exist in the eternal present, which the intentional work of sacred psychology brings into time. So you will find yourself remembering, and it will seem to you that you are being helped in your memories.

A commitment to the transformational work of sacred psychology states formally and dramatically the evolutionary fact of your readiness and willingness to be born into an extended body, an amplified mind, a compassionate heart, a deepened and active soul, and a new life of high service to whomever and whatever comes your way. High service is never exclusive; it serves the God-in-Hiding in all forms of life, in every opportunity. Thus you are reborn with a much fuller instrument to be a citizen in a much larger universe, with the response-ability to help co-create the culture of extended reality, wherever you are.

PART TWO
Basic Practices

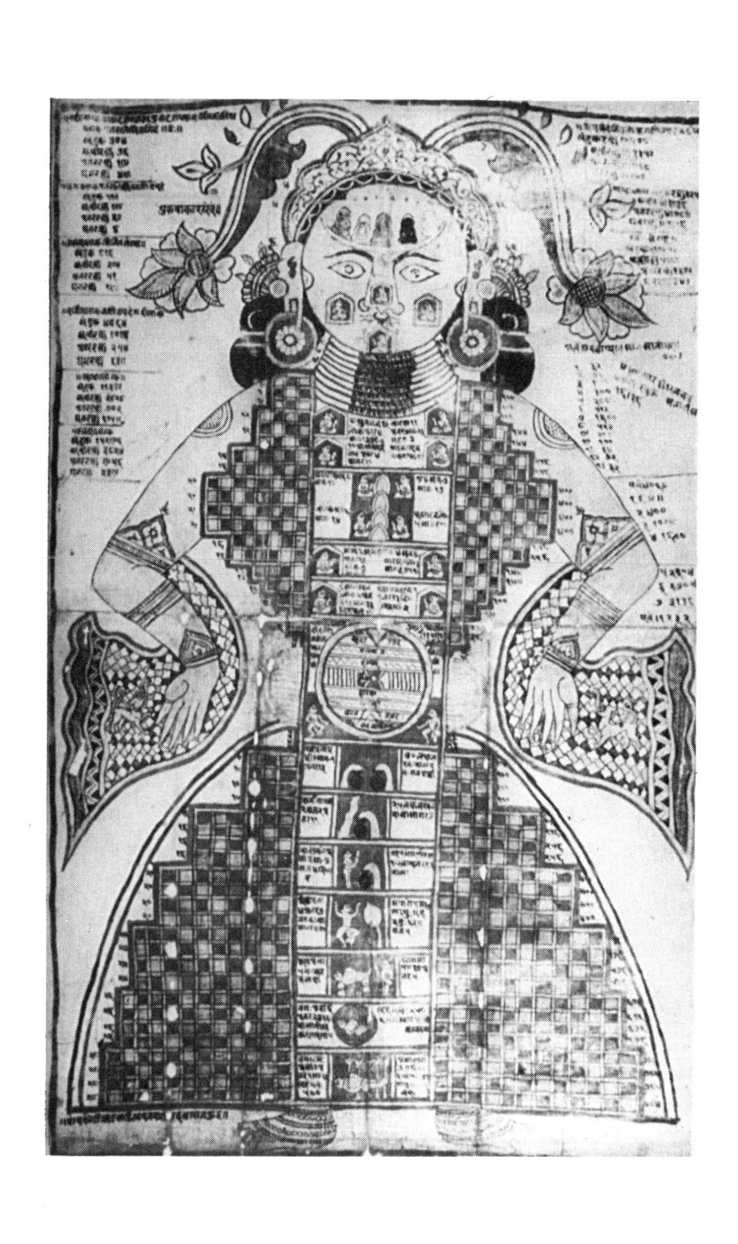

Overleaf: The torso of this Cosmic Person contains the heavens and the lower body contains the hells; the earth dwells in the middle world of the waist. The realm of liberated souls—the goal of life in Jain philosophy—corresponds to the head. Gouache on cloth, from Rajasthan, India; artist unknown; ca. A.D. 1800.

4

GUIDELINES TO BASIC PRACTICES

Sacred psychology is a practice, a way of perceiving and experiencing reality that can become internalized only through experience.

To evoke and develop your capacity for the practice of sacred psychology, this section is devoted entirely to processes that I have used as basic-foundation practices in my seminars. They have been used, separately and together, in all my teaching as initial preparation for the depth explorations elaborated on in Part Three and the journeys set forth in Part Four. The most important injunction that I can offer is: *Do the practices and processes.* Reading by itself is not an adequate substitute for the actual experience, no matter how vividly you read. You must also be willing to devote quality time to the practices. Doing them mindfully and with close attention to their physical, psychological, and other effects is equivalent to learning to drive a car before you head off on a cross-country trip, or like jogging five miles a day before you send in your application for the Boston Marathon. Just as learning to drive or jog will stand you in good stead whether or not you set out on a greater challenge, so, too, will consistent work with these practices enhance your functioning in many areas of life. Their greater aim, however, is to enable you to develop an awareness of and ready access to inner and outer realms that may have hitherto been unconscious and dormant.

These practices provide the training to be awake to every moment. This is an aspect of the *via positiva* nature of sacred psychology. The *via positiva* promotes growth and transformation through gaining the ability to orchestrate and integrate different states of consciousness, to use the senses and the body with greater awareness, and to tap the enormous richness of the imaginal realm. Thus you acquire patterns of knowledge expansive enough to incorporate multiple realities, and you come to recognize their spiritual genesis.

The *via negativa*, on the other hand, focuses attention on a single point or a special mantra until consciousness is totally without an object and enters into union with Being. Both paths lead to the same goal, and mystics and creative minds have often used a blending or alternation of these two methods.

One of the marvelous things about being alive today is that we enjoy a harvesting, not possible before this time, of the genius of many cultures. And from this diversity of genius, we are discovering universal forms of training for the practice of sacred psychology. A modern sacred psychology can draw on these universal patterns in ways that many of the earlier sacred psychologies could not, bound as they were to a specific locale and tradition. What is offered in this work is not a series of wholesale borrowings from other cultures and times, but rather the creation of new practices that seem appropriate to our time, drawn from the great common themes and ancient patterns of awakening.

The order in which the practices are presented is developmental, evoking a continuously deepening skill at contacting the sacred as a state of consciousness and a way of being, and integrating it richly and fully into your daily experience.

Each practice is preceded by a discussion of its relationship to the tradition and practice of sacred psychology. After you have worked with the practices in the order presented here and have gained a sense of familiarity and confidence about them, you can adapt them to any particular situation you may choose.*

GUIDELINES FOR DOING THE PROCESSES

INITIAL PREPARATION

It is essential to have a real familiarity with the introductory material of Part One of this book and also with the introduction to each process. Out of context, the practices can become trivial and meaningless, as can most activities. Within the context of sacred psychology, of ritual process, they assume their power and serve as deep training in transformational development.

*If you are new to this kind of work, you would be wise to explore, preferably within a small group, the more basic introductory exercises in my previous books: *Mind Games* and *Listening to the Body* (coauthored with Robert Masters), *The Possible Human*, and *Life Force*. All of these works are available in paperback.

ADAPTING THE PRACTICES TO SPECIFIC SITUATIONS

I would suggest that you do these practices initially as presented here. They have been tested and used in this form over the years in many diverse situations. After you are familiar with them, modify them to suit the group and situation. As you become familiar with these practices, you will find yourself co-creating them, imbuing them with new life and meaning so they do not become stale or routinized. Thus, for example, after an initial experience with evocative sound in the I AM, WE ARE, THIS IS ME process, you may choose to chant alone for ten to fifteen minutes as a daily practice, or with others at the beginning of each group meeting. You might also choose to select a portion of the work on extending the senses or the imaginal body and use it to shift perspective before tackling a particularly difficult situation.

THE IMPORTANCE OF DOING ALL THE PRACTICES

Change comes from engaging the variety of these processes, and doing them regularly. Since they work together, apparently interacting at depth levels, it is important to *do all of them,* not just those which have the most immediate appeal.

WORKING IN A GROUP

Sacred psychology is best practiced in a group. (This, like anything else I might say, is not true for everyone. If you are a natural hermit, skip to the next section.) Indeed sacred psychology has always been the practice of a community. This community may take any form: your family, friends, colleagues, students, clients. A consistent commitment to the group will enhance the experience for all.

People in community stimulate, support, and evoke each other. In their diverse reactions, they prime a diverse set of responses on the part of all. Groups also help to eradicate the tyranny of the dominant individual's perception—reflected in such smug statements as "If it is good enough for me, it is good enough for you," or "What's sauce for the goose is sauce for the gander," or "Outside of the Church there is no truth." I do not deny the importance of consensus and commonalities, but I am suggesting that our differences are enriching. Thank God I need not be limited to my own experience but may share in yours! As we recognize the enormous variety and richness of the realm of the sacred in others, we are more able to drop simplistic judgments and stand in awe before the abundance and variety of life.

By practicing sacred psychology in a group, you also bypass one of the greatest and most insidious human potentials—the potential for sloth. Self-discipline and good intentions have a way of evaporating without some consistent external commitment to and challenge by other members of our species. Why do people go to exercise classes when they can more easily and cheaply listen to a tape? To avoid the formidable foe of entropy! The practice of sacred psychology, which challenges well-entrenched habit patterns of the mind, psyche, and body, requires allies. Resistance to change is natural, maybe even healthy, but the only way I know to overcome it is through regular participation in the loving, celebrating company of co-journeyers.

In forming a group, try to involve people who, in their faith in the future of humanity and the planet, are willing to work together with constancy and caring to develop and extend the sacred in daily life. Narcissists, psychic exhibitionists, and "poor me's" may offer more challenge and distraction than you need.

CREATING SACRED TIME AND SACRED SPACE

Setting aside a regular time and place for working on sacred psychology allows for a greater integration of the material. You meet one evening a week, one weekend a month, or according to whatever schedule works best for all concerned.

Remove irrelevant clutter from the space so that it is relaxing and soothing. Mood can be established through the appropriate use of music. When specific pieces or styles of music are needed for the process itself, this is indicated at the beginning of the instructions under "Materials Needed."

Many of the basic practices have a strong ritual component that, when recognized, imbues them with new meaning and power. The word *ritual* comes from the Sanskrit *rita,* which refers to both art and order. Like all real art, ritual provides organic order, a pattern of dynamic expression through which the energy of an event or series of events can flow in an evolutionary process toward larger meaning or a new stage or level of life. It offers ways in which your transitions are illuminated. When occurring in time and space that are prepared and understood as sacred, ritual has the power to help you move to the next stage of your life journey. Once arrived, you know by the difference you perceive in yourself and your surroundings that you are there.

If you're going to engage the nervous system in the work of growth and transformation, you've got to get the more recalcitrant parts of the brain to comply with your wishes. Otherwise you will be stuck in the usual conditionings and habituations of the older parts of the brain. The need for ritual, encoded in the old, reptilian brain, is insistent in its demands for expression. The reptilian brain also needs security and repetition, the old mammalian midbrain needs emotional charges, and the cognitive neocortex needs intellectual stimulation. If you court all these parts of your brain, your body will listen to you! A ritual engages the fullness of your whole being.

One significant element of ritual is the use of sacred repetitions, mantras, zikrs, affirmations. These function as rhythms of awakening, songs sung to lure the consent of the creature self.

Ritual is also created through the body. Imbuing your gestures with sacred intention restores balance and presence. Aligning your body movements with patterns of nature and cosmos can invoke the participation of archetypal beings, and of your own high self. You cannot be in "low self" at the same time that you are performing sacred movement.

Other ritual procedures may be conducted to remind the deeper recesses in each person participating that the time and space are "sacred." Such rituals put everyone "on notice" that they are safe to take the inward journey, and they help to evoke the personal feelings that signal the psyche to open the doorway to the inner realms. These procedures might include a provision for ritual washing, a cleansing of the space with incense, or a group creation of a sound field through the simple chanting of "OM." An agreement to limit conversation and to practice the art of mental, emotional, and vocal silence is also suggested for supporting the sacrality of the space and time. This latter practice is a challenge for all those who erroneously believe that their existence is predicated upon the constant, and often meaningless, movement of their thoughts, feelings, and tongues. A final technique for creating a mood of the sacred is to greet each other according to the Hindu tradition of prayerfully folding your hands before your heart, looking into the eyes of another, and quietly saying, "*Namasté.*" This greeting means, roughly, "The god within me greets the god within you."

THE ROLE OF THE GUIDE

The role of the guide is critical. This role may be held by one person or shared among members of the community. Although you will discover what works best as you go along, remember that the guide needs to be

- thoroughly familiar with the material,
- committed to sacred psychology,
- attentive to the timing of the group,
- respectful of the experience of everyone.

The guide is not to interpret the experience of others, but rather to trust the process and the enormous individual variations that are possible.

In group work it is important that you do not take the role of therapist and that you caution everyone involved against doing so. Professional therapists may find this very difficult, but it is important that they practice their profession only during regular working hours. Comments overheard, despite repeated injunctions to refrain from making them, include "You really are blocked!" or "I can see some enormous anger stored up there." Such comments are inappropriate because the acceptance of people for who and what they are is critical to the practice of sacred psychology. Each person is perfectly capable of interpreting his or her own experience and can invite the comments of others if desired. If a person should consistently want more response from the group than is appropriate, encourage her or him to set up an outside appointment with one or more group members.

WAYS OF IMAGING

The guide should know that everyone images in different ways. Some may actually see images as though they were on a screen; others will "sense" them; still others may feel they "get nothing at all." Often those who seem to "get nothing" later find themselves deeply integrating the practice of sacred psychology into everyday life. Fabulous mythic images that astonish you and cause envy in your more prosaic colleagues may entertain and titillate, but they are not necessarily the emblem of "success." Success, if there is such a thing, lies in your capacity to incorporate the processes of sacred psychology into your daily activities and to evoke the God-in-Hiding in those you meet along the way.

DEEPENING AND INTEGRATING YOUR PRACTICE

After the process has been completed, you may take some private time to reflect upon and record your experience. Your understanding of sacred psychology will deepen as you keep a journal, upon annotating your recollections with drawings, musings, quotes, questions, and whatever else asks to be written down. This kind of expression will engage you in the most fascinating kind of conversation there is—the conversation with the inhabitants of your own inner crew.

In a group, the experience may be shared with one or two others, or, if the group is small enough, with the group as a whole. While some may feel reluctant to share in this way, I have found that the process of verbal sharing deepens the experience for all concerned, and a situation that allows for maximum expression and participation should be encouraged.

This personal sharing is often enhanced by your journal work. If a group works together for a number of sessions, it can be valuable for everyone if each person occasionally chooses an insightful passage from his or her journal to read aloud to the entire group.

WORKING ALONE

Warnings against working alone have already been abundantly stated, yet certainly there are those for whom this is an appropriate path. Having at least one other person with whom you can consistently share your experience will help to keep you from the traps of isolation and inflation. Persistent and thorough journal writing is doubly important to the person working alone.

To give yourself the complete experience of these sacred psychology processes, tape record the longer ones before you begin. As you read the exercises into the tape recorder, try to imagine them vividly so that you allow sufficient timing in the pauses for the performance of part of the exercise.

REASONS FOR DOING THE PROCESSES

The processes are designed to help you amplify your natural potential and your capacity for experiencing the sacred, and to restore your connection to the deep source levels of being. Through them you learn to prepare the mind and body for the receiving of "transcendent" experience. Thus work with these practices is intended to train you in the extended use of your sacred birthright, allowing you to be present consciously in the splendor of your being.

While it is impossible to attribute specific results to any one practice, consistent and committed work with the whole has led many to report the results that follow here.

An expanded and deepened perception may lead you to experience what previously appeared ordinary and routine as extraordinary and novel. When you have extended your imaginal sensorium, your physical sensorium may be refreshed and move away from automatic, allowing you to experience the sensory world more enthusiastically. Having been a great bird in your imaginal body, the patterns and texture of the wind, sky, and earth may be imbued with greater meaning. Some find that a sense of wonder and delight is restored as vitality is renewed, and much that has been relegated to the unconscious becomes available again. When you incarnate the archetypes, irritating problems seem to seek their own resolution as another level of reality offers a new perspective. You may feel yourself to be more capable than you had previously thought yourself to be.

Newly discovered capacities and powers, however, must be bridged to everyday consensual where they are joined to compassionate service and rigorous practice of daily living as spiritual exercise. Unless there is this grounding in service, love, and discipline, the local personality can run amok.

5

EXTENDING THE SENSES

We have lost the wonder of the inner and outer worlds that is our legacy and our vehicle to extended realities. It is essential to your practice of sacred psychology that you restore your inner and outer sensing to a fuller use so that you may look upon the world with wonder and astonishment and appreciate all others in the fullness of their human and divine essence. To touch the sacred you must touch the divinity of skin and bark; to see God you must sense the numinous in all things. The divine-human perception becomes reciprocal. Or, as Meister Eckhart, that great mentor of sacred psychology, once put it, "The eye by which I see God is the same eye by which God sees me."

There is much to suggest that more "primitive" peoples used their sensorium with much greater awareness than the "civilized" humans of today. Jean Auel, in *The Valley of the Horses,* reminds us of this in her description of a woman of the Paleolithic era:

> All her senses were alert. She listened for sounds of breathing or small scufflings; looked to see if there were any telltale signs of recent habitation; smelled the air for the distinctive odors of carnivorous animals, or fresh scat, or gamey meat, opening her mouth to allow her taste buds to catch the scent; let her bare skin detect any sense of warmth that might come from the cave; and allowed intuition to guide her as she noiselessly approached the opening. She stayed close to the wall, crept up on the dark hole, and looked in.[1]

It is only a metaphorical quarter turn from this heightened awareness to the sensing of unseen information, taking in with inner proprioceptors the information that may be coming to you from a flow-pattern of electrons, or "feeling" an evolutionary pulse coming to you from beyond the ordinary dimensions of space and time.

Without finely tuned senses, both your inner and outer life become sterile, robotized. "Nothing" ever happens to you, because you have dulled your capacity to perceive—and dulled conception is not far behind. On the other hand, people who feel more, listen more deeply, have greater vision, and embrace the richness of their inner and outer lives experience a creative universe in which they find themselves daily partners of Creation.

Thus, in this process, you will evoke the power of "in"-sight as well as outer vision, learn to listen to your inner guides as well as freshen your sense of sound, remember how to be deeply touched as well as develop your tactile sense. So, too, will you enhance your "sense" of space and time, extending your capacity to reach out and harvest your heritage across the boundaries of calendrical time. In doing so you will release the learned constraints of the local self, bringing to consciousness those perceptions that you may have had as a child but which have been conditioned out of you, and restoring your sense of wonder and connectedness. With this restored and extended sensorium, one of the doors to the realm of sacred psychology is opened to you.

The Kinesthetic Body

In this process we will be using what I have called the "kinesthetic body" (from the Greek: *kinema*—motion, and *esthesia*—sensing). It is the body image encoded in the motor cortex of the brain, but which is experienced as the *felt* body of muscular imagination. The experience of the kinesthetic body is familiar to athletes and musicians who rehearse inwardly when not actually performing their respective skills. Many of them seem to have an experience in this kinesthetic rehearsal almost as vivid as the actual physical engagement. Sometimes, too, watching an artistic or athletic event will so engage you that you will feel kinesthetically that you are actually participating in the event. Thus the boxing match or the adventure movie or the tenor reaching for high C can leave you physically elated or exhausted.

You may want to practice using the kinesthetic body if you are not already familiar with this phenomenon. (The theory behind the practice of using the kinesthetic body is discussed at length in my book *The Possible Human,* and exercises are provided to help in its development.) The exercise below is a brief developmental practice similar to that found in *The Possible Human*. In preparation for the more complex kinesthetic aspects contained in the process "Extending the Senses," it is advised, in any case, that the individual or the group practice the kinesthetic body even if they are already familiar with its tenets.

TIME: 20 minutes.

MATERIALS NEEDED: You will need only a small area of clear floor space and comfortable clothing. Wear soft, flexible footwear, or go barefoot so you can more easily sense the movement throughout the body.

INSTRUCTIONS FOR WORKING ALONE: If you are working alone, you will want to read these instructions onto an audiotape, pausing to leave time for the movement. If you are the guide in a group, you will want to remain constantly alert to the time required by the participants for the movement.

SCRIPT FOR THE GUIDE: Before you begin, stand up, get a sense of your body as it is, at rest, quiet, ready to experience.

Now raise your *real* right arm over your head and feel the stretching of muscles throughout the arm and the torso as you do so. (Pause, allowing time for complete feeling.) Now lower your arm. Repeat this process of raising your right arm several times, remembering to concentrate on the feeling of the movement within the body.

Now sense your right arm as clearly as you can with your muscular imagination (pause), and then stretch this *kinesthetic* right arm—that is, the arm of muscular imagination—over your head, trying to experience it as vividly as you sensed the real one. Now lower your kinesthetic right arm.

Alternate several times between stretching with your real right arm and your kinesthetic right arm. (Longer pause.)

Do the same thing with your real left arm and your kinesthetic left arm, always remembering to experience your kinesthetic arm with as much reality as you had when stretching your real arm.

Do the same thing, alternately stretching your real and kinesthetic arms.

Let your real shoulders make circular movements forward, down, and around, like spinning windmills, remembering to concentrate on the *feeling* of the movement.

Now do the same thing with your kinesthetic shoulders, trying to feel the same forward circular movement that you felt with your real shoulders.

Alternate between real and kinesthetic movements.

Let your real shoulders circle in a backward movement.

Do the same thing kinesthetically.

Alternate.

Now with your real body, make a fencing lunge to the right. Come back to center. Repeat this several times.

Now lunge to the right with your kinesthetic body. Come back to center.

Alternate several times between your real and your kinesthetic body as you lunge to the right and back to center.

Do the same thing with a fencing lunge to the left.

Follow this sequence:

Real body lunges to the right. Back to center. Real body lunges to the left. Back to center.

Kinesthetic body lunges to the left. Back to center.

Real body lunges to the left. Back to center.

Kinesthetic body lunges to the right and comes back.

Real body lunges to the right and comes back. Real body lunges to the left and comes back.

Now, at the same time, your kinesthetic body lunges to the right and your real body lunges to the left. Back to center.

Now lunge with your real body to the right and your kinesthetic body to the left. Come back to center.

Now alternate lunging simultaneously with the kinesthetic body in one direction and the real body in the other. Do this a number of times.

Rest.

(Feel free to experiment with this process, utilizing as many different movements as you like. Movements can include jumping up and down in your physical body, followed by jumping up and down as vividly as possible in your kinesthetic imagination. Another kind of practice could involve going back and forth between the real and the kinesthetic bodies while raising and lowering your arms, spinning slowly in one direction and then in the other, and so forth. Gradually you will notice the sense of the kinesthetic body getting stronger until it is almost as vividly sensed as the actual physical body.)

The Extended Sensorium

With this kinesthetic preparation you are ready for the more complex exercise in the extended sensorium. While it is designed to be developmental, and therefore to be done as a whole, the earlier parts of the exercise may be adapted as a part of your daily practice. They are particularly effective for alerting the brain and body when you first wake up or when you are feeling stuck or tired. After a while, even playing the same music used in the exercise will restore your sense of well-being.

The Guide for this process (and any other process in this book) should review the "How-To" section above and be familiar with the material she or he will be guiding. In this particular process the guide must adjust the pace of speaking to maintain a focused and mindful mood throughout, being careful to allow sufficent time for the different processes to be experienced. As with all these processes, observing the participants in the exercise is the key to appropriate timing.

TIME: 35–45 minutes.

MUSIC: Suggested music is Jean Michel Jarre's *Equinoxe* followed, where indicated, by Vangelis's "Eric's Theme" from *Chariots of Fire*.

INSTRUCTIONS FOR WORKING ALONE: Modifications for doing the exercise alone are included in the notes within the exercise. You will need to tape the exercise, as well as the accompanying music, before you begin. A mirror will be useful.

PART 1
Parting the Stars and Giving Yourself Away

SCRIPT FOR THE GUIDE: (To be read aloud, slowly, with constant attention to "right timing.") We are now going to enhance and refine the senses, both inner and outer. Then, with these senses, the extended being that is you will be able to meet and see the extended being in the other. Find a place in the room where you have enough space to extend your arms in all directions.

(Note: Begin music, the opening passage of *Equinoxe* here.) You begin by becoming the source of creation at the center of the universe. Standing and becoming fully balanced, close your eyes and begin to focus on your breathing. Sense each inhalation filling you with *prana,* the energy of the life force, of Creation itself. (Pause, waiting until all are breathing easily.)

Now bring your arms to shoulder level and, placing your hands facing outward on your chest, begin to part the stars as you slowly extend your arms in a vast arc until they meet behind you. As you do this you will feel and image the planets and the stars flowing from and through your fingers. Reach back and clasp your hands behind you and bow partway in reverence to Creation, your clasped hands rising behind you toward the ceiling.

Straighten up now and come back to center. Again, bring your hands to your chest and slowly part the stars, feeling planets and creatures and life in myriad forms flowing from your fingers. Reach behind you and clasp your hands, these hands of creation, and bow even more deeply in reverence to Creation, letting your clasped hands rise above your head.

Come back up to center. Again parting the stars, feel realities flowing from your fingers. Stars and planets, whole galaxies even, streaming from your hands until they are clasped behind you. And bow as deeply as you can in reverence to Creation.

Come back up to center. Step out with *your right leg toward the rightward worlds* and part the stars, feeling the life of planets, the life of suns, streaming from your hands. Reaching behind you, clasp your hands and bow as deeply as you can in reverence to Creation, raising your clasped hands behind you.

Come back to center. Step out now with *your left foot to the leftward worlds* and part the stars, feeling the planets, the suns, the galaxies, and new forms of life stream from your hands. Reach behind you and clasp your godly hands, bowing as deeply as you can, raising your clasped hands behind you as high as they can go, in reverence to Creation.

Come up and become centered. Place your right hand over your heart and make a fencing lunge to the right as you fling your right hand outward from your heart, giving yourself away.

Come back now to center. Once again, lunge and fling your hand out from your heart, giving yourself away. You give yourself away in service to the universe, and you grow from the giving. Come back to center.

Now in your kinesthetic body, fully imagine giving yourself away. Feel the movement just as vividly as you would if you were doing it physically. And come back to center. In your real body, lunge and fling your right hand out from your heart, giving yourself away. And come back to center. And in the kinesthetic body, do the same, giving yourself away.

And now let your physical body lunge into your kinesthetic body, so that you have the two bodies, the physical and the kinesthetic, there together.

Now extend your physical hand into the space in front of you, continuing to keep your eyes closed. As you move your physical hand, feel your kinesthetic fingers move way out beyond your hand so that you can caress the walls. Raise your physical hand toward the ceiling and feel with your lengthened kinesthetic fingers the texture of the ceiling. Extend your physical hand to the wall and kinesthetically sense the walls. Now do the same with the surface of the floor. Let your kinesthetic hand extend beyond your physical hand, moving out in an arc over the other people here, feeling their heads and their hair, caressing their heads with your kinesthetic hand.*

And now come back to center and bring your left hand to your heart; and, with a great lunge to the left, fling your left hand away from your heart, giving yourself away. And come back. And again, as a god, give yourself away, for that is what gods do: "Here, take all of me!" Give yourself into Creation. And come back to center.

Now in your kinesthetic body, give yourself away. And return to center. And in the physical body, give yourself away. And back. And in the kinesthetic body, give yourself away.

Let your physical body now move into your kinesthetic body. The kines-

*If you are doing this exercise alone, you may wish to touch kinesthetically various objects in the room that have special meaning for you.

thetic body grows inches and feet beyond your physical body so that you feel the wall with your kinesthetic fingers as you extend your physical hand toward the wall. Now do the same toward the ceiling and the floor. Now with your kinesthetic left hand, feel the heads and shoulders of all the others present.

(Note: Again, if you are doing this alone, adapt this part of the exercise to your situation.)

PART 2
Extending the Five Senses

Guide: Come back to center. Bring your hands, palms facing each other, an inch apart and sense the flow of life between your hands, consciously sending suggestions to strengthen the energy flow between your hands. Allow the hands to move slowly apart and then toward each other again to stimulate the flow. (Allow sufficient time for this.)

Bring those charged physical hands up to your eyes and, without touching your eyes, let the kinesthetic fingers lengthen and gently reach into your physical eyes, massaging them, improving them, sharpening your physical vision. Also let them enhance your inner vision as well, the vision that enables you to sense the great patterns and meanings behind things. The life energy working through your hands, real and kinesthetic, reaches deep into the sensory centers, the brain centers of the eyes, sharpening both outer and inner vision.

Now bring your fingers to about a half inch from your ears. Reach with your lengthened kinesthetic fingers into your ears, activating the sense of hearing and also activating your ability to listen on many levels, on many frequencies, so that you can hear the rhythms of awakening coursing through the land. Activate hearing now so that you can listen with the ears of the heart, the ears of the mind, the ears of the soul. With your kinesthetic fingers activating hearing, clarify your capacity to listen deeply to others, to truly hear what is being said: the messages in the rain, the rhythms of the planet, the music of the stars, the voice of the gods, the heartbeat of Creation. And know that it is so.

Reach now into your nostrils with your kinesthetic fingers, clearing and activating the full use of your nasal passages and olfactory centers and exercising the capacity to sniff out a variety of interesting aromas. Clarify these capacities so that air as *inspiration* can be taken in deeply, in great clear draughts. Prana, the vital air of Creation that moves throughout the universe, is also taken in so that each breath activates the life force within you. Breathe in deeply now, knowing that the air is also the vital life force of Creation, so that clarifying breath and creative life are being taken in with each breath. And all knowing is going in through the nose.

Now open your mouth and place your fingers about an inch from your tongue. Let your extended kinesthetic fingers reach in and activate the taste buds so that your palate of taste buds is like a palette by Michelangelo—so many subtleties of taste, as if microscopic master chefs are in each taste bud.

Extend now the sense of inner taste, savoring the pleasures of your inner knowing. Actually taste this pleasure now.

Since the tongue is the instrument of expression, of words, clarify your ability to communicate. Just stick your tongue out and tap gently on it, both with your real fingers and kinesthetically, and feel that the tapping is like a keying—like the coding of a great biocomputer—so that you are tapping in the capacity to be filled with high speech, filled with the communication that you need to express. Tapping, tapping, and actually touching new keys, new keys of transmission of communication, releasing what you really wish to say from your depths. And feel the tongue extended, connected with the source level of knowledge that can communicate through your tongue the fullness of your knowing.

And now begin to move your physical and kinesthetically amplified hands over your skin so that your tactile sense, your sense of being in communication and resonance with the pressures and the caresses of the universe is amplified. Reach out and touch another person who is nearby. Now kinesthetically touch someone who is not in the room, who may be distant both in space and time so that your touch can transcend both space and time—knowing that your hands have the touch of gods. And feel your own skin and sense of touch being deeply activated so that you can both receive deeply and send fully.

PART 3
Improving Other Functions

Guide (continuing): *In the next minute of clock time,* reach into other organ systems—the reproductive system, the digestive system, the lungs, the liver—and give abundant life wherever you may need it. Reach in with your hands kinesthetically, and begin now to improve the quality of whatever organ systems need enhancement. If, for example, some internal organ or process is not functioning well or you have a health problem, reach in kinesthetically to the relevant part of your body and have a sense of activating its capacity for health.

And now, with your kinesthetic fingers, reach into your heart, massaging your heart, holding your heart in your kinesthetic hands, and feeling your hands holding your heart. You are holding the heart that is beating the core of Creation and of existence, that is sending out love to all beings, beating rich blood without blocking, feeling the heartfulness of life, giving and receiving emotion. Boom-boom. Boom-boom. Give-receive. Give-receive. And know yourself as Great Heart, O Noble One!

Now reach out and feel the fields of life around you. Open yourself to these fields, filled with information, which can pour into you the necessary extensions of energy and knowledge you need. Actually hold your hands like a great cup, a great Grail, about twelve inches from your head and feel that your hands are receiving that energy of life and light and information and knowing and reenergizing. Feel that you are being flooded and filled with these energy fields that are giving you the appropriate knowledge to live in the fullness of your being.

And come back now to center, filled with these extended perceptions.

PART 4
Extending in Time and Touching the Lives of the Ancestors

Guide (continuing): Know that as you can extend yourself in space, so, too, you can extend yourself across time. Bring your hands together now, let us meet and harvest the essence of the lives of our ancestors. The right hand represents the World of the Fathers. The left hand, the World of the Mothers.

Bring your hands about a half inch apart in front of you and slowly, slowly bring them apart. Find yourself caressing and harvesting and blessing the essence of the lives of your ancestors, the world of your father's side on the right, the world of your mother's side on the left.

Let this blessing occur so that you are bringing a glory of recognition, of perspective, and a rich and noble honoring to these ancestors. Your hands, gradually moving out, moving out, go back a hundred years to your great grandparents and to their ancestors before them. Find, somehow, the textures of these lives as you caress all these different cultures, all these different kinds of lives—the lives of farmers and shopkeepers, serfs and saints, rowdies and kings, bakers, masons, and fisher folk—touching and honoring them all.

Caress their lives, honoring and giving them the deep empowerment that perhaps they never knew—so that in some sense, back there in the seventeenth or the thirteenth or the fifth century, or 3000 years ago, they stop hoeing in the field, look up, and think, "Some god has touched me! And my life feels better now. It feels like it has some purpose." And it is you, reaching into their time, who is the god doing the honoring now, as you touch and illumine the lives of your ancestors.

Harvesting, caressing, blessing the lives of your ancestors, continue until you stand with your chest out and your arms way behind you like a great ship borne up on the sea. You are the prow of the Ship of Ancestors, carrying the lives of thousands of years. Feeling yourself proud, borne up, take several steps forward, knowing that with this harvest of the richness of so many lives, you can go forward now. And walk now several steps into your future.

Slowly now, bring these ancestors into your present life. Slowly harvest the essence of their lives by bringing your arms together until your hands are crossed on your chest. And you have brought home and recognized, honored and deepened the genesis that has made you, the ancestral world that confirms you and says, "You are now the prow of the Ship of Ancestors." And know the poignancy of all these lives that have now been taken into your own, giving you of their mystery, their wisdom, their pain, their craft, their knowing.

PART 5
Dancing the Extended Life

Guide: Now with your eyes closed, let your hands come to your sides. Filled with the Greater Story, filled with a thousand stories, you have amplified and extended your latent senses—your eyes, your ears, your taste buds, your nose, your tactility, your fields of life, your heart, your liver, your inner organs, and your mind. You have harvested the genius and journeys of your ancestors. Now, filled with life, begin to dance backward and forward with your eyes closed. Dance and feel the great connections of life among and through you, using your arms to sense the now-extended life fields of others. (Let the dancing continue for about five minutes.)

(Note: If you are doing this exercise alone, continue to dance for a while, sensing the fields around and within yourself as you move, letting your extended awareness flood every cell of your body. After five minutes or so [having taped the music so that *Equinoxe* ends after about five minutes and "Eric's Theme" from *Chariots of Fire* or other celebrational and joyous music begins] you will slowly open your eyes and stand in front of a mirror. See now the person in the mirror as if for the first time, seeing in that being the God-in-Hiding. So, too, that being in the mirror will recognize you as the God-in-Hiding.)

Guide: Slowly, continuing to keep your eyes closed, find a partner and dance with that partner, touching the fields of life around one another. Continue dancing together for the next several minutes with your eyes closed.

(Note: If partners are not found within several minutes, the guide can help by bringing partners together, reminding the participants not to open their eyes.)

PART 6
Meeting Another in Extended Space and Time

Guide: Continue to keep your eyes closed and become still, standing close together. In a few moments, but not yet, this music will end and other music will begin. When the other music begins, I want you to take each other's hands, staying very still together. You will then open your eyes and see each other from the perspective of one looking now with extended senses and ways of knowing. You will see in the other all of time, all of history, all of the expressions of human existence. You will sense the Ship of Ancestors behind each person. But mostly you will see and be seen as the eternal human and the godseed in the world.

When the music changes, open your eyes, and without speaking, receive the fullness of humanity that is in the other, receive the godseed in the world.

Now open your eyes, in wonder and astonishment before the other, and see the godseed, the divine essence inherent in the humanity of the other.

("Eric's Theme" from *Chariots of Fire* is used here.)

Guide: When the music ends, sit with your partner and share what you have just experienced.

Allow from ten to fifteen minutes for sharing the experience. At the end, the guide may choose to invite the pairs to share with the larger group before formally closing the practice.

6

TRAINING THE CREATIVE IMAGINATION

Critical to any practice of sacred psychology is training in multiple imageries to facilitate the inner realism of journeys of the soul. In Eastern religious traditions, which include an integrated practical psychology and philosophy, many techniques are used to develop creative imagination.

In both Mahayana and Vajrayana Buddhist practice, for example, one learns to build up the most precise and complex images of Buddhas and Boddhisattva figures so that the interior image has as much reality as if that image were seen and known externally. Then these "living" inner divine teachers become one's guides to the deeper levels of human and divine experience. The meditative experience of these Buddhist schools developed the most intricate system of focusing on internally held symbols and sounds thought to have evolved from the archetypal depths of human consciousness. This focusing, when developed, has the effect of taking the student back to those depths for renewal and spiritual awakening.

As we shall see in the story of Jalaloddin Rumi, Sufi practice also, taught intensive modes of actively engaging the imaginal realms of the *alam al mithal* wherein one was able to "live" and learn in archetypal realities. In many esoteric schools, from the ancient Egyptian mystery schools to modern theosophical movements, training in internal imageries is critical to their practice of engaging the inner gnosis.

With the rise of Jungian and archetypal psychologies in the Western world, the creative imagination, once thought to be dangerously hallucinatory, is again being extolled and probed for its inherent wisdom. So recent is its return to legitimacy, however, that most Western people find that they have little skill and less success in activating imagery. What used to be second nature to the majority of humankind now has to be relearned in its most basic essentials. But the benefits of this relearning provide us with an important and valuable mode of accessing knowledge.

The following process is a basic training in relearning imagistic thinking. It is presented as a dyadic form, for we have found in our research that people will learn these processes better if they occur as challenge and response, rather than as guided imagery or hypnotic induction. The learning is progressive, beginning with the five senses, going on to more complex and compound imagery, and ending in a mutually shared journey like those practiced by sacred psychologies the world over. The final journey prepares one to access the inner gnosis of archetypal realms. The dyadic form, in which two people are directed to enrich and evoke each other's quest, minimizes the potential for stuckness and psychic recalcitrance often experienced by the pilgrim on a solitary journey.

Relearning Imagistic Thinking

For the purpose of demonstration, this process generally requires that there be two guides, or a main guide and someone who demonstrates the process with him or her. If this is not possible, then the guide will assume two roles for the sake of demonstration, playing the parts of both A and B. The process cannot be performed alone but needs two people to be successful. If you are doing this with one other person, both of you should familiarize yourselves with the Guide's demonstration as described below, and take each other through the process of developing inner imageries.

TIME: 1 hour.

MATERIALS NEEDED: None.

Guide: Find a partner and sit opposite each other. Begin by breathing together and attuning to each other's presence. We want you to ask each other to sense or imagine a variety of sensory images in the manner we will demonstrate. Most people tend to have certain senses for which they have strong imagery, as well as senses with weaker imagery. Whenever the sense image is strong, try to sense it as if you were actually seeing or touching or hearing or tasting the image. Wherever the inner sensing is weak, try as vividly as you can to imagine how it would look, feel, sound, and so on. We will start with visual images.

Partner: B, I want you to see or imagine your own bedroom. . .

Partner: A, I want you to see or imagine a sunset. . .

Guide: B, I want you to see or imagine a weeping willow tree. . .

Partner: A, I want you to see or imagine your own shadow stretching out in front of you on the ground. . .

Guide: Now everybody go to it, challenging each other with visual images. Make sure you give each other several moments to actually see or imagine each image as it is suggested. Begin by addressing each other by name as you ask your partner to see or imagine a visual image (2 minutes).

Guide: Now we will give each other auditory images. B, I want you to hear someone singing in a very high soprano. . .

Partner: A, I want you to hear a car engine starting up. . .

Guide: B, I want you to hear a cowbell. . .

Partner: A, I want you to hear a great storm. . .

Guide: All right, now will you all give each other auditory images (2 minutes).

Guide: Now we will go back and forth suggesting different tastes to each other, addressing each other by name. B, I want you to taste strawberry ice cream.

Partner: A, I want you to taste a crisp, juicy apple.

Guide: B, I want you to taste an angel food cake topped with minted dark chocolate mousse and gobs of whipped cream.

Partner: A, I want you to taste a potato salad filled with pickles, eggs, and mayonnaise.

Guide: Now everyone, with your partner go back and forth on tastes. You can make them as simple or as complex as you wish (2 minutes).

Guide: Now we will give each other images of touch. B, I want you to touch a baby's skin.

Partner: A, run your hand over the bark of a tree.

Guide: B, feel what it's like when you take a very hot followed by a very cold shower.

Partner: A, dig for buried treasure with your bare fingers in the stony ground.

Guide: Everyone now give each other tactile images (2 minutes).

Guide: Now we will explore images of smell. B, I want you to smell a freshly mown meadow.

Partner: A, smell bread baking.

Guide: B, smell a cow barn.

Partner: A, smell the kitchen of an Italian restaurant.

Guide: Everyone now with their partner, give each other smell suggestions (2 minutes).

Guide: Now we will challenge each other with moving images. B, you are walking along the beach and happen to look up and see a transparent cube falling from the sky toward you. Regard this cube, seeing its different sides as it tumbles down, turning over and over.

Partner: A, you are standing by a railroad track and a train with many cars passes right by you.

Guide: B, you are watching a bowling ball as it rolls down the alley and then strikes and knocks over all of the pins.

Partner: A, imagine a three-ring circus with trapeze artists flying through the air, clowns cavorting on the ground, and a lion leaping through a fiery hoop in the center of the ring.

Guide: Now everyone give each other moving images (2 minutes).

Guide: Now we will give each other complex images that involve multiple senses. B, you are riding down a busy street on a bicycle with a great wad of bubble gum in your mouth, passing by a chocolate factory.

Partner: A, you are sitting by a stream with your feet in the water, on your right side holding the hand of a very old man, and on your left, the hand of a very young child while you recite a poem that you learned as a child.

Guide: Now everyone give each other complex, multisensory images (2 minutes).

Guide: Now we will do together a mutually created composite image. Observe as we do it. B, we find ourselves in a great prairie with tall grasses waving in the wind.

Partner: A, there is a herd of buffalo grazing in that prairie.

Guide: B, on the bluff above the prairie there are several Indian braves carrying bows and arrows and looking at the buffalo.

Partner: A, the Indians begin to climb quietly down the bluff.

Guide: B, they are distracted when they hear a freshwater perch jumping in a nearby stream.

Guide: Now, at this point, I will say stop. B and I will stop and be in the scene for a while. After you have shared about six images in the composite image, one of you will say stop, and then you will take about a minute to silently be in the scene and let it unfold naturally. After the minute is up you will share your experience of what happened to your composite image in the intervening minute. You will see if the composite image began to unfold its own story, its own narrative. Now begin to give each other a composite image, remembering that it does not have to be a fantastic image. It can be an ordinary, mundane scene. Then, after you have shared around six images or so, one of you will call a stop, and then you will take about a minute to live in the image, seeing if it has a story that unfolds. Then, after a minute, share what has happened. Now begin (3 minutes).

Guide: I am going to give you another five minutes to do the same process again, creating other composite images. Try to go through several sequences of images in the time allowed, remembering to stop after about six shared images and to live for a minute in the scene created by the two of you.

Then share what has occurred for each of you. Do this now several times (5 minutes).

Guide: Now we have sufficient experience in imagery to do one of the more complex tasks of sacred psychology: the taking of a shared inner journey. In this process we will give each other images of a journey in search of wisdom, or a great inner teacher, or some profound place of power and enlightenment in the imaginal world. We will share and live in the images we give each other, talking back and forth and participating together in the shared inner reality which we are co-creating. We will do this for some time until we both feel that we have reached that place or that being of sacred power and knowing. We will now give you a demonstration of the beginnings of such a journey.

Guide: B, we find ourselves walking into a closet, pushing the clothes back and discovering that there is a door in the back of the closet. We open that door and find that it leads to a very ancient stone staircase which winds down and around to we-know-not-where. The light is dim, and so we carefully descend down this staircase, going down and around, a step at a time, careful not to fall, descending deeper and deeper into the earth.

Partner: A, we now reach the bottom of the stairway and find ourselves standing at the edge of a dark river, where a small skiff comes sailing toward us. A heavily mantled figure stands in the boat and beckons us to enter. We enter the boat and are given strange clothes to wear, with many symbols sewn on to them.

Guide: B, the boat sails through a narrow tunnel which seems to go on forever. The strange figure who is standing in the boat reaches out to the sides of the walls of the tunnel and pulls away some fungus-like growth and gives it to us, indicating that we should eat it.

Partner: A, after we have eaten the fungus we notice that our senses have become much more alert and that we are curiously exhilarated. There is a light at the end of the tunnel and the boat approaches that light. . .

Guide: That is an indication of how we work together in taking a shared inner journey. Now we will all begin our own journeys with our partners. To begin, lie down on the floor together, not side by side but rather with your feet in opposite directions so that your ears are close together. Talk for a few minutes back and forth about where you would like to go in order to find wisdom or knowledge or whatever else you may wish to discover. Is it a wise person you wish to discover, or an archetype or a god or goddess? Is it a potent traditional symbol like the Holy Grail, the Philosopher's Stone, the Pearl of Great Price? Or perhaps it is a symbolic place of knowledge like the Hall of the Akashic Records, which is said to contain all the wisdom of all the universes. Perhaps it is a sacred place of mystery like Avalon, or ancient Atlantis, or a planet inhabited by high beings like certain African tribes believe exist on a planet around the star Sirius. Perhaps it is a place or person you have never heard of but whose call draws you into their mystery. Wherever or whatever or whoever it is, try now to come to some agreement about the nature of your quest (5 minutes).

All right, to begin, breathe together for several minutes, and then let one of you begin the shared inner journey by suggesting some initial image that will begin the journey—for example, as I suggested the image of the secret door in the back of the closet that led to the winding stone staircase. Find your own image, however, and begin there. Your partner will then add to the story by suggesting another image. You will have *thirty minutes or so of clock time* to experience your shared journey (30 to 45 minutes depending on how the participants seem to be doing).

After the time has ended have the participants share their experience of their journeys with others in the group.

7

DEVELOPING THE IMAGINAL BODY

Having extended your senses, both inner and outer, and having stimulated your imagination in the previous chapters, you will learn now to develop the imaginal realm further, thus equipping yourself for the journeys ahead. Think of this process as a preparatory practice, one that can be done, in part or as a whole, on a daily basis. After you have mastered the initial process, you will find ways to adapt it to many situations, becoming increasingly adept at building bridges between the imaginal realm and your everyday existence.

Had you been born in a different time or space, many of these practices in developing your imaginal capacities in order to enter the realm of the sacred would be familiar to you. Modern Western education has, however, focused almost entirely on the mastery of the objective and measurable world to the exclusion of the depth levels of reality, the underpinnings of all our "worlds." Thus dread and anxiety haunt Western consciousness, as it is faced with a reality that is at once unsupported, unpatterned, unfriendly.

These exercises seek to remedy this lopsided focus and restore your birthright of access to the many levels of essence and existence. You no longer need to feel like a stranger in a strange land, or a visitor to Flatland, but rather a participant in a richly textured reality, full of support and meaning, which invites you to play the high game of co-creation on all possible levels.

The practice of sacred psychology often makes use of the meticulous and effective creation of an imaginal body that houses your consciousness so that you may effectively identify with symbolic and archetypal forms. The concept of the imaginal body belongs to an ancient and extensive tradition, both Eastern and Western. It suggests that each individual has a second, nonphysical, or "subtle" body composed of more subtle matter and energy than that of the corporeal body. While the body identified in these traditions may be related to the kinesthetic body, the former is created by your imagination and is not based on muscular memory. You will try to "see" this body as vividly as possible. Because it is imaginal, it can do anything—shrink, expand, radically change shape, or whatever else you can imagine. It is not constrained by gravity or normal laws of body function, and it is extremely flexible and responsive to suggestion.

Critical to sacred psychology is the ability to incarnate or incorporate a variety of identities and personalities. This may allow you to access the knowledge and experience of different life forms as well as gain the compassion and understanding that comes from getting inside another person's reality. You learn to operate with leaky margins, and osmotically assume the persona of another.

Traditional psychologies of the sacred have always taught this facility for "incarnation." In the shamanic traditions particularly, the apprentice learns to "become" various animals or qualities of nature, like wind, fire, and water. In T. H. White's *The Once and Future King,* the great wizard, Merlin, trains the young Arthur for sacred kingship by having him serve apprenticeship in various animal, fish, and bird forms. Even athletes are known to utilize this phenomenon in their creation of an inner optimal athlete whose muscles and joints, breathing, skill, and timing are such that the athlete's "inner game" is always training his outward performance. Mahayana and Tibetan Buddhism contain practices in which one builds up a most complete internal mage of a Bodhisattva, especially Kwan Yin or Avalokiteshvara, and then joins with this image, taking on some of the Bodhisattva's power and compassion. This aspect of sacred psychology teaches the ability to assume, when appropriate, the archetype of the god or goddess. Divine identity carries evolutionary enhancement. You take on the body, the mind, the spiritual resonance of the god—or, if you will, of the next stage of evolution. You enter into the lure of becoming and acquire aspects of the extended physical, mental, emotional, and spiritual capacities of the archetype.

In the fourteenth and fifteenth centuries, many books entitled *The Imitation of Christ* were written. Essentially they dealt with taking on the archetype of Jesus in order to develop an extended sensibility. Some of the exercises of St. Ignatius, which are critical to Jesuit training, involve entering into a vivid and active imagining of the Passion of Christ. This can result in a catharsis of the small and negative qualities of one's local self; if one can go through the Passion experientially, local toxicity tends to fall away.

The protagonists of mythic journeys, including those in Part Four of this book, require for their transformation a wounding and trial, a death or depletion, and a resurrection or restoration as well-defined stages of growth. In the experience of identification with these protagonists you, like them, die in some sense to those local habits and patterns that have outgrown their usefulness. You see life anew from the vantage point of the archetype, and you return to your ordinary reality refreshed and invigorated by the experience of having gained a larger perspective and a renewed sense of vision and commitment.

Using your imaginal body is a somewhat different experience from working with your kinesthetic body. Whereas the kinesthetic body involves more of an internal muscular sensing, the imaginal body is a separate, externalized image. Working with the imaginal body is not unlike observing yourself in a dream and occasionally discovering that you are both observer and observed as you slip in and out of the dream body.

You will use your imagination to create a "second body," one that you will manipulate as though it were another person. The process begins by doing simple, traditional psychophysical movements with the imaginal body only. You will then observe the effect of the movement of your imaginal body on your physical body and you may be astonished to find what effect a "merely" imagined movement has on your physical body. The demonstrated power of the imagination to change physical reality may suggest to you what could happen if you were to vividly imagine a wound being healed or some other desired physical change. The process is designed to take you slowly into a fuller use of the imaginal body, activating the senses of the imaginal body and making the image clearer and stronger as you work with it in many ways.

The process becomes more complex as you learn to let your imaginal body take on other forms—those of animals, birds, and fish—and perceive the world through these incarnations, gathering your animal wisdom.

Finally, you will allow your imaginal body to assume the form of your personal entelechy and integrate this entelechy with your physical being. Again, the skill developed in this process is one that will be used in a variety of ways later in this book.

The process is followed by an extension into archetypal shape-shifting, discussed and demonstrated at the conclusion of this process. It will allow you, through the use of the imaginal body, to perceive reality from the vantage point of these great mythic forces, revealing patterns and perspectives that the "local you" might not have consciously considered. Shape-shifting will be much more effective if you have developed the psychophysical imaginal body work first.

Here again we struggle a little with the difficulty of translating what is an oral tradition into a written mode. Although doing the process will take you only forty-five minutes, the instructions are lengthy because they must be very specific to engage fully the development of the imaginal body. Once the experience is familiar, you may, of course, shorten and vary the process in a variety of ways. Doing so initially, however, would rob you of the fullness of the experience and the development of the skill-to-be.

Evoking Your Imaginal Form

Part of this process is adapted from the work of Robert Masters. You will need either a guide or a tape to do this process. But the guide, as well as the person putting the process on tape, must remember to pause after each instruction to allow the participant sufficient time to perform the indicated movement ten to twenty-five times. All general instructions about the exercises apply here also. During this exercise, however, you are asked questions from time to time and are free to respond aloud or silently. The questions are meant to help you focus on changes in body functioning. There are no right or wrong answers, and responses may vary greatly from one to another.

It is best to sit comfortably on the floor with your spine straight. You may be more comfortable with your back against a wall. It is also possible to do most of the process seated in a straight-backed chair.

TIME: 45 minutes.

MATERIALS NEEDED: None.

MUSIC: "Space Fantasy" from Tomita's *Kosmos*.

INSTRUCTIONS FOR WORKING ALONE: If you must work alone, you will need to put this exercise on tape for yourself in advance, remembering to pause long enough for execution of the movements.

NOTE TO THE GUIDE: *Pause* after each instruction, to allow time for the movement to be made. Each movement should be made from ten to fifteen times in the imaginal body. This process will take from ten to fifteen seconds.

SCRIPT FOR THE GUIDE: To begin, be seated comfortably and focus on your breathing with your eyes closed. Imagine that you are sitting opposite yourself.

Now actually get up in your physical body without opening your eyes and sit opposite from where you had been sitting.

Now get up again and sit where you were before, and imagine yourself sitting opposite yourself.

Repeat this process a number of times. After each move, try to have as concrete a sense of yourself as if you were actually there.

Now physically reach out with your real hand and shake hands with your imaginal body. You may notice a kind of electrical charge tickling your palm. Try to make that handshake as vivid as possible.

Reach over with your physical body and give your imaginal body a kiss on the cheek and be kissed in return.

Still sitting opposite yourself, imagine the consciousness attributed to out-of-body experiences. For example, you may have at some time fallen asleep and suddenly found yourself on the ceiling looking down at yourself. You are now shifting your consciousness so that you're looking down at your physical body sitting there. Look down at the top of your head. Note the shape of your head and whether your hair is combed. What does your body look like when viewed from above? (These questions allow you to focus on details that increase the clarity of the imaginal body.)

Now I am going to ask you to imagine yourself in the form in which we are going to work. I want you to imagine that you are lying down somewhere in front of yourself, on your back, with your hands at your sides. Your palms are down and your feet are separated by twelve or thirteen inches. We are going to work only on the imaginal body. You will keep your physical body still as you do this.

Turn the right foot of your imaginal body on its right side and bring it back to the middle. Keep doing it. Notice that as you rotate your right imaginal foot you will be rotating your right imaginal hip as well. Bring the outside of the right foot as close to the floor as you can and then bring it back. Be aware of the sensation of the right hip as you rotate it and bring it back. Be aware of the outside of the foot as it touches the ground. Then stop.

Now just flex and extend the toes of the right foot of the imaginal body. Actually sense them. Flex and extend the toes. Stay focused in that imaginal body.

Then flex and extend the ankles a few times. Really be aware of that flex in the imaginal body, which is lying out in front of you. Flex and extend. Do nothing with your *real* body. The awareness is entirely related to the body that is lying there before you.

Now make some circles with the right imaginal foot by rotating the ankle. Circle in one direction and then circle in the other direction.

Now bend both legs of your imaginal body, so that your feet are on the floor. Rap with the ball of your right imaginal foot on the floor. Rap. Rap. Rap. Rap. Rap. Rap rather vigorously. Place your imaginal foot so that the movement is easily performed. Then rap with the heel. You will see that you have to bring your foot into a different relationship to your buttocks in order to rap well with the heel. Where you rap best with the ball of the foot is not where you rap best with the heel. Notice that.

Now just pick up your imaginal foot and put it down a number of times on its bottom. Keep the leg bent. Raise the foot and put it down. Now let the right imaginal leg stand next to the left one. And let the right knee fall over to the right side so it approaches the floor as closely as it can. Then bring it back. Keep doing that. Be aware of the movement in the hip joint and the arc of the right knee going through space, going over to one side and then coming back to the middle. Just keep doing that for a minute. And stop.

Pick up your imaginal right foot and make circles with the right knee in the air. Circle in one direction for a while and then in the other. Then stop.

Bring the right leg back toward you, so that the top of the right thigh approaches your rib cage, and then return the foot in a forward motion to the floor. Be sure that what you feel are the sensations of your imaginal body and that you are doing everything with reference to that body. Be aware of the sensations—the raising of the leg, the pull in the thigh, the sense of the foot returning to the floor. Keep doing that for a while. Stop. Now allow your right imaginal leg to lie on the floor.

Now rap with your imaginal right hand. Leave the right arm on the floor and raise your hand from the wrist, bending the wrist, and rap with the hand. Rap. Rap. Rap. Rap. Rap. Be aware, not just of the bending of the wrist and the rapping of the hand, but also of the sound that your imaginal hand makes when rapping on the floor. Listen in your imaginal body to that sound.

Now continue rapping with the hand on the floor, but do it by picking up the entire imaginal arm. Keep the arm extended, raise it several inches off the floor, and bring the hand down so that you can make even louder rappings. Listen to the louder rappings with your imaginal ear. Then stop.

Slide your imaginal right hand up and down on the floor. Feel the floor beneath your hand and arm. You are using your imaginal sense of touch as you feel the floor. You are using your imaginal sense of muscular movement to feel the movement in the shoulder, the hand, and the arm. You are also using your visual sense as you look down at that body and observe the hand moving up and down the floor. So for a moment you make your consciousness multiple.

Now bend your imaginal arm at the elbow and make many circles with the arm and the hand, rotating the elbows. Make a number of circles in the imaginal body in one direction, and a number of circles in the other direction. Small ones and big ones. Just experiment. Quick ones. Slow ones. Feel what is happening in the elbow and the movement of the hand and the arm through space. Really feel it in your imaginal body. Then stop.

Now put your right imaginal palm on your right chest and raise and lower the elbow toward the ceiling like a flapping wing. Keep doing that. See how quick and light you can make that movement. Now slide your elbow along the floor toward your waist, and then up along the floor to shoulder height, keeping your upper arm on the floor. Continue this other kind flapping until the movement is also quick and light.

Now lie down on the floor and scan your physical body, seeing if you can tell whether the two sides are the same. Let your arms lie at your sides. Try to see if the two sides are the same or whether one side feels longer or tilts more or can be seen more clearly. You have only been moving in your imaginal body, not in your actual physical body. So turn your attention now to your physical body and see what you feel.

Is there any difference in the clarity of the right and left sides? Compare your right eye with your left eye. Your right hand with your left hand. Your right leg with your left. What do you notice?

Now get up and walk around and see what else you notice. Does your right side feel different from your left side? Really try to define. What is the difference? How does your left side feel? Don't worry; you will be balanced out. Your left side is how you normally experience your body.

Now go back and sit down. Make yourself comfortable and focus on your breathing, breathing in and out in a regular and relaxed way, keeping your eyes closed. And breathe through the center of your actual body. Breathe very deeply so that you get a sense of your breath being pulled up through the middle as you inhale and then down as you exhale. Get a good sense of this movement.

Continuing this process, imagine your imaginal body sitting opposite you. While you are doing this breathing in your physical body, do the same thing with your imaginal body. If you have difficulty being aware of breathing in both bodies, be aware first of one, then the other, shifting your awareness back and forth until the two are breathing together.

Now bend your physical legs so that your feet are standing on the floor. Let your imaginal body do the same. Continue to breathe together, letting the right leg of your imaginal body drop over to the side and bring it back. At the same time, take the left leg of the physical body, the mirror image of the right leg of your imaginal body, and drop it over to the side and back. Be aware of the left leg of your physical body doing it and the right leg of your imaginal body. See if you can do both of those things together without sacrificing the awareness of your imaginal body. Be aware of both legs going at the same time. Stop.

Scan your physical body as you sit there, and see whether the right side is still clearer than the left. What do you notice? Are you more balanced now?

As you remain seated, let your imaginal body get up and walk around. Actually feel your imaginal body. It will step around the physical bodies sitting there and see the other imaginal bodies walking around this room. Let your imaginal body go outside now and walk around, feeling the ground beneath its feet. Stay very focused. Stay awake. Stay alert.

Now let your imaginal body walk in the sawdust on the floor of a circus. Then let your imaginal body walk along the seashore. Feel the sand, being aware of the sea currents, the freshness of the ocean breeze. Your imaginal body is also using its eyes. So look out through the eyes of your imaginal body at this seashore scene. At the same time, be aware of looking down at your imaginal body and watching it walk. So you are in your imaginal body as well as being an observer, conscious of your imaginal body as it is walking along the seashore. Stay focused. Stay alert. Be aware of every sensation—the contact of the foot with the sand, how the ankles bend, how your knees move, the hip joints. What are your hands doing? Are they carrying anything? How are you holding your elbows? Your shoulders? How are you carrying yourself? How are you breathing? Be as completely aware of both yourself and the environment as you can be.*

Come back now, returning fully to this place. As you sit in your physical body, make yourself comfortable. Now we're going to work very rapidly on the left side. We can do this much more rapidly because of the generalization phenomenon in the brain: if you learn something in a meticulous manner on one side, you can, by working in the imaginal body, transfer it rapidly to the other side.

Still keeping your eyes closed, place your imaginal body on the floor in front of you where you worked on it before. Let it lie down. Your imaginal legs are lying out straight. Your imaginal arms are at your sides with their palms down. Take the left leg of that imaginal body over to the outside. Rotate the hip so that the outside of the foot approaches or touches the floor beneath you. Bring it back. Continue rotating the left imaginal hip joint, doing that as vividly as you can. Now flex and extend the toes of the left foot. Flex, extend. Sense very clearly what you are doing. These are all movements that your mind and body have experienced. Flex, extend. Good.

Now flex and extend the left imaginal ankle several times. Now bend both legs of your imaginal body. Place the feet on the floor. Rap with the left imaginal heel. Place the foot at that distance from the body that allows you to rap easily with the left imaginal heel. Now rap with the left imaginal ball of the foot. You'll have to place the foot somewhat differently.

Now stop that and let the left imaginal knee drop over to the side. Drop it over to the side and bring it back to the middle. Continue to let it go as far as it will, dropping over to the side and coming back. Keep doing that. Now straighten your right imaginal leg and when you take the left imaginal leg over to the left, let it come up and over the right one until it lies across the right leg, perhaps even goes past it to the floor. Go all the way over to the left, and all the way over to the right with your imaginal leg. Keep doing that. Very good.

*Here the guide may wish to insert an experience that draws on the material from the story the group may be studying. The following is an example of such an extension used during an exploration of the ancient Celts.

Now allow your imaginal body to don the white robes of the Druids, and find yourself in a Druid rite in ancient Stonehenge. You walk over the ground around the great megalithic pillars in the full sunlight. Two ravens are flying overhead in the great open temple. You can hear the chanting. You feel the brush of your clothes on your body. You feel yourself raising the the Sword of Enlightenment with one hand and offering the Cup of Possibilities with the other. Your imaginal body is walking around the megalithic pillars of the temple carrying the Sword and the Cup. Be aware of how you carry yourself, of how you breathe as an ancient Druid. And look out through the eyes of your imaginal Druid body at this place.

Then, coming back, just stretch, with your eyes closed. Be aware of energy currents charging you, flowing through your body, perhaps coming from that place of the great megaliths.

Now bend your right imaginal leg so that both feet are standing on the floor. Rap on the floor with your left hand just by bending the wrist. Rap. Rap. Rap. Rap. Rap. Actually hear it. Listen to the rapping. Then make it louder by raising the entire arm and slapping the left imaginal hand against the floor. Then let the left arm rest at your side just like the right one.

Make some circles with the left hand on the floor. Have the palm of your imaginal hand inscribe circles going in one direction and then in the other direction. Now raise that left imaginal hand and let it make sweeping circles in the air. First go in one direction and then in the other direction.

Now place your imaginal hand and arm back on the floor and move your left arm up and down, sliding along the floor. Do that by raising your shoulder up and down. You sense the feeling in the shoulder. You feel the surface beneath the hand. Use your tactile sense. Feel the floor, and now feel what your hand is feeling, shifting back and forth between sensing your hand and sensing the floor.

Now place your left imaginal hand on your chest, with your elbow out at shoulder height. Raise the elbow toward the ceiling, flapping the arm like the wing of a bird. Flap it up and down.

Now put your right imaginal hand also on your chest and perform the same movement, so that both arms are flapping up and down like a bird. Think of the bird flapping its wings. Think about the special muscular, wing, and bone structure of the bird while you are flapping your arms.

As you continue to flap your imaginal arms, discover that your body is now the body of a *bird,* flapping your strong wings. You are a great bird, soaring through the heavens. (Pause.)

Feel your wings flapping and the body of the bird soaring in the sky. See what else you feel. You might even be aware of what kind of bird you are and what you look like. Enjoy the feeling of strength and the cushion of air as you flap your wings, as your body soars on the wind currents of the sky, looking down with incredible precision and vision at the land beneath you. Do you see that tasty worm down there 1000 feet below? Swoop down and get it. Do you see that high pillar? Sit on it and look at the landscape around you. Stay alert. Stay awake. Stay focused. Stay in the body of your imaginal bird. Now fly off again. Soar and glide. Sometimes just let the wings be extended, floating along in the sky. Enjoy the experience of flying. (Pause 15 seconds.)

Then cease this movement and let your consciousness hang suspended without form. Now find yourself in the body of a large *cat*: a tiger, a lion, a panther, whatever you wish.

Move in this wonderful, supple, graceful, strong, lithe body of the great cat, be it lion or tiger or leopard. Be aware of the tremendous power and grace of the body you are now in. Make a great leap to a rock. Bound across a plain. Climb up a mighty tree. Feel the strength of your claws or your hind quarters as you pull yourself up. Growl hugely. Just go around now and enjoy being in that graceful, powerful body that moves so lightly. Look out at the world through the eyes of this great cat. Feel its consciousness. (Pause 15 seconds.) Compare being a cat with being a bird.

Lose that body. Let your consciousness hang suspended. Find yourself in the body of a *mosquito,* wings going very fast, whirring along, looking for something tasty. Buzz around your own physical body in this room. Buzz around and notice that tasty forehead there. And then go to the forehead of your physical body and have dinner. What is the mosquito thinking as it puts its prober, its proboscis, under your skin? Fly off again, into the world of the mosquito.

Lose that body. Let your consciousness hang suspended.

Find yourself in the body of a great *snake.* Feel that body as it undulates and slithers along the earth with its tongue darting in and out of its mouth. How do you sense the earth as you undulate and wiggle and slide along the earth? Every stone, every crevice, every blade of grass is felt sensuously against your undulating body. As you slide along the earth, stay awake, stay alert, stay focused. You are a snake. Look out at the world from snake consciousness. (Pause 15 seconds.)

Lose that body. Let your consciousness hang suspended once again.

Now find yourself in the body of an *elephant.* Feel that enormously massive body with its head high up off the ground, with its great ears flapping, its little tail, and its wonderful, heavy, calloused flesh, its extraordinary nose. Feel what it is like to have a nose that helps you to eat, to give yourself a bath. Find a stream or a pond, take a great snort of water, and let the dust wash off of you. Find a great patch of green juicy grass, wrap your nose around it, pull it up, shake off the dirt, and put it in your mouth and chew away. Find yourself enormously attracted to another elephant and feel what it is like when an elephant falls in love with another elephant. How does the world look to you as elephant?

Lose that body. Let your consciousness hang suspended.

Now transfer into the body of a *dolphin.* And be in the dolphin with a great school of dolphins talking to each other in high-pitched sonic songs—rolling and leaping and playing. See a great group of sharks, your natural enemies, not feeling fear, but knowing that you have a duty. And with your tremendously strong, bony head, go and just bump the sharks away. Then go back to your playing and rolling. Understand the subtle communications among dolphins. Know what it is to be a dolphin.

Lose that body. Let your consciousness hang suspended.

Once again find yourself back in the body of the great *bird,* flying high and looking down on the elephant and great cat and the mosquito and the snake and the dolphin. Enjoy the feeling of your wings flapping and gliding. As you glide, you are gliding now in *your own human form.* You can fly. You can move your arms like a bird's and see that they will carry you through the sky.

Shamans fly. They say that Buddhas fly. Flying through the air, look down at the ground and see the shadow that you cast, like a strange cross on the land.*

Now you have *two minutes of clock time,* equal subjectively to all the time you need to assume other, different forms, be they the forms of people, animals, fish, or whatever. Transform your imaginal body into other forms, and identify in your imaginal body with the forms you assume as completely as possible. You have two minutes of clock time, equal subjectively to all the time you need, beginning now. (Pause 2 minutes.)

Now place your imaginal body on the floor again and let your imaginal body rise up and walk around this room. Sense its movements and sensations very clearly. And see if it has become easier to be in your imaginal body. Run and leap now in your imaginal body. Now lie down and roll and roll and roll. Now jump up with your imaginal body and whirl like a dervish. Just whirl and whirl and whirl and whirl. Let your movement be agile and free. Pay attention to the feelings and sensations of the imaginal body because it makes it easier and easier to be in it.

Now for the next minute of clock time, equal subjectively to all the time you need, take your imaginal body to whatever environment you wish. Give it interesting, pleasurable experiences—perhaps a splendid meal or a wonderful plunge in a mountain lake. Pleasurable sensory experience reinforces and strengthens the creative process that helps produce your imaginal body. It creates the desire to go into it. So for the next minute of clock time, give the imaginal body interesting and delightful experiences, beginning now. (Pause 1 minute.)

Now let your imaginal body stand up. And as it does that, let the High Self, your deep High Self, loaded with possibilities for your unfolding, join with your imaginal body in its rich unfolding. Stay alert. Stay awake. Your imaginal body is filled with the High Self, filled with light, filled with your tremendous possibilities; it is a body of wholeness, of fulfillment.

Let your imaginal body, filled with the High Self, come over to you and sit opposite you. And let that imaginal body sitting opposite you reach into your mind and into your body and help effect physiological, emotional, and mental processes of healing and of evolutionary quickening. Let the loaded, coded imaginal body reach into you, giving healing, forgiveness, and the potentiation of evolutionary qualities wherever they are needed. Your imaginal body, with its sense of union and communion with the High Self, knows a great deal about

*Once again the guide may wish to insert here an experience related to the material the group may be exploring. Here is another example of how this might be done:

Become *Arthur,* the Once and Future King, and move in the body/mind of Arthur. And let that go. And become now *Morgan le Fay,* the great priestess of the in-between realms who knows the faery knowledge. Know what it is to be Morgan le Fay. And release her. Become *Merlin,* the Druid, the wise one, the one who has the knowledge of the sea and stars, of classical culture and Druid knowings, and a great wisdom and compassion of heart. Merlin, the wise one. Then let that being dissolve.

what is appropriate for you. So in the next minute of clock time, equal subjectively to all the time you need, receive the healing, the wholing, the loving, the quickening evocation. (Pause 1 minute.)

Open your eyes now. Stretch. Reflect quietly on how you feel and what you now know. In a few minutes some music will begin, and you are free to dance the celebration of the creation and partnering of the imaginal body or, if you would rather, to sit quietly and reflect further.

(In about three minutes put on celebrational music from *Area 3,* like "Space Fantasy" from Tomita's *Kosmos*.)

Archetypal Shape-shifting

The extension of the kinesthetic body and imaginal body into the mythic realm allows you to prepare for the exercise that follows. In the imaginal-body exercise, you experienced reality from the perspective of different animals and perhaps different mythic personae, and you moved from place to place in the physical realm. Here we enter more explicitly the realm of myth and archetype, using the skills you have gained in working with the imaginal body. Now you will learn to engage, with a more expanded imaginal experience, both god identities and archetypal perceptions. These are yours for the having, since they live just below the surface of consciousness.

If you do this exercise carefully, you may notice a considerable change in feeling and perception as you move from one archetypal identity to another. The genius of the shape-shifter within you can be used with as many additions and variations as you like, to enrich the perceptual-conceptual continuum of your own knowings. To have such empathy with archetypes is not only to gain the eyes of Athena, the taste buds of Dionysius, or the tactile sensations of Aphrodite. It is to release oneself from the perspectives of local space-time; it is to gain the ideas of gods and prepare oneself for the rigors of *therapeia*.

As you shift into these archetypal perspectives, you will see the experiences of daily life in terms of larger patterns, each unique to a particular archetypal entity, each able to yield its wisdom to you. In this process you will be working with major archetypal figures and motifs that have risen in most cultures. Identification with these in one way or another have proven essential to the practice of sacred psychology in many places and times. Seven of these archetypal figures are presented here.

While no archetype can be fully defined, each seems to have its own constellation of more or less universal characteristics. Because of their universality, these archetypes are thought by many psychologists and mythologists to be accessible to all, symbols that exist in everyone to evoke the soul. While it is possible to list the chief characteristics of each archetype, I have found that this only hinders your own spontaneous access to the richness and variety of expression inherent in your own unique contact with these symbolic forces.

TIME: 20–30 minutes.

MATERIALS NEEDED: None.

MUSIC: No music is needed, although you may wish to use any evocative piece of music that speaks to you of mythic powers. Much of the music listed in *Area 2* would be suitable here.

INSTRUCTIONS FOR WORKING ALONE: If you are working alone, put this exercise onto a tape before you begin.

SCRIPT FOR THE GUIDE: Sitting comfortably and relaxing totally, follow your breath for the next few minutes, all the way in and all the way out. With each breath cycle let your local identity become more porous and permeable. Allow yourself to be in a state of leaky margins so that you can more readily experience the god-selves that are waiting to be assumed.

Now let there rise in you from the imaginal realm the archetype of the *Great Mother*. Feel the body and being of this archetype stream into your own being, so that you find yourself becoming the Great Mother. Now move in the body and being of the Great Mother. Know what it feels like to move as the Great Mother, and then look out at the world with her compassion and senses and knowings (1 minute).

Now release the Great Mother and let there rise in you from out of the imaginal realm the archetype of the *Wise Old King*. Feel the body and being of this great archetype enter fully developed into your own being, so that you find yourself becoming the Wise Old King. Now move around as the Wise Old King and know what it is to look out at reality with the responsibility and the perspective of the Wise Old King (1 minute).

Now release the Wise Old King and let there rise in you from the realm of imaginal forms the archetype of the *Young Redeemer*. Let yourself become the Young Redeemer, feeling his energies and form stream into you so that you do not know where you begin and he leaves off. Move as the Young Redeemer. Know the world as the Young Redeemer knows it. Even sing as the Young Redeemer (1 minute).

Now release the Young Redeemer and let there rise in you from the imaginal realm the archetype of *Dionysius,* the god of wine and of intoxication, of excess and too-muchness. Let the fullness of body and the sensory appetites of this god fill you to the brim. Laugh and snort as Dionysius, reach for the ripe grapes, drink deeply from life's many pleasures, and know yourself as Dionysius (1 minute).

Now release Dionysius and let there rise in you from the imaginal world the archetype of the *Great Snake*. Let yourself receive the sinuous twisting form of this archetype, your voice becoming a hiss, and your mind a mystery that remembers all earth magics. Move and be and know as the Great Snake (1 minute).

Now release the Great Snake and let there rise from the imaginal world the archetype of the *Trickster*. Let yourself become the Trickster, with his subtle form, his movements like quicksilver, his mercurial disposition. Now, filled with whimsy and mischief, consider what you as Trickster can do to the reality around you (1 minute).

Now release the Trickster and let there rise in you from the realm of the imaginal the archetype of the *Holy Child*. Let that little body move into yours, and feel yourself as that small, that complete, that innocently wise. Wholly becoming the Holy Child, look out at reality with the innocence, wisdom, and grace of this archetype (1 minute).

Now let your own local identity return to you, quickened by the knowing that you are a One who contains the Many. Know, too, that each of these great symbolic figures, as well as many others, dwells within you and can be engaged deeply and felt imaginally, granting you access to both their perspective and some of their capacity.[1]

Individuals may want to discuss and share the archetypes they discovered, or they may want to sit quietly with music playing as they reflect on their capacity for archetypal shape-shifting.

8

THE FRIEND IN COURT AND THE THREE REALMS OF BEING

Having entered imaginal and archetypal reality, we can bring this perspective to bear on our local reality, which often suffers from too limited a story. All archetypal tales serve to remind us of the limits of the purely human realm, no matter how great the resources of the particular mortal in question.

Let us consider, as an example, one of the most resourceful heroes ever extolled in myth and literature, the adventurer-warrior Odysseus. The first lines of *The Odyssey* say: "This is the story of a man, one who was never at a loss." He is a "man of many devices"—the man who has seen everything, can do everything, and (at least with his intellect) understand everything. He is in some sense the first modern man, for although he is cunning and brilliant in the known ways of the world, Odysseus, like other modern humans, has somewhat ignored his own deeper nature. Necessarily, then, his learning must come out of the deeps, which he has mishandled. From these deeps will come most of his adventures and a larger experience of reality. And, of course, he will get himself into some pretty deep waters, marooned on some very remote islands with some very weird companions. He will experience ten more years of adventure and despair, lostness and foundness, mute tragedy, and terrifying triumph. And all he really wanted to do was go home to Ithaca. Perhaps the story sounds familiar.

Chastened and at the end of his resources, with no identity remaining except bare consciousness, Odysseus stays for many long years as the kept man of a minor goddess on an isolated island, yearning for home. So, too, you may have found yourself marooned in second-rate jobs and relationships after long and arduous journeys into the deeps, unable to get to the place where your yearning tells you that you belong.

But grace is a function higher even than the remedial power of the deeps, and his education has gone far enough. The great change in Odysseus's fortunes is occasioned by his "Friend in Court," the goddess Athena, pleading his case before her father Zeus and the gods of Olympus.

Athena, the goddess of heroes and innovators, of those who live life to its fullest and at its edges, has been present throughout the entire story. But it is not until Odysseus has fully exhausted his human resources that she is able to intervene. She speaks of his cleverness and of the sacrifices he made to the gods on the plains of Troy, of his present trouble and sorrow, imprisoned in the middle of the sea. It is now almost twenty years since Odysseus has seen his home. He has first spent ten years in Troy, subsequent weeks wandering from one harrowing adventure to another, and a year with Circe, before finally landing with Calypso for seven full years in the great stuck place of his life. It is perhaps some small comfort to note that, like most of us, the actual famed adventures took only a few weeks and the rest of the time he was stuck in the middle of nowhere. Thus, like most of us, he bides his time waiting, longing, hoping for something to happen so that he can get on with his life. Athena reminds the gods that this fate has befallen him because he incurred the hatred of the sea god Poseidon for putting out the single eye of his son Polyphemos, the Cyclops. Poseidon, the god of the sea, of the unknown, the mysterious, the unfathomable, is clearly the one god who has it in for Odysseus. But Poseidon is away in Ethiopia at a party in his honor, and so the gods are free to act in favor of Odysseus. Ably and convincingly, Athena argues that after all he has patiently endured, it is time for the gods to help him to return home. She herself will go to Ithaca to begin the preparations for his homecoming and to give heart to his son Telemachus. The other gods in turn agree that they will dispatch Hermes to Calypso's isle and make her release Odysseus.

Twenty-eight hundred years after it was written, this episode of the archetypal Friend in Court still serves as a telling model of what it is in us that helps us out of our stuck places and illumines our transitions. Often some quickening agent of the life force, some stimulus from the archetypal world, is needed to help us *get on with it.* This can be interpreted perhaps as the entelechy in us, the most potent and personal of evolutionary principles, which constantly seeks to remind us that we are that grand intersection between cosmology and biology, and that the universe seeks to grow in our own becoming.

How, then, can you make contact with this agent, this guide and guardian? How can you, like E.T., "phone home" before your resources are exhausted?

Most of this book is dedicated to answering this question in a variety of ways. Here, however, I present a basic and deceptively simple exercise in which you *become* that guiding archetype, observing with both great compassion and detachment the mortal that you are. Essentially, instead of trying to contact this other realm, you will allow yourself to incarnate this realm directly. You will find that force within yourself that guides and protects you, that serves as your ally and champion, and it is from this place that you will view your life.

The earlier exercises with the imaginal body and archetypal shape-shifting have given you the skills and practice to incarnate whatever you choose to incarnate. You will now take this a step further and become your friend in the court of the gods.

On the existential level, this exercise offers the opportunity to greatly increase the *perspective* of your own life, allowing you to release negative and derailing habit patterns and to choose consciously those steps that lead to a life of growth, courage, and creative action.

It is important that while playing the role of the Friend in Court, you fully enact the archetype with appropriate change of voice, gesture, language, and energy. This means that you will make full use of your imaginal body, sensing yourself garbed as the archetype, and without equivocation or doubt, bearing the power and knowing that belong to this realm.

Incarnating the Friend in Court

The process will begin with a chant, for chanting prepares you to dissolve the barriers that surround the local THIS IS ME self, and allows the archetypal energies and personae of the WE ARE realm to be identified with and engaged. After the chanting, you will come together in groups of "godded" beings and present the case of your mortal.

TIME: 45–60 minutes.

MATERIALS NEEDED: None.

INSTRUCTIONS FOR WORKING ALONE: After reading the instructions for the guide below, so that you have them thoroughly in your mind, begin with the chanting and let it slowly carry you into a meditative movement in which you feel the forces of the archetypal realm rising within you.

After some time with this, be still and seated with this deep knowing, and begin to speak *aloud* of your human. Sense the presence of other witnesses from the archetypal realm as you do this. When you have finished, come again to stillness and allow time to hear what the unseen others may wish to add. After some consideration, make a final summary statement.

To deepen and enhance your experience, record what has happened in your journal.

You may also want to do this exercise with one other person, perhaps a person with whom you are having some temporary difficulties, to allow both of you to shift perspective and bring a higher wisdom to bear on the situation.

SCRIPT FOR THE GUIDE: You will begin by chanting, allowing your consciousness to shift as you move into the rhythm and the resonance of the chant, calming and quieting your "local" mind.

The chant is from Holderlin's poem, *Patmos,* and sets the stage for the coming of the archetypal Friend in Court.

> Near is, but difficult to grasp, the God.
> But where there is danger, the saving powers also rise.

As you repeat this chant, move throughout the room until you begin to sense "the rising of the saving powers." (Allow several minutes for this.) Still chanting, begin to allow the god of the deepest wisdom in you to be expressed through dance or movement. This symbolic entelechy principle or "god" should be personal and unique to you, and need not belong to the roster of known gods or symbolic forces. Dance the god and let the god dance you. (Let this continue until the chanting and dancing peak and subside.)

Now gather in groups of three of four. This is the Court of the Gods. Each person will incarnate the archetypal Friend in Court, speaking for the needs and needed transmutations of his or her own local life, referring to the local self in the third person. In this role you speak for the life of your human from an archetypal and even Olympian perspective. Allow yourself as god or goddess to observe the causal weave of circumstances that informs the life, the strengths and weaknesses, the lacks and the possibilities of your human. Observe where he or she is coming from and where they could be going. Above all, state what is needed in the life to get on with it, what in Odyssean terms would enable your human to get off the island of his or her stuckness and get home. Should it be that your human is not stuck, then you as god or goddess might deal with the state of transition that your human may be in, and the help that he or she needs with this transition.

The perspective of the gods is always a helpful and empowering one, and you have to be careful not to let your god share in your local human's current negative view of him- or herself. Here is an example of what *not* to do.

Goddess: "Consider my human Doris. What an awful wretch! Most of her life she has been betrayed, cheated, disliked. She has no talents and little hope. Nor is there any good reason why she should have any. Doris is a real loser, and you'd think that as a goddess I would have been given someone less pitiful to work with. I think I'll trade Doris in for a new edition."

It would be far better for the Friend in Court to see her client from the perspective of the rich gifts inherent in every human being, and which the larger perspective of the "god" can discern. Here then is another version of the Friend in Court speaking for the same human.

Goddess: "Consider my human Doris. What a strange and interesting life she has had. So many tests, so many challenges, so much learning experience. But Doris has prevailed and become wiser than she knows. That is why so many people seek her out for counsel, for she has the wisdom that has come from suffering. And so compassionate too. Why just last week Doris helped her nephew through an episode of traumatic doubt and brought him to a place of wanting to live again. Doris's rich harvest of experience makes her deeply sensitive to the developing patterns in the lives of others. She shows all the makings of a midwife of souls. Clearly a new role in life is calling her. Tell me, gods, how and what you see this role to be? For Doris is rare among mortals, and her present unhappiness is but the passing emotion of the striving soul whose abundance of being has not yet unfolded. How can we help Doris?"

The other "gods" will listen with attention and compassion and offer only helpful, thoughtful, and high-minded suggestions. They speak only out of High Self and they never try to "do therapy." After one god has finished speaking for his or her human (10–15 minutes), the next god assumes the role of the Friend in Court for his or her human. (The guide should indicate the end of the allotted time for each god's statement.)

(After all three gods have finished speaking for their human, the guide will give the following directions.)

In the light of further reflection and the briefs of the other gods, each god is now allowed several minutes to give an overview and a summation of the life and needs of his or her human charge. (The guide will keep time and allot 2 minutes for each god's summation.)

(At the conclusion of this process, the guide may advise each member of the court to give thanks and honor to the other members for their support. The court can close with a dance of the gods and a resuming of human identification.)

Sacred Sound: Evoking the Three Realms of Being

As we discussed in the first section of this book, sacred psychology is based on three realms of being, each having its own kind of reality. The opportunity and challenge, then, is to become a citizen of all these realms, at home as a full participant and co-creator. In this exercise, we will set up those resonant fields of sound that can help you in doing that. One significant element of many sacred psychologies is the use of sacred sound in the form of repetitions, mantras, zikrs, affirmations. These function as evocateurs and reminders of the larger reality of which we are a part, and give us access to this reality and its transformational power. There is no question that these practices have neurophysiological power. Indeed, there have been many studies demonstrating the power of chanting in reorganizing the nervous system, centering consciousness, and providing for pathways to the deeper Self.

In various advanced cultures there are creation myths in which the world is described as being brought into being by the utterance of the God-force in a certain frequency. These are the great myths of the Edict, and they tell us a great deal about the nature of our creative intentions in the re-formation of ourselves. In the following practice we perform our own myth of creation; we incarnate frequency, and chant ourselves into an identity with all the realms that inform our being.

You will chant in a slowly accelerating rhythm in order to identify with and bridge the realms of I AM, WE ARE, and THIS IS ME.

After doing this process initially for thirty or forty minutes, you may wish to do it for five minutes several times a day. It will be especially effective if you do it upon awakening and before going to sleep. It is also useful at times of stress to bring you back to your own center, while, at the same time, enlarging your perspective.

TIME: 30–40 minutes.

MATERIALS NEEDED: A gong with a deep resonant sound. If you do not have a gong, you may use a good drum or a deep bell. In the instructions, reference is made to a gong, but obviously you will use whatever instrument you have.

INSTRUCTIONS FOR WORKING ALONE: Although this is best done initially in a group, you can do it alone by reading the instructions thoroughly, doing it with your kinesthetic body as you read, and then actually doing it physically.

SCRIPT FOR THE GUIDE: Begin by sitting up straight and getting very comfortable. Breathe slowly and deeply while you listen to the instructions.

I will strike a gong, and together we will chant a long extended "IIIIIIAaaaaaammmmmmmm. . . ." As you chant these words, know them and feel them, not just as sounds but as a realm of being. You will become the realm of I Am, letting yourself he filled with the fullness of the god realm that is the I Am. You will become Being Itself.

Then the gong will sound again, and we will chant an extended "Wwwwweeeeeee Aaaaarrrrrreeee. . . ." Again you will identify with what is implied in the words *We Are*. Thus you will become gods and goddesses, archetypes and mythic figures, with all their potent forms and messages. You will become the great creative forms and principles underlying creation—Christ, Buddha, Athena, Vishnu, the Good, and the Beautiful. Feel the marvelous richness of this great inner archetypal crew as you chant the words.

Then I will sound the gong for the third time and we will chant "TttthhhhiiiissssIiiissssssMmmmeeee. . . ." This time you will identify totally with who you are in everyday space and time—your name, your profession, your gender, your interests, and all of the other identifiers and functions that pertain to daily existence in our culture.

Then I will sound the gong again and go back through the I Am, We Are, This Is Me, over and over again for a period of fifteen minutes or so. At some point,* the gong will begin to sound at shorter intervals and there will be a gradual speeding up of the chant until it is a continuous, rapid I-Am We-Are This-Is-Me I-Am We-Are This-Is-Me I-Am We-Are This-Is-Me. . . . This will allow for a confluence and flow between these different states. We emerge from this with a deepened sense of access to the weave of these three realities.

(The guide now carries out the instructions with the participants, allowing about twenty minutes or longer, depending on time available for the whole process.

At the end of the accelerated chanting, the guide will slow down the process to the original speed and end with one last cycle of I Ammmmmmmmmmmmmmm Weeeeeeeeeee Aaarrrreeee Thiiiiiiss Isssssssss Meeeeee.

Allow now a few minutes of silence to deepen the sensation of sounds.

In many cases, discussion may not be appropriate immediately. After a break, participants can discuss this experience. Everyone should be urged to practice on a daily basis, and this can be discussed at your next meetings.

*At the discretion of the guide.

Again, responses differ from person to person, and all are valid. Some report a sense of deep centering and peace; others report that the chant seems to continue even when their consciousness is apparently elsewhere; still others report a sense of continuity between realms that enables them to move through situations with greater clarity and compassion than they had previously known.)

PART THREE
Basic Themes

Overleaf: Representing a shift from the old to the new paradigm, an earth-spirit goddess rises from the ground, welcomed by the spirits of new life and love. The satyrs have broken open the ground to allow the goddess to rise; the erotes fly in attendance. Terra cotta vase, detail; Hellenic Era, ca. 375 B.C.; Museum Royaux d'Arte et d'Histoire, Brussels.

INTRODUCTION TO BASIC THEMES

Many of the major themes of sacred psychology have to do with the quickening of the larger story and the movement of the human agenda from the personal particular to the personal universal. To demonstrate this, I have chosen three critical themes which, in my practice, have been found to encourage a rich and complex development for both individuals and groups. Taken together they reveal the movement from the THIS IS ME realm of our everyday story, to the WE ARE archetypal realm of our more universal story, and finally to the I AM realm of union with the Beloved, the god self within.

The first chapter of this section deals with the nature and relevance of story and myth to the finding of the personal entelechy. The exploration of the "pattern that connects" within our own particular stories and myths signals the deep self that we are ready to embark upon a journey of transformation.

In the second chapter, which deals with the immensely potent themes of wounding and betrayal, we discover ways to effect the healing and resolution of those areas in our lives that have kept us caught in static anguish. By probing our own tragic dimension for its deeper story, as well as raising it to a mythic level, our wounding becomes the vehicle for grace and we become spiritually charged and able to live a larger and nobler life. This life consummates, as we show in the third chapter, in our seeking and finding the Beloved of the soul, thereby partnering spiritual reality in order to bring the great creative patterns of possibility into the world of space and time.

9

OF STORY AND MYTH

The destiny of the world is determined less by the battles that are lost and won than by the stories it loves and believes in.[1]

—HAROLD GODDARD

Sacred psychology calls for the recovery and deepening of our personal story. A deeper story sustains and shapes our emotional attitudes, provides us with life purposes, and energizes our everyday acts. It offers us both meaning and momentum. Everything coheres when a deeper story is present.

CONNECTING WITH GREAT STORY

Life is a treasure hunt for story. Gregory Bateson describes story as "a little knot or complex of that species of connectedness which we call relevance."[2] Thus we seek, consciously or unconsciously, for those people and ideas whose stories seem relevant to our own. Their stories illumine, run parallel to, and fill in the missing gaps of our story. Human connections are deeply nurtured in the field of shared story.

When I begin my seminars, I always tell stories—stories that have been key to my being and becoming. These tales set the stage for the work the participants and I are to do together, and they serve as living metaphors for the processes I am about to teach. For example:

When I was eight years old, my father, a comedy writer, invited me to go with him to deliver a script to Edgar Bergen, the ventriloquist whose weekly radio show he was writing at the time. I loved visiting with his dummy, Charlie McCarthy, who was very friendly to me (although evidently not to Ed's daughter Candice, to whom he felt deep sibling rivalry.) Ed didn't hear us as we knocked at his open hotel door; he was sitting on the side of a bed deep in conversation with Charlie. My dad shrugged. "He's rehearsing." But then we heard what Ed was saying. He was asking Charlie ultimate questions, like: "Charlie, what is the nature of love? What is the meaning of life truly lived? What really comprises the good, the true, and the beautiful?" And Charlie was answering! Pouring out pungent, beautifully crafted statements of deep wisdom. This funny-faced little dummy was expounding the kind of knowing that could only have come from a lifetime of loving study, observation, and interaction with equally high beings.

After several minutes of listening to this wooden Socrates, my father, embarrassed, coughed. Bergen looked up and somewhat shamefacedly greeted us. "Hello, Jack, hi, Jean. I see you caught us."

"Yeah, Ed," my father said. "What in the world are you doing?"

"I'm talking to Charlie. He's the wisest person I know."

"But Ed," my father expostulated, "that's your voice and your mind coming out of that dummy!"

"Yes Jack, I suppose it is," Ed answered quietly. But then he added with great poignancy, "And yet, when he answers me, it is so much more than I know."

At that moment my future was set. I had no choice but to pursue a path and a career that would discover ways to tap into the "so much more" of the deep knowledge that we all contain but rarely contact. These ways are offered in my seminars, not to produce more ventriloquists, but to enable people to inhabit more levels of themselves.

I use story also to illustrate the work of sacred psychology, which, among other things, provides a way to expand and enrich a shrinking story. For sometimes our stories are too small and we find ourselves caught in the morass of being wedded to what seems to us a tale of trivia. Sometimes, too, in despair or crisis, our story suddenly ends or seems bereft of meaning. We may break down, succumb to inertia, experience defeat and a kind of death. But if we can continue to remember and value story, then the grace of story will rise again, gifting us with a deeper narrative and a deeper journey, filled with patterns of connection and felicitous engagements that seemed impossible before.

How, in the midst of loss, can we remember story? By consciously and conscientiously seeking Great Story, inviting its power to pour into our lives. Great Story is like a force field, charging the many incidents of our personal history with meaning and significance. Great Story plays upon our minds like a symphony, activating different tones, themes, feelings, and fancies, illuminating parts of ourselves we didn't know we had. When we join Great Story we align our lives with evolutionary forces that carry us beyond old agendas into new ways of being.

By Great Story, I mean story that enables us to see patterns of connections, as well as symbols and metaphors to help us contain and understand our existence. I mean story that contains a rich mytho-poetic language whose power propels us beyond the personal-particular focus of the local life toward that realm I call the personal-universal. Great Story contains images that are historical, legendary, mythical, ritualistic, and archetypal. In the mythic and symbolic dramas of Psyche, Prometheus, Parsifal, Oedipus, Antigone, Odysseus, Isis, Rumi, Jesus, Buddha, Faust, and Coyote, we can discover the broad patterns of our own lives, finding ourselves changed and charged. For in this time of the democratization of consciousness and psyche, extraordinarily interesting and useful things can happen to those who tap into Great Story. We become ones who herald "the prophetic moment, the annunciation of a new myth, and the beginning of a new culture,"[3] as William Irwin Thompson describes it.

Consider those teachers who see the child as the pattern of infinite possibility, a crossroad of biology and cosmogony; they work with passionate commitment to call forth the wonder dwelling within that child. And consider the cook who marries available ingredients to the styles of many cultures to create a planetary cuisine at the local cafe. Consider the judge who sees the dynamic relationship between society and the offender, and works to heal the whole. In each of these instances, a larger story has entered, more energy has been released, and new connections have been revealed.

Great Story is powerful and primal, capable of unlocking levels of the deep psyche. Engaging it produces an intense force, which in turn produces a mutation in consciousness. You become who you really are—and you know it. At those times when you are open to a sense of your own deeper story, "coincidences" multiply; suddenly there is energy for even tedious tasks; everything feels haloed with meaning. And you gain opportunities for opening to larger and larger stories, to an awareness that everybody and everything is replete with story. That is the Pattern that Connects.

To know the pattern is to know a loadedness of connected stories: What is it that connects the starfish on the beach, the two-month-old human embryo, the sainted ecstatic wandering the streets of Benares, and the Sequoia grove, to one another and to you? What is a seed but a loaded story waiting for its unfolding? What is that tiny embryo but a potent and potentiating story? All primroses and coconut palms, starfish and stars are connected through story.

HOW THE MIND STORES STORY

Observe your own imagery long enough, and what emerges? Lots of stories with beginnings, middles, ends, and even new beginnings. In our own research we discovered, for example, that first-level imagery is random sensory-level raw data—a purple snail, an elf, your mother-in-law, the tiles on the bathroom floor. Then, as you watch your images, invariably they go from a sensory, random level to a psychological level and become storied. Random things—a park, a face—coalesce and you have a person with that face walking through a park, meeting someone, and something happens.

If you continue to watch these stories long enough, or if your level of consciousness deepens, the story becomes even more profound. No longer random, personal, psychological stories, they become mythic. The park becomes a magical landscape and there is something to be found, something forgotten and buried in the sand that you begin to search for—perhaps a "Pearl of Great Price." Before you know it, you have a myth.

If you continue the story long enough, what happens? It becomes integral and spiritual. The treasure that you have found becomes a source of illumination. You have arrived and are accessible to all Story.

This developmental progression of imagery, which I have found to be universally available, suggests that these four levels—sensory, psychological, mythic, and integral—are built into the innate story lining of the brain/mind system of each of us.[4] As you move through these levels, or as they move through you, you travel from the personal-particular to the personal-universal levels of Story, taking on widening contexts and deeper formulations.

There is a tale about a man who passionately loved his computer—a great, extraordinary, mainframe computer capable of analyzing millions of bits of data in microseconds. One day, filled with yearning for deeper communion, he typed on his keyboard: "Do you compute, O Beloved, that you will ever think like a human being?" The computer hummed in response, and then a line appeared on the screen—"That reminds me of a story."

HOW WE USE STORY

Helen Luke, veteran explorer of the nature of story, enables her clients to raise their own stories to mythic dimensions. She writes:

> A real story touches not only the mind, but also the imagination and the unconscious depths in a person, and it may remain with him or her through many years, coming to the surface of consciousness now and then to yield new insights.[5]

Luke reminds us that story is like a time-released capsule. Not an ephemera of the moment, it works deeply within us as a potent structuring force.

Storytelling is the oldest form of teaching, and the basic vehicle for the transmission of culture from one generation to another. Jesus taught through parables. The Hindu lives in a culture knit by the great stories of the *Mahabharata* and the *Ramayana.* The Sufi is trained through the stories of Nasrudin. All of these great teaching stories are available on multiple levels, simple enough for the child, yet complex enough to engage the deepest levels of reflection.

Many educators have recognized this truth. Story is at the heart of the Waldorf Schools, which are based on the philosophy of Rudolph Steiner. There teachers tell their students *The Odyssey, The Iliad, The Quest for the Grail.* In these schools, the practice of sacred psychology is a way of life.

An acquaintance of mine, John Simon, created a school in New York, the Dome, for teenage boys whose lives promised little more than years in prison. One of his techniques was to read the great tragic dramas to his students and have them act out the story. He'd have them play out Oedipus, and identifying directly with the story, they'd say—"Yeah, in my family we've got a situation like that too." Suddenly their local, devastating personal story was played out in terms of the grand speech, grand tragedy, grand emotions, and grand depths. Some of them went on to become scholars, and, in the best sense, gentlemen—"people of the gentle airs"—instead of "people of the violence." For they were activated by Great Story—and great nurturing too, I might add.

The hearth and the campfire have served as the sacred site of storytelling for millennia. Gathered around a flickering fire, surrounded by the darkness of the night, people have come together to share their stories, to listen again to the old ones informed by the new experiences of the active day. Thus they have been re-sourced, connected again to meaning, to pattern, and to one another.

We must restore story. It is a shame that so many grandparents have moved to sunnier climes and are no longer available for the telling of stories. In this era of radical mobility, we have no hearth for storytelling, so we have lost the pattern of connection, the knot or complex of relevance that serves as a force field to illuminate and play out the human story. No hearth, no heart.

Nowadays, the hearth has been supplanted by the television set, which often tells aborted, abbreviated stories. This may be one reason that many are so bored and find life meaningless. If you watch—

> disconnected pieces of news: blip
> soap opera: blip blip
> situation comedy: blip, blip, blip

—interspersed with the big-blip commercial, then finding the Pattern that Connects is a major challenge. All too often the television is turned on to escape from complexity and the pattern-making mind.

Story is living and dynamic. Stories exist to be exchanged. They are the currency of human growth. Stories conjugate. Alone you are stuck. In the exchange, both you and the story change. Stories need to be told and retold, heard and reheard to reveal their meaning. We go to therapists to tell our stories, to remember them, to dig into their deeper meaning. We check in with our best friends to swap stories. Indeed, old and close friends tell each other stories of their lives *ad infinitum,* and to the outsider, often *ad nauseam.* However, friends are not boring each other; rather they are working together to reveal the facts of the story, to call forth its illumination. This exchange of story is at the heart of sacred psychology.

The quality and nature of the story we will tell is determined, in part, by the one to whom we tell it, for we want our stories to be recognized, approved. When this does not happen, we are subtly diminished.

We are also selective about the specific content of our stories, depending upon who the listener is. If I were your physician for instance, you might tell me a story about your childhood bout with whooping cough and frequent head colds and occasional pneumonia, for you would be asking me to give meaning to the story of your health.

If I were a Freudian psychiatrist, you would tell me about what your father did, what your mother didn't, the envy you felt at baby sister, the anxious love of Mama, the fear of Papa, the repressed sexuality, and the neurosis before the Other, who reminds you of Papa. Eventually, if I pressed you, you might finally tell me a story remarkably similar to the Greek tragedy of Oedipus Rex. For this you would have my smiling approbation, and your story would bloom into meaning.

If, however, I were a Jungian therapist, you would surely tell me your dreams and archetypal stories, about wise old men who dwell on the inner planes, about anima figures, and other symbolic forms from your deep psyche—all woven together as a rather esoteric story.

If I were your seatmate 35,000 feet up, chances are you would tell me the story of your profession, or of where you just came from and what you are about to do. This story is not likely to go far.

If I were a priest in a confessional, you might tell me about recent anxieties, fears of unworthiness, and sinful behavior—all seen as story. You want absolution so that this particular story can end.

If I am someone you are courting, you may tell me a glorified story of where you came from and where you are going in this golden universe that you are willing to share with me.

If I were a child, you might tell me the stories of your own childhood. And finally, if I were a brilliant microbe, traveling to all these places embedded in your skin and hearing all these different tales that you tell and not knowing that context creates story, I'd probably think you a liar and an untrustworthy character.

For in each case, story is verified and vivified in the telling and the hearing. It builds a bridge between the teller and the listener that transcends all factual accuracy.

HOW STORY USES US

Resistance to Story is a great and present reality for many. The seductive lure of homeostasis, the steady hum of the even keel, urges you to "stop the world and get off." This resistance is supported by your culture and your tribe, which are often quick to remind you to follow the tribed and true.

A great deal of current "positive thinking" is premised on selecting, by means of affirmation and visualization, only that aspect of your story that relates to your apparent prosperity and getting what "you" want *out* of life. The problem with this is: Which one of the polyphrenic "yous" is doing the wanting? Which "you" is being used, and which of the "yous" is getting abused? Those denied aspects of yourself, shadow and all, are having their stories rendered impotent and unseen. Inevitably they will rise in revolt. And then, suddenly, you will have to make many desperate and mindless affirmations against shadow forces that you earlier affirmed do not exist.

And still Great Story seeks you in many guises: falling in love with the "wrong" person, a chance encounter with the unknown, a strange and disturbing dream that will not leave you, a phone call out of the blue, or any one of a number of events that do not fit in with the current small story. As storytellers always tell us: "The plot thickens." You can avoid the story as much as you wish, but the story has a remarkable way of coming back to seek you.

These days, stories, little local stories, have an almost revolutionary way of ending. Marriages end, people lose or change their jobs, whole communities change their demography within a few years, obsolescence occurs overnight. No longer does "happily ever after" offer a real vision of the future. Story is accelerating.

In the face of this unprecedented acceleration, you may go to Story, kicking and screaming all the way and saying, "I don't want to see! Please, I don't want to see!" This protest arrives when the thickening plot suggests a story that you do not like, that you find inconvenient, that seems devastating. Yet devastation, or at least radical surprise, is an inevitable and central theme of Great Story, which always engages us at our most fragile and wounded edges. Then, suddenly, in these events that wound, the ensuing holes make us holy, allow more information, more interchange, and more stories to come in. (This theme of awakening to

Larger Story through wounding and devastation will be explored in depth in Parts Three and Four.)

As you are broadening your story, if you are also deepening and amplifying your patterns of connection by extending the capacities of your body, your mind, and your spirit, then quite simply, you evolve. Sometimes you evolve exponentially; that is, you grow into deeper patterning, connection, communication, and networking of mind, soul, and being—into deeper integration with the complex of interrelated realities waiting for your engagement. Facilitating this conscious participation in your own evolution is the whole purpose of sacred psychology.

WHAT HAPPENS WHEN STORY IS LIMITED

The limiting of our stories, by ourselves or by others, inevitably has tragic consequences. What is any kind of illness, mental or physical, but a limiting of story?

Cancer can be seen as a limitation of story, a limitation in the relationship between cells, so that one limited but imperialistic story proliferates. On the simplest level, the cure is the burning or cutting out of the imperialistic story. The more complex cure is the finding of ways for the richer, deeper stories to rise within the organism.

My associates and I have worked with people whose physical illnesses seem to have been precipitated by narrowing stories. Our work has been to rediscover the connections with a larger story, inner and outer. The discovery of these stories apparently works to orchestrate, on cellular levels, the whole organism. Illness can then be seen as an invitation, albeit an often unwelcome one, to inhabit larger story.

This idea is not new. Among the Native Americans of the Southwest, healing has been accomplished by reciting and chanting the Long Story (the tale of the creation of the world and its creatures) over the body of the sick person for as many as seven days. The family, and even members of the community, participate in this process under the guidance of the community shaman. This story of origin, of creation, sometimes accompanied by a sand painting on the body, releases those energies inherent in creation to restore life and health.

This is not to suggest that death is to be denied or avoided. For all peoples who have the time and place to listen to the story of nature, death is not the end of story; it is, rather, a change in the status or level of story. Thus "Life and Death" are known as a never-ending story.

Part of being skillful in sacred psychology is knowing when to allow the story to shift when death, or some other form of transition, is appropriate. Our hospitals and nursing homes are filled with people plugged into life-support systems whose story in local space and time has already ended. The work of Elisabeth Kübler-Ross and those involved in the hospice movement is dedicated to illuminating this transition of story. Again, this idea is not new. The *Tibetan Book of the Dead* testifies to an ancient tradition of providing storied transition for the great journey of the soul at the time of death.

When my mother-in-law was dying, painfully and reluctantly, I sang to her, in sequence, the songs she had heard and loved during her lifetime from the year 1902 to 1976, beginning with lullabies and nursery rhymes, ending with the Beatles, and including many hymns along the way. She was able to die with the story line of her life, heard in these songs, carrying her through the transition.

Many of you are probably in the helping professions and have listened for thousands of hours to neurotics. And what do you hear? The same old story, over and over again. Neurotics cannot seem to move beyond their story to broader contexts and deeper formulations. Your work is clear. It is not to *change* the story, for this is to deny it; it is, rather, to *expand and deepen* the story, thus releasing the energy bound within it. (Future chapters of this book address the "how-to" of this process.)

Similarly, when one ideology, be it religious, political, psychological, or economic, imposes its limited story on another culture, the culture is maimed, if not decimated.

In various places around the world, missionaries, of both the technical and religious varieties, often impose their own particular and limited story, with little or no exchange of Essential Story. The result is an inhibition of the local story. Invariably there will be a revolt as the repressed story seeks to reassert itself. Certainly this has happened in Iran, where a twentieth-century high-tech story was imposed from above on a people whose richly storied culture was ignored and bypassed. Other examples of such attempts and their consequences are legion. The imperialism of a limited story may appear to be efficient, but it is, at best, a short story. Should such impositions be successful (which is unlikely, since Essential Story itself is a more powerful force than gold), there would be a tragic diminution of planetary Story and planetary soul.

Such domination, however, is true not only in our dealings with other nations; it is true in all relationships. Sometimes apparently "advantaged" service professionals, with the best of intentions, unconsciously impose their limited stories on those they purport to serve, often crippling them and impoverishing their psychic ecology. The same "imperialism of story" often exists in the therapeutic process, in the parenting process, and in the teaching process. Indeed, it exists whenever you have the One who tells you and shows you the "right" thing to do.

All healing, helping, and consulting professions are more effective when interactive storying can occur, when each story is enriched and all of Story can grow. Basically, imposition of story is a human anomaly. For any kind of creation must be a *co*-creation. Thus much of the work of sacred psychology is done in dyads and triads so that it will be co-creative. Together, you con-verse and create a richer pattern of story.

All over the globe we find people increasingly available to the myth and metaphor, the magic and mystery of story. You who are reading this book may very well have become involved in the renaissance of story, be it through interest in other religions or fascination with symbol and myth. If so, you are a part of a rising planetary phenomenon.

THE EFFECTIVENESS OF STORIES

Because Great Stories implicitly engage all manner of human function, while seducing us with the passion and promise inherent in narrative, they are far more effective vehicles for transformation than volumes of didactic and theoretical material. If I say: "Now this is the way you change your brain, change your brain, change your brain. This is the way you open your heart, open your heart," and so on, one superficial level of you would learn a lot of techniques, and you might be very happy—for a while. But you would not have stories or deep connecting patterns both within you and between you and other human beings.

If the same techniques are taught within the context of a Great Story, more of you would be engaged because Great Story taps deep levels and provides for connections across categories. When I began teaching human capacities fifteen years ago, I taught brain exercises, sensory expansion, imagery, and psychophysical reeducation, but not in a storied context. Although the teaching was "successful," I have found that the work of human growth and deepening is much richer and more enduring if it is storied with the great plots and patterns that live in our psyches.

OF MYTH AND PSYCHE

All Great Stories draw their power from an archetypal world, the world of pattern, the world of the soul's authority, which is common to people of all cultures and all times.

As the body and mind extend in capacity, the psyche becomes more available to explore in a healthy and creative manner its roots in mythic dimensions. Go as far as you can, take as many paths as you want on the journey into psyche, and you will inevitably find yourself in the realm of myth.

What is myth?

I have asked and sought, lost and found, fought and pleaded with this question for many years. This journey has sent me all over the world to take depth soundings of the psyches of those whose lives have touched mine. It has greened me in the wasteland, and it has wasted me by its sudden turns and shocks when I thought I was in the green land. It gives me knowledge, even occasionally wisdom, but remains elusive.

To attempt to speak about myth, one has to use metaphor and reach through the back door or side window of thought. (And so I say, paraphrasing Mr. Browning, "A man's reach must exceed his grasp, or what's a Meta Phor?")

Myth is something that never was but is always happening. It is the nuclear cell in the entelechy, the wake-up call from Central: "It's time! Time to wake up now!"

Fairy tales are essentially narrative complexes that collapse many mythic archetypal structures into one story.[6] Myth, however, has a more universal formulation that speaks to the codings of the deep unconscious. Thus myth is not just an ancient narrative designed to entertain benighted souls during the long winter evenings; it is an imprint in the psychic and spiritual DNA. Can I "prove" this? No. Do I believe it? Absolutely.

Joseph Campbell has perhaps dug more deeply than any other figure in our century into the mythic loam from which our humanity grows. In the opening pages of *The Hero with a Thousand Faces,* he writes:

> It would not be too much to say that the myth is the secret opening through which the inexhaustible energies of the cosmos pour into human cultural manifestation. Religions, philosophies, arts, the social forms of primitive and historic man, prime discoveries in science and technology, the very dreams that blister sleep, boil up from the basic, magic ring of myth.
>
> The wonder is that the characteristic efficacy to touch and inspire deep creative centers dwells in the smallest nursery fairy tale—as the flavor of the ocean is contained in a droplet or the whole mystery of life within the egg of a flea. For the symbols of mythology are not manufactured; they cannot be ordered, invented, or permanently suppressed. They are spontaneous productions of the psyche, and each bears within it, undamaged, the germ power of its source.[7]

Myth orchestrates the culture and consciousness of entire civilizations.

And a new myth is indeed rising now. Consider how many of you have become fascinated with myths and symbols in the last few years. From the acoustically amplified, mythically cloaked rock group to the proliferation of drugstore paperbacks with mythic themes, there is a growing awareness that just beneath the surface crust of consciousness are cornucopias teeming with myths and symbolic stories. "Mythological symbols," Campbell writes, "touch and exhilarate centers of life beyond the reach of vocabularies of reason and coercion."[8]

Embedded in the psyche itself, myth engages the depths because it expresses in its own imagery and on its own terms the symbolic figures and actions, not just of the unconscious, but also of what is often called the superconscious. Myth is a kind of lensing system for the mind of God. It carries the codings of existence.

Proximate to the creative principle itself, myth can be tremendously evocative of individual creative forms, for in moments of high creativity, people often run into some powerful, mythic, imaginal force that so quickens them that they say, "Here I am, and here is more of me, and more upon that, and still more. . . ." And in being more, they are seized by the forms, forces, and dimensions of their own creative power. Out of this seizure comes a book, a play, a project, a friendship, a new way of being.

Campbell has observed how mythology serves four major functions:

1. *It provides a bridging between one's local consciousness and the* mysterium tremendum et fascinans *of the universe—the sheer, vast, overwhelming environment of being.* It reconciles local, historical space-time with transcendent realms and eternal forms. One might say, for example, that Thomas Jefferson, Benjamin Franklin, and the other American Founding Fathers believed that theirs was a mythic moment in which they were enabled "to create the world anew."

2. *Myth provides an interpretive image of the relationship between local and universal consciousness.* It provides, in artistic and religious form, the "revelation to waking consciousness of the powers of its own sustaining source." The Hopi Sun Dance, the Passover ceremony of the Jews, the Christian celebrations of Easter and Christmas, the Dragon Festival of the Chinese New Year—all of these employ the ritual art and spirit of the remembrance of who we are, where we came from, and why we continue to be.

3. *Myth empowers the moral order and brings about a reconciliation between the individual and his or her environment, climate, geography, culture, and social group.* For example, if you are an inheritor of the Judeo-Christian tradition, you follow certain ethical precepts because Moses received them on the tablets at Mt. Sinai millennia ago. If you are a Navaho, you know how to live a spiritual life because many moons ago Spider Woman gave your ancestors directions and prescriptions for "walking the pollen path."

For those societies in which the local mythology works, there is "the experience both of accord with the social order and of harmony with the universe." Being several times removed from that harmony by virtue of industrialization and the shattering of natural rhythms, we long for that universe of which we were once so intimately a part, that realm of nature and deep belonging. Myth assures us, however, that the universe fits together, even though we may live in towering glass houses and get our dogma from the editorials in the newspaper or the preachers on television.

When mythological symbols no longer work, we experience a sense of alienation from society, often followed by a desperate quest to replace the lost meaning of the once-powerful myths. Consider the recent widespread interest in exploring the myths and rituals of the Native American, the mysteries of Egypt, the practices of Tibetan Buddhism, and the shamanism of Central and South America. This kind of exploration has offered an extended perspective and allowed us to find valuable commonalities. Perhaps we had to leave our heritage to see it, to widen and deepen our perspective. Now we can return, renewed and refreshed, both to harvest the bounty of our own stories and to link all the stories of the planet; for surely, for the first time in history, we are on the verge of a planetary mythos.

4. *Most importantly, myth "foster[s] the centering and unfolding of the individual in integrity," with himself (the microcosm), his culture (the mesocosm), the universe (the macrocosm), and finally with the ultimate creative mystery that is "both beyond and within himself and all things."*[9]

Myth is always, in some sense, about soulmaking and about the pathos that accompanies the journey of the soul as it travels from outmoded existence to the amplified life in the Kingdom. Thus the fascination of the depth psychologists, especially Jung and his followers, with the parallels between the structure of myth and the process of individuation.

To be true to myth, we must also speak to its autonomy. The great stories and actions of the soul function within each of us seemingly quite apart from our own directives or even our awareness. These stories emerge as spontaneous creations, full and richly detailed realities glimpsed in dreams, in visions, in moments when the walls between the worlds are let down.

Indeed, a new story is beginning to emerge in our time. A new story of mythic proportions is trying to enter from the Pattern that Connects. The journey of sacred psychology is the journey to the new story in which you and the emerging story become one.

10

THE SACRED WOUND

Call the world, if you please,
The veil of Soulmaking.
Then you will find out
The use of the world...
—JOHN KEATS

Sacred psychology is the process and practice of soulmaking; and soulmaking, as you may have discovered, is not necessarily a happy thing. Critical parts of it are not. As seed making begins with the wounding of the ovum by the sperm, so does soulmaking begin with the wounding of the psyche by the Larger Story.

Soulmaking requires that you die to one story to be reborn to a larger one. A renaissance, a rebirth, occurs not just because there is a rising of ancient and archetypal symbols. A renaissance happens because *the soul is breached.* In this wounding, the psyche is opened up and new questions begin to be asked about who we are in our depths. These powerful questions need not lead to alienation and withdrawal, but can lead to the seeding of the world with the newly released powers of the psyche. A larger story is revealed by the wounding. When psychological energy is no longer bonded to social forms, then, uncensored, depth images and archetypes can have their day. Whether they serve to madden or illumine is up to us.

The classical Renaissance was a golden time when internal and external realities flowered together. The internal world knew the cosmos for its own, and the external world became "psyche-tized." The spillover of psyche's abundance into the outer world primed the creation of vital and resonant arts, sciences, history, statecraft, and philosophy.

So, too, is your wounding, the breaching of your soul, an invitation to your renaissance. Our woundings tell us that old forms are ready to die, however reluctant the local self may be to allow this to occur, and that hitherto unsuspected new forms are ready to flower.

As the "ties that bind" loosen in our culture and in our psyche, the incidence of woundings accelerates and comes in many guises. Consider your *physical* woundings: illnesses, accidents, birth or genetic defects. Consider the *acts of violation* upon your person: rape, incest, child abuse, torture, robbery. Consider the *losses* you have endured: the loss of a deep relationship to death, the loss of a job, the loss of a marriage, the loss of sanity, the loss of self-esteem, the loss of status, the loss of financial security. Consider those *woundings that have afflicted cultures and nations:* famine, plague, enslavement, war. The list seems endless.

Wounding involves a painful excursion into pathos, wherein the anguish is enormous and the suffering cracks the boundaries of what you thought you could bear. And yet, the wounding pathos of your own local story may contain the seeds of healing and transformation. The recognition of this truth is not new. In the Greek tragedies, the gods force themselves into human consciousness at the time of pathos. It is only at this time of wounding that the protagonist grows into a larger sense of what life is all about and is able to act accordingly.

The wounding becomes *sacred* when we are willing to release our old stories and to become the vehicles through which the new story may emerge into time. When we fail to do this, we tend to repeat the same old story over and over again. If you have a neurosis or psychosis, it probably originated in pathos that was not worked out to its source in a Larger Story. If we would only look far enough and deep enough, we would find that our woundings have archetypal power. In uncovering their mythic base, we are challenged to a deeper life. As Carl Jung has reminded us, it makes a difference whether we serve a "mania," which is detestable and undignified, or a "god," which is full of meaning.

An abundance of sacred wounding marks the core of all great Western myths and their attending gods and humans: Adam's rib, Achilles' heel, Odin's eye, Orpheus's decapitation, Inanna's torture, Prometheus's liver, Zeus's split head, Pentheus's dismemberment, Job's boils, Jacob's broken hip, Isaiah's seared lips, Persephone's rape, Eros's burnt shoulder, Oedipus's blinding, Jesus' crucifixion. All of these myths of wounding carry with them the uncanny, the mysterious, the announcement that *the sacred is entering into time.* Each prefigures a journey, a renaissance, a birth or rebirth, a turning point in the lives of gods and mortals. In sacred psychology, the possibility for therapeia, for healing and wholing, seems to require acknowledgment and understanding of our deepest wounds.

Wounding involves the *breaking* or *penetration* or *opening* into the human flesh or soul by a force or power or energy coming from beyond our ordinary recognized boundaries. The violation of these boundaries makes us vulnerable to be reached by larger forces, Larger Story. Would there be much of a story around Jesus if he had been left to preach around Galilee and ply his trade as a carpenter? Only by being wounded unto death could he be prepared for the resurrection. In the Gospel of John, we are told: "I am the true vine and my Father is the vinedresser. Every branch of mine that bears no fruit he takes away, and every branch that does bear fruit, he prunes that it may bear more fruit." In our woundings we are forced to stop, to shift, to move in new directions, to face what had been hidden to consciousness, to be pruned of our primal growth so that we may bear fruit.

Instead of discrediting the phenomena of the myth as does a normative psychology, sacred psychology shows the ingeniousness and therapeutic power of myth in its ability to illumine and redeem the sacrality of the phenomena around wounding that occurs in our lives. It is not that the *myth* is wrong, but rather that we are ignorant of its contents. Without pathos, the larger story that the myth is trying to tell would not be whole. Myth allows both hearer and teller to see the Pattern that Connects. Similarly, in our own existential times of wounding, pathos can tap us directly into the deeper topographical levels of the psyche, where we both reflect and join the Larger Story.

In times of suffering, when you feel abandoned, perhaps even annihilated, there is occurring—at levels deeper than your pain—the entry of the sacred, the possibility of redemption. Wounding opens the doors of our sensibility to a larger reality, which is blocked to our habituated and conditioned point of view. Consciousness that had been previously well-robotized and trained to the consensual perspective of our particular culture is excruciatingly sensitized and has a vastly extended sensorium. Pathos gives us eyes and ears to see and hear what our normal eyes and ears cannot.

Wounding is the traditional training ground for the healer. The shaman-healer is often wounded and marked as part of his preparation. Those who have, through accident or illness, vividly confronted the reality of their own death often return to life with a renewed sense of wonder and strength. Moshe Feldenkrais developed his revolutionary methods of awareness through movement initially as a way of living with his badly damaged knees. F. Mathias Alexander, once a Shakespearean actor, developed his approach to proper body use from observing the postural causes of his own chronic laryngitis. Addicts who have managed to overcome their addiction have served as powerful guides to those caught in the throes of addiction. The god-man Asclepios was said to walk with a crippled leg; the Fisher King, who bears the secret of the castle of the Grail, has a wound that will not heal. Consider how your own wounding may be offering training in compassion and deepening.

Disconnected from the myth, from the Larger Story, and from the sacred, we seek to "understand" our pain, or find relief from it as quickly and comfortably as possible. Or we resort to blame and seek to avenge the wrongs done to us. Thus we turn our backs on the knocking at the door of our souls.

Sacred psychology offers an alternative: not always a comfortable one, or even always a "safe" one, but a very powerful one. Sacred psychology invites you to allow your wounds to stay open; to take off the Band-Aids and cover-ups; to allow the engagement of the Great Story; to link the local self to universal patterns; and to sacrifice the old story to which you were bonded so that the new story may become manifest through you.

This is *not* an invitation to self-pity, self-flagellation, victimization, or martyrdom. It is *not* an invitation to court disaster or revel in inauthentic suffering. Nor is it an invitation to the realm of Pollyanna. Suffering is real and soul-rending in our time. Despair, hopelessness, burnout, and a radical experience of impotence strike many who are most committed to offering alternatives.

And yet . . . And yet . . . The myth reminds us that the Phoenix rises from the ashes, burning bushes speak when all hope is lost, the blind Oedipus becomes the revered wise counselor of Athens, the Grail is ultimately found, and the Fisher King and the wasteland are healed.

In the cosmos of the psyche, our lives are governed by mythic and symbolic categories, and myths have their own patterns and logic, independent of individual ego processes. The sacred wound is the critical act through which the mortal achieves divinity. Christ must have his Crucifixion. Dionysius must boast to attract Titanic enemies. Persephone must be carried down to Hades and married to Darkness. Artemis must kill him who comes too close. So, too, must you breach that story that denies your full unfolding. You may deny and resist this truth with all the strength you can muster, but the woundings will continue, sometimes relentlessly, apparently meaninglessly, until you agree to wake up.

The two stories in Part Four serve to illustrate the power of wounding to deepen and extend both the story itself and all of those beings who play a part in and are touched by the story.

Before turning to them, however, you may need to re-vision and re-member your own wounding so that its larger pattern is revealed. We have been tyrannized by the local historical psychological story. While there is nothing wrong with this story, which carries its own level of truth, as the *only* story it is extremely limited, limiting, and isolating. In the process offered here, you are going to explore your own wounding, one that is central to you at this time, and allow it to unfold the greater dimensions and perspectives of which it is a part. Thus you will take your story from the THIS IS ME level to the WE ARE level, allowing the I AM to guide the process. Through the local story of your particular wounding, you will open the door to the Larger Pattern, the mythos itself, that is trying to enter your life.

It is essential that you ask the terrible and unavoidable questions: "Where and by whom were you wounded?" and "What or who is trying to be born in you from that wound?" In engaging these questions you may find the gestations of your own possibilities, the stigma that could well be the stigmata, the moment of your election to a larger reality. The process given here allows you to explore the broader implications and the depth story hidden in your wounding.

From Pathos to Mythos: A Therapeic Dyad

In this process you will raise your pathos to the level of myth, revisioning a time of personal loss and tragedy as an evolutionary and transformational event. While there is no effective way to erase past trauma, nor would it be wise to do so if there were, the past can be "remythologized" to reveal its deeper meaning. Beginning with the familiar story line of the THIS IS ME level of experience, you will, with the help of your partner, be enabled first by a series of questions and answers to explore the nature and pattern of your wounding. Then, moving deeper into the WE ARE realm of the story inherent in your own historical experience, you will be led to discover ways of understanding the events and patterns of your life mythically so that you may experience the power of redemption and transformation inherent in the Larger Story of your life.

It is important to remember that myth, like poetry, cuts quickly to the essence and tends to contain a great deal of information in symbolic form. Myth also exists beyond the parameters of local space and time. For this reason, details of dates, addresses, and the specifics of everyday life are not relevant in the telling of the myth. Each figure and situation in the myth is archetypal. Thus a soldier becomes the Warrior, a young girl is the Maiden-to-Be-Rescued, an animal may be the Ally, and a serpent the Guardian of the Gates. The child is always Holy, if unrecognized, the circumstances of birth extraordinary; the family is always poor but honest, or of the highest nobility (there is no bourgeoisie in the land of the myth); an elderly person is the Wise One; the one who yearns is the Lover, the one who seeks, the Hero or Heroine. In the language and structure of myth, details slide away and essence is revealed.

As we have seen, although wounding is central to the myth, the mythic movement continues beyond the wounding to the redemption of both the protagonist and his or her world. Thus the wounding serves as a necessary chastening and deepening for the central figure.

In doing this exercise, you will be enabled to tell your story mythically through and beyond your point of wounding to your place of resurrection and ennobling, even though historically that may not yet have happened in your own life. In teaching this exercise to thousands of people, we have found that the very act of telling a story of ennoblement and reempowerment that takes one beyond the wounding often establishes a new pattern for transformation and deepening in a person's life. The shifting of perspective is critical, but it is more than a mere reframing of your story. It is a way of accessing an innate transforming metaphor that seems to rise from the entelechy of yourself, giving you the finest story line available from the cauldron of possible stories. The gaining of a deeper story is a kind of grace when it comes, and it can only be evoked, not fabricated. Thus you are not just "making up" a story to "fix up" the wounds of your life. Rather, you are availing yourself of the deep intention of the Godseed Story that is yearning to emerge.

At the end of the process you will be asked to dance your myth, thereby allowing the myth to be more fully embodied in your physical reality. For those of you whose take on the world is more kinesthetic than imaginative, the dance is critical and often leads to a sudden realization of the deeper implications of the myth. For everyone it enhances and deepens the experience.

TIME: 90 minutes to 2 hours.

MATERIALS NEEDED: Boxes of tissue should be on hand to be passed out if needed.

MUSIC: Background music to be played during the process is music from *Area 1*, such as Kitaro's *Silk Road*. For the dancing of the myth, use music from *Area 3*, such as Pachelbel's *Canon in D* repeated twice.

INSTRUCTIONS FOR WORKING IN A GROUP: Before beginning, the participants should be thoroughly familiar with the material presented in the chapter up to this point, including the preceding introductory remarks for this process. They can have read it prior to meeting, or the material can be read and discussed at the meeting itself. If appropriate, each person might bring a favorite myth to share briefly with the group, thus creating a context in which the essence of mythic form would naturally become apparent.

The guide will firmly remind everyone that what is revealed in the course of this experience belongs to sacred time and sacred space. Under no circumstances is it to be discussed in any way beyond the confines of that space. Should you be so foolish as to go home and say to your friends or relatives, "You wouldn't believe the story I heard today!" and then give a juicy account of someone's story, certain consequences are bound to follow. You may forget for a while this "minor" betrayal, but the universe will not. And will it ever "dump" on you! Each person is free to disguise the particular events that have occurred as he or she tells the THIS IS ME story, if that seems necessary. However, being as specific as possible enhances the reality of the THIS IS ME realm.

Everyone should also be reminded that he or she is not engaging in therapy. No matter how emotionally involved people may become, the process must be allowed to continue as directed by the guide. Professional counselors must guard against their natural tendency to guide or interpret. For example, should one of the partners tell an emotionally loaded story that causes them to weep or respond strongly, the questioner does not offer comfort or interpretation, but continues to sit as high witness, repeating the question and listening with dignity. When the time comes to change roles, regardless of how emotionally involved the participant may be with his or her own story, he or she will rise to the occasion and with dignity ask the given question of his or her partner. In this way sacred space is maintained, and the process can unfold in a manner appropriate to therapeia.

INSTRUCTIONS FOR WORKING ALONE: If you are doing this exercise alone—and it is preferable that there be two people—read the instructions below and be sure that you understand the process fully.

Before you actually begin, write each of the questions on a separate sheet of paper on a page in your diary. Put on the music suggested here, or other meditative music, and do whatever else allows you to create an atmosphere of centering and clarity. Then write the answers to each of the questions. When you have completed the writing, read the answers aloud as though you were reading to a friend. On a separate piece of paper rewrite your story as a myth. Again, with full resonance and power, read your myth aloud. An alternate way of doing this is to ask and answer the questions into a mirror, as well as telling your myth into the mirror. Then put on the music and dance the myth you have just written and read.

SCRIPT FOR THE GUIDE: To begin, find a partner, preferably not someone you know very well.

Sit down together and touch hands, breathing slowly and deeply in unison for several minutes, setting up a resonance of breath, touch, and empathy.

Now decide who will be the first questioner and who the first answerer.

Each of you will now review silently the woundings in your life, allowing to rise to the surface of your consciousness that wounding which at this moment appears most critical. Go back to some of your earliest memories and let these guide you.

(Allow several minutes for this.)

I am going to give you a series of questions. The first questioner will repeat the question after I give it, and the first answerer will answer. At the end of five minutes, you will switch, and the person who has been answering the question will now ask the other the same question. Again there will be five minutes for responding.

We will repeat this process for each question. I will let you know when five minutes have ended and you need to switch roles, and then I will repeat the question so that both partners have a chance to ask and respond to each question.

If the person who is answering finishes before the 5 minutes have ended, then the questioner will repeat the question so that the answerer may enlarge upon his or her response. It is essential that you who are asking the question maintain your capacity to listen as high witness, with no commentary, no matter what you hear.

Unless there are any questions, we will begin now.

The first question: "What happened? How were you wounded?" Questioner, repeat these questions to your partner.

(After 5 minutes): Now will the person who has been answering ask the same question: "What happened? How were you wounded?" And the person who was asking now becomes the answerer.

(Allow 5 minutes for response.)

The second question: "What did you feel when you were wounded?" Questioner, repeat this question to your partner.*

(After 5 minutes): Now will the person who has been answering become the questioner and ask the same question: "What did you feel when you were wounded?" (Again, allow five minutes for response.)

The third question: "What were the full consequences of this wounding in your life, for good and ill?"

Remember that often our woundings allow us to reach out to others, beyond our stuck places, gaining experience that we would not have sought if we had not been wounded. This question, therefore, is a very important one and implies that there were many consequences, not just bad ones, that resulted from the wounding.

Again, the question is: Questioner, repeat this question to your partner.

(After 5 minutes): Now will the person who has been answering become the questioner and ask the same question: "What were the consequences in your life of this wounding, for good or ill?" (Another 5 minutes.)

The fourth question: "In the light of this, what do you want?" Questioner, repeat this question to your partner.

(After 5 minutes): Now will the person who has been answering become the questioner and ask the same question: "In the light of this, what do you want?" (Allow time for answers.)

*Note to Guide: Although this question may seem similar to the first, it allows the respondent to deepen the memory and understanding of their wounding.

The fifth question: "What does all this mean? What pattern is playing itself out here?" Questioner, repeat this question to your partner.

(After 5 minutes): Now will the person who has been answering become the questioner and ask the same question: "What does this all mean? What pattern is playing itself out here?"

(When this has been completed, the guide will continue as follows:)

You have been telling your story in the specific details of your existential life. Soon you will tell it again. But this time you will "re-member" it as a myth, assuming the role of myth-maker and telling it in the third person, not as "I," but as "she" or "he" or "it." Your protagonist may take any form that appears appropriate—mortal, animal, plant, or god. Allow the myth to go beyond the wounding to its natural resolution. The important thing is that the story have mythic and symbolic dimensions and be more universal in character than the story you have just told.

In telling your story existentially, you might say:

> Well, I was born into an average family. My mother was a schoolteacher and my father worked as conductor on the railroad. As the youngest child, nobody paid much attention to me. My mom was away working all day and my dad was away for days at a time. So one day I ran off to the woods and stayed there for three days and just enjoyed being with the squirrels and rabbits and birds. And when I got back, my father beat me with a strap until the blood came. My brothers and sisters wouldn't talk to me, and my mother didn't seem to care. I began to fail in school, and the teachers told me I was stupid.

Told mythically, the story up to this point could sound something like this:

> Once upon a time, there was a very special child, born with a promise and a light within him that was so bright that it blinded all others and they did not dare to look at him. Even his mother, who knew of the Ways Things Work, and his father, who officiated on Caravans to Distant Realms, could not see him. Only in the Forest was he known and recognized by the animals and birds. He stayed there once for a long time, experiencing the joy of being truly known and accepted for what he was. When he returned, he was tortured until he forgot his true identity. It seemed years that he wandered lost in mists, occasionally bumping into giants who would try to squash his tiny form. Crushed and broken he continued in this manner, until one day. . . .

Whatever kind of myth you tell, allow the story to well up from deep inside of you, not consciously creating it or trying to determine its details ahead of time. This will allow for the Larger Story, the Entelechy Story, to emerge. Allow yourself to be surprised by the gift and the grace of the Larger Story as it comes through your mouth.

You who are the listener will be present as fair witness, listening deeply to the myth that is about to unfold. Again, do not engage in any discussion or commentary. Simply stay present in deep listening.

You will have 15 minutes for the telling of this myth. If you are finished before the time given, stay seated together in silent communion.

Let the person who was the first questioner say: "Tell me your story as a myth, beginning 'Once upon a time . . .' and taking the story past the wounding to the place of transformation."

(After 13 minutes the guide says): You have two more minutes to allow your myth to come to its natural ending.

(At the end of the 15 minutes, the guide says): Let the person who has told the myth become the questioner and say to their partner: "Tell me your story as a myth, beginning 'Once upon a time . . .' and taking the story past the wounding to the place of transformation.

(After 13 minutes, the guide says): You have two minutes to allow your myth to come to its natural ending.

(When this has been completed, the guide continues): Now stand and individually dance the myth you have just told, enacting the stages of your myth in the dance. Know that frequently the dance releases other aspects of the story that were not there in the telling. Now let the music start and the dance of your living myth begin."

(Play the music for about 10 minutes. After the music is finished, the guide concludes): Return now to your partner and give thanks for what has been given and what has been received.

This process can be followed by a general discussion of what has been discovered and experienced, or time can be given for journal writing.

BETRAYAL

Betrayal, of all the woundings that may be suffered by the soul, can be the greatest agent of the sacred. This wound has always had an awful and luminous quality surrounding it. It marks the end of primal, unconscious trust, and forces upon us those terrible conditions that accompany the taking of the next step. In all the great stories, scriptures, and myths of betrayal, we find the loss of a simple and wholehearted faith in the Primal One, the bringer of justice, stability, and comfort. The condition of this trust has been a subtle and powerful binding that blocks the fullness of the greater consciousness needed to respond to new situations—situations that cannot be met within the old conditions.

Trust always contains the seeds of its own betrayal; the taboo implies and requires its own transgression. Betrayal allows for the coming of reflection and therefore of consciousness. And with consciousness you can trangress, transcend, deceive, evoke, evade, create, enter, and exit—in other words, you can get somewhere. The loss of primary attachments permits the entry of the "gods," the entry of the More, of insights and knowings that you could not assimilate before. The message of betrayal is always that things are much more than they seem.

Consider the two great myths of betrayal that dominate the Western mind. One is the myth of the Fall. Adam and Eve apparently betrayed God, but the story can also be read as their betrayal by their creator. There they are, living on welfare in paradise. They have a naive, total faith in God, and they obey all His wishes, even the one concerning the great forbidden act—to eat of the Tree of the Knowledge of Distinctions. Along comes the snake who has all the lines, offers all the temptations, and carries the call to complexity. When Eve eats of the Tree of the Knowledge of Distinctions, the trust is broken. Yet the snake was in the garden from the beginning. Is this a setup? Much closer to home, how or why have you set up the conditions for your own betrayal?

Eve and Adam are thrust out of the primal Garden and are on their own. They have to begin living by their wits, using and growing their bodies and minds as they challenge their environment and struggle for survival. Their conversation improves as does their pluck and cunning. They compound the distinctions even further, and in so doing, create culture and civilization and become more fully human. The story has grown.

The second great Western myth of betrayal is the betrayal of Christ. As James Hillman suggests, the key mystery of this story is not the Crucifixion; it is the Betrayal.[1] Throughout the narrative in the New Testament, Jesus is very sure of his primal bonding with God the Father. "I and My Father are One" is his repeated assertion. Even throughout the week of the Passion, although he is a man of sorrows, his primal trust is not shaken. You can see it in his behavior before Pontius Pilate. He even asks forgiveness for his tormentors.

But as the theme of betrayal unfolds its dark and mysterious course, it is raised to high ritual drama. It occurs in threes: by Judas, by the sleeping disciples, and by Peter. Peter's betrayal is itself repeated three times. That number tells us that something high and holy is going on. In each of these betrayals Jesus is forced to the terrible awareness of having been let down, failed, left alone. His love has been refused, his message mistaken, his call unattended, and his fate announced. Then, in the final moments when he is riveted to the cross, denied and abandoned by everyone—although not by his mother and the other women—he feels the full human depth of the reality of the betrayal, and cries out: "My God, My God, why hast thou forsaken me?"

The charismatic miracle preacher is gone, and the full human is born. At the end of primal trust, Jesus is available to the fullness of the human condition. In the Christian mythos he can die, gestate for three days, and be reborn. A fuller love, a fuller beingness comes into existence.

This is also true of ourselves. Look back over your life and note the holy and evolutionary qualities of betrayal. You will remember that trust and betrayal always contain each other. Therefore, it was the close relationships that more often than not carried the fullest agony of betrayal: betrayal by the parents who did not fulfill their promises; betrayal by the lover who finds another; betrayal by the child who never calls home; betrayal by the close professional associate who abandons the dream or project you had together. Betrayals mark the expulsion from our Eden of complete trust into the empirical but evolutionary world of consciousness, growth, autonomy, and responsibility. We only really begin to grow when, through betrayal, we lose our sense of intimate linkage with the other—be it mother or father, family or friend, profession or ideology—and are thrust out into an unprotected existence.

Yet this leap into the greater reality is not always made. Sadly, at the point of betrayal, you can instead become calcified in the hard shell of alienation and unforgiveness, unable to love, and given to one or another kind of sterile choice and distrustful fixation. The sterile choices are familiar; indeed, we see them in the soap operas of television, read about them in thrillers, and play them out in our own lives.

James Hillman provides a list of the many life-denying forms that we choose.[2] The first is revenge: an eye for an eye, a tooth for a tooth, a betrayal for a betrayal. You become so consumed with thoughts of revenge that you court evil as a state of mind. All that can be said for revenge is that it may occasionally provide for some limited abreaction of emotion; otherwise it has the most abysmal shrinking effects upon consciousness, leading to an obsession that is anything but magnificent. I think of a woman I know whose husband had an affair with another woman. She spent the next six months brooding upon ingenious methods to arrange for his "accidental" death. A higher, and largely unconscious, force stopped her, but it certainly was a debilitating way for a highly creative woman to spend her time. You cannot grow and be in a state of revenge. Yet it plays a central role in many of the popular myths we see on television and at newsstands. Our constant ingestion of this material can only have an insidious effect, as revenge is reinforced and made to seem a thrilling and honorable form of behavior.

Another self-defeating choice is denial. If you have been disappointed in a relationship, you may totally deny the value of the entire relationship: "I never loved him/her anyway . . . ." "I knew all along . . . ." "They may seem okay on the surface, but at the core they're rotten . . . ." Before the betrayal all was light, but now you see only the dark side. In choosing denial, you annihilate a whole part of your own story. Since there is no "happily ever after" (at least not the one you hoped for), you flee from the fullness of the experience and cling instead to a childish innocence and ignorance, refusing to see the polarity and ambiguity inherent in life. So you leave the unconscious Garden of primal trust for self-conscious alienation in the world.

Or you may choose cynicism, which can also take the form of broken idealism. The most meaningful things in your life are now seen as cheap, hollow frauds—the friendship, the church, the political cause, the profession—all pretense and fakery dedicated to setting you up for shooting you down. You'll stay on the ground from now on, thank you, and like Cynis the dog, chase your own tail. To justify this choice, you will call it "realism."

Ultimately the refusal to accept the opening offered by betrayal leads you to self-betrayal. You betray yourself in belittling your deepest hopes, values, ambitions, and story. The plans that you had so carefully made are dismissed as mere "castles in the air." The dream, the ambition, is laughed away. It is the "nothing but" syndrome; you belittle your deeps, and you become less as a consequence. Self-betrayal finds its modern apotheosis in certain forms of psychological analysis, where we are encouraged to categorize ourselves negatively in the meanest and most sordid terms. We are asked to assume not the archetype of aspiration but the archetype of denigration. We are handed over to the enemy within, and the nebbish has his day. People who are given to self-betrayal court the crash in themselves and in others. They are remarkably skilled at giving others and themselves a litany of why things won't work. Refusing to become what they can be, and cheating themselves with escapes and excuses, they often go into what Jung calls *uneigentlich leiden,* inauthentic suffering. Real suffering at least leads to wisdom and deepening. The suffering wrought through chronic addiction to your own self-betrayal is merely erosive and uninteresting.

The supreme disease of betrayal is paranoia. All human actions and affairs are seen under the rubric of betrayal as the constant for everything all of the time. This is surely the most dangerous disease in the world today, for the active practice of paranoia among powerful nations can lead to a combination of revenge, denial, cynicism, and self-betrayal that involves the ultimate betrayal of planetary life itself. Paranoia is no longer a livable option.

How, then, can we change the pattern and transform the suffering? Transformation occurs in the discovery of the Larger Story. Often that means that the healing cannot happen for a long time, not until the context is larger, until the Pattern that Connects is manifest. (In the Christian mythos, the world waited for redemption, for the coming of the More, from the time of the fortunate fall of Adam and Eve until the coming of Christ. In the long waiting, however, humankind grew and, by inference, God also grew. Ambiguity was compounded, consciousness expanded, culture and civilization developed.)

Time is thus essential to the healing of our betrayals. Time reveals the Larger Story, hidden to primal consciousness, in which we must play a part. Looking back on your own betrayals, you may notice how they have given you the necessary shove, the unwelcome but needed kick in the pants to invite you to get on with it, to release patterns and attachments that need to die, so that the world may be grown again and a deep and conscious trust may be born.

But the key to redeeming our betrayals is forgiveness. Anyone can forgive a petty matter, but if you have been involved in a situation of deep trusting, of mutual flowing into one another, of rich coherence in which you have shared your soul—and then have been betrayed—forgiveness takes on a momentous and evolutionary potency. Such a forgiveness will allow you to return to the Garden after the gaining of complexity and to enter into fully conscious partnership with the creative principle. When this forgiveness is fully known and experienced in the soul, you can recognize the "betrayer" as the instrument of the Larger Story. Indeed the betrayer and the betrayed are classically bound together in a mutual story of unfolding, and chances are, if each of their separate stories were to be followed, you would find that their rhythms and weavings are astonishingly alike, even though they may never see each other again. Each has served as a mediator of divinity for the other.

This is why betrayal is such a strong theme in all the great religions and myths. It is the human gate to higher religious experience; it gives us the experience perhaps of God. In our betrayal, the other becomes the instrument of God, bringing us to a tragedy that needs our ennoblement in order to understand it. And the only way to be ennobled and to forgive truly is through love. In giving much more than one thought one could, one discovers that one has much more still to give. This is the mystery and miracle of love, and it changes the very fabric of reality, the very structure of our lives. When we are able to *give forth*, to give of ourselves beyond our protective shell and see the other in wonder and astonishment (regardless of how unskilled another's behavior might have been), then something evolutionary happens and we and the betrayal are not the same. Then love is restored, revealing the larger consequence and the deeper unfolding.

Thus, for all of its agony and suffering, betrayal is a necessary advance over primal trust; for its challenges and vicissitudes extend the universe, bring love into darkness, and grow the world and ourselves.

Yeats reminds us in "The Second Coming":

> Turning and turning in the widening gyre
> The falcon cannot hear the falconer;
> Things fall apart; the centre cannot hold;
> Mere anarchy is loosed upon the world,
> The blood-dimned tide is loosed, and everywhere
> The ceremony of innocence is drowned;
> The best lack all conviction, while the worst
> Are full of passionate intensity . . .
> And what rough beast, its hour come 'round at last,
> Slouches
> towards Bethlehem to be born?

When betrayal and subsequent disaster have ripped us from our moorings, when the known world lies in a shambles around us, will we recognize the rough beast within, slouching toward Bethlehem to be born?

Betrayal and Forgiveness

Although this process has much in common with the preceding one, I have found that focusing on betrayal, in and of itself, leads to the development of compassion both for the self and others, releasing the capacity to love.

The two processes presented in this chapter should not be done one after the other, but at different times (at least several hours apart, but preferably several days). It has been my experience that the healing of pathos and wounding must include experiences of real work and play in the world so that the resulting changes can become integrated into your daily life.

Each process has a somewhat different intention, although both invite you to a larger perspective of the personal story—which is, after all, what sacred psychology is about. The first, as we have seen, allows you to move from local wounding to larger myth; the second allows you to bring love and forgiveness to traumatic events. Both processes, however painful, are profoundly healing. Both help the work of therapeia, which instead of focusing only on the problem, releases the energy stored in the wounding or betrayal for development and transformation.

TIME: 70–90 minutes.

MATERIALS NEEDED: The guide will need a box of tissues to distribute when needed. Please do so as unobtrusively as possible.

MUSIC: Use music from *Area 2* here. We have found the first side of Vangelis' *Ignacio* to be particularly effective for this process. As the music will undoubtedly finish before the end of the experience, it is important, if you are using the tape version, to rewind it in order to play it again, or to prerecord it twice.

ROOM SETUP: Clear a fairly large space, provide subdued lighting or candles.

INSTRUCTIONS FOR WORKING IN A GROUP: Everyone should be familiar with the material on betrayal before beginning this process. Begin the session with some form of group experience—singing, chanting, performing together the Zikr of Communion (Chapter 13), or whatever else the guide might select—to coalesce and center the energy of the group.

The role of the guide here, after giving the initial instructions, is to stay present as fair witness to the process of all. Except under the most extraordinary conditions, it is unwise and unnecessary to intervene in anyone's experience.

INSTRUCTIONS FOR WORKING ALONE: If you are doing the exercise alone—and again, a partner makes a profound difference here—read the instructions carefully before you begin. Prepare the music and allow yourself to become centered, relaxed, and focused. It is important that you physically walk backward with your eyes half-closed as instructed, speaking of your betrayals as you pass through them. Then sit and write, letting your journal be your partner, and answer the questions. Limit your time for doing this so you do not become self-indulgent. Then continue with the exercise, walking forward. At the end, celebrate the experience by dancing, walking in nature, or performing a kindly action.

SCRIPT FOR THE GUIDE: Choose a partner, preferably someone you don't know very well.

Sit together and listen as I explain what we are about to do. As in all of our work together, it is essential that you honor the privacy of what you may hear from each other. As you explore the role of betrayal in your life, remember that betrayal often has consequences not just of pain and suffering, but also of widening the contexts and opportunities in your life.

Now you will take turns remembering your betrayals and discovering your capacity for forgiveness. Thus each person will be taken through the entire process before the other person has his or her turn. Take a moment now to decide who will do the remembering first.

You who are not doing the remembering now will serve as guide and high witness to the other.

The rememberers will close or half close their eyes, and their guides will face them with their hands on the rememberers' shoulders, gently steering them as they walk silently backward through their lives from the present to the past, feeling time enter their bodies through their backs.

As the person remembering passes through lesser betrayals, you will both stop, and the rememberer will comment briefly on the nature of that betrayal.

Then continuing and stopping at lesser betrayals, you will walk backward until the rememberer reaches a major betrayal. This point is usually very clear because the visceral and emotional response is stronger than it is with the lesser betrayals. It can also rise up from any time in your life, from last week, or from when you were a child. With this major betrayal, do not speak about it as you have done with the others. Rather, at this point you will sit down together and remain in silence until I give the high witnesses a question to ask his or her partners.

You who are the high witness, remain centered throughout the entire walk, maintaining a loving and supportive silence except where questions are indicated. Commentary and discussion, no matter how caring, only dilutes the power of the experience.

Are there any questions? (Allow a brief time for questions if necessary.)

All right. Now standing together with the high witness holding the shoulders of the one who is to remember, begin to guide the rememberer backward and say: "Tell me about your lesser betrayals."

(Start the music now.)

You who are rememberer, stop at each of your lesser betrayals, commenting briefly before you continue backward to the next one. Now begin.

(After about 7 minutes, when most couples are seated, the guide will say:) For those who are still walking, allow yourself one more minute to reach the point of a major betrayal and then sit down with your partner.

(The guide will allow one more minute and then say:) You who are rememberer, now tell about this major betrayal in as much detail as you wish to give. High witness, do not act as therapist or comforter, but stay in the role of compassionate witness to what is being told. If you need tissues, signal and I will bring them, but stay focused on your partner. You will have 10 minutes for this process. Begin now.

(After 10 minutes, the guide continues:)

The high witness will now ask: "What were the consequences for good or ill of this betrayal?" You have ten minutes to consider this question, beginning now.

(After 10 minutes, the guide continues:) The high witness will now say: "In the light of what you have just told me, try to see me as the betrayer, and grant me forgiveness if you can."

You who are rememberer will try to do this, perhaps giving a gesture of some kind that indicates the forgiveness. Even if you cannot do this at this time, act "as if" there is forgiveness present. Often this quality of acting "as if" has the effect of evoking the capacity for forgiveness.

(When this process has been completed, the guide says:) Now rise and walk forward together through the life of the rememberer with the high witness serving as guide with one arm around the waist and the other holding the arm of the rememberer.

As you do this the high witness will say: "As we walk forward, see if you can forgive the lesser betrayals that we encountered before. If you can, speak aloud your willingness to forgive each lesser betrayal."

And begin this now.

(The couples do this, and the first half of this process ends. After a short break, the couples reverse roles and repeat the process using the script above.

After this process has been completed, the couples sit and reflect together on what has occurred and what they feel happening in themselves. A group discussion or healing circle can conclude this experience.)

11

THE SEARCH FOR THE BELOVED

Oh, night that guided me,
Oh, night more lovely than the dawn,
Oh, night that joined Beloved with lover,
Lover transformed in the Beloved!
Upon my flowery breast,
Kept wholly for himself alone,
There he stayed sleeping,
And I caressed him,
And the fanning of the cedars made a breeze.
The breeze blew from the turret
As I parted his locks.
With his gentle hand he wounded my neck
And caused all my senses to be suspended.
I remained, lost in oblivion,
My face I reclined on the Beloved.
All ceased and I abandoned myself,
Leaving my cares forgotten among the lilies.

—ST. JOHN OF THE CROSS,
The Dark Night of the Soul[1]

In all the great spiritual and mystery traditions, the central theme, the guiding passion, is the deep yearning for the Beloved of the soul. This yearning for union with the Beloved lies at the heart of sacred psychology, for it is this profound longing, which transcends the desire for romantic love, the nourishment of parental love, and all the multiple and marvelous varieties of human loving, that calls us to the Source.

The passion of St. John of the Cross for the Divine Lover, the Beloved of the soul, is one of the most ecstatic and exquisite statements of the mystery of divine-human loving. It recalls the yearning of Isis for Osiris in the Egyptian mystery, of the love songs of Orpheus in the Orphic mysteries, of the spiritual and fleshly erọs in the *Song of Songs.* The search for the Beloved and the ecstatic joy when the One is found are central to Sufi mysticism (witness the poems of Jalaloddin Rumi), and the Hassid is never more himself than when caught up in the ecstatic dance of love with God. In the gospels, both gnostic and orthodox, union with the Divine Lover is the metaphor for the mystery of personal transformation and human consummation. Christianity arose amid a tide of spiritual eros upon the bleached and empty shores of Roman civic religion. Most of the mystery religions fermenting at that time were caught up in yearning for the Divine Lover.

Nor is this yearning limited to the experience found within the major world religions. One of the most moving accounts of this longing is found in Laurens van der Post's account of the "dance of the great hunger" of the Bushmen of the Kalahari. He writes:

> [It] is the dance of a hunger that neither the food of the earth nor the way of life possible upon it can satisfy. It is a dance of the Bushman's instinctive intimation that man cannot live by bread alone, although without it he cannot live at all . . . .
>
> Whenever I asked them about this great hunger they would only say, "not only we dancing, feeling ourselves to be raising the dust which will one day come blown by the wind to erase our last spoor from the sand when we die, lest others coming and seeing our footsteps there might still think us alive, not only we feel this hunger, but the stars too, sitting up there with their hearts of plenty, they too feel it and feeling it, tremble as if afraid they would wane and their light die, on account of so great a hunger."[2]

There is a wonderful Greek word to describe this yearning: *pothos.* It is a magical, mysterious word that speaks volumes but brooks no translation. Only an example can point to its richness, so let us again turn to that great exemplar of the human sojourner, Odysseus. You recall that when we first meet him in *The Odyssey* he is weeping on the shore of Calypso's island, staring at the sea and *yearning* for home. Odysseus is in the most acute state of *pothos* for Ithaca. And others in Ithaca are in as serious a condition of *pothos* for Odysseus. His wife Penelope, his son

Telemachus, his father Laertes, his swineherd Eumaeos, even his ancient dog Argos, live in a state of acute yearning or *pothos* for the missing adventurer. It is this accumulating intensity of *pothos* that bestirs the conscience of the gods and prompts the Goddess Athena to initiate the actions that will bring Odysseus home. Thus *pothos* is that state of soul in which the barriers between ourselves and the archetypal world are broken. The how and why of this process are part of the message of sacred psychology. *Pothos* has a profound and profoundly engaging assumption: everything and everyone belongs somewhere and to someone. And somehow, somewhere, the Kingdom of Heaven is at hand. Generations of popular songs have spoken poignantly to this longing. "Somewhere over the rainbow" is my true home where I will be known for who and what I truly am. Somewhere, somehow, my true love awaits me. And sometimes I almost remember. . . . "I saw you standing in the same way then, but I can't remember where or when."

James Hillman, who has investigated the classical origins of *pothos*, writes:

> Plato defines it . . . as a yearning desire for a distant object. Its associations in the classical corpus are with longings for *that which cannot be obtained:* yearning for a lost child, or a beloved . . . longing for sleep and for death. As late as the Church Father, Gregory of Nazianzus, *pothos* was described as a striving power in plants. It is the "vegetable love," a *via naturalis* of which Andrew Marvell has written, or "the force that through the green fuse drives the flower drives my blood" of Dylan Thomas.[3]

The greatest ancient exemplar of *pothos* was Alexander the Great. He is said to have invented the phrase "seized by *pothos*" to account for his indescribable longing for something beyond, a longing that carried him beyond all borders in a horizontal conquest of space. Alexander had merely to sit upon a riverbank and gaze into the distance to be seized by *pothos*. Space and distance became the images that released his yearning.[4]

Hillman reminds us that in classical etymology *pothos* was the third member of the three persons of *eros*: *himeros* was physical desire, *anteros* was answering love, and *pothos* was the longing for that which transcends and goes beyond the other two. "If *himeros* is the material and physical desire of love, and *anteros* is the relational mutuality and exchange, *pothos* is love's spiritual portion. *Pothos* here would refer to the spiritual component of love or the erotic component of spirit."[5]

Hillman describes *pothos* as the archetypal force that drives the wanderer ever onward toward what can never be fulfilled in local space and time. In this guise it informed the ecstatic longings of the great courts of love of the twelfth and thirteenth centuries wherein the courtly couple sublimated the sexual possibilities inherent in *himeros* and *anteros* so that they both might know the spiritual-erotic joys of *pothos*. It is the divine force behind all our ceaseless wandering, behind the apparent foolishness that sends us in pursuit of the improbable. It is the nostalgia for God-Knows-What, and it will not leave us, regardless of how ephemeral its form or absurd its calling.

Pothos is an impetus to all our evolutionary striving. Its basis in the human soul is very deep, for it is the memory of a union that fails to go away, a union that can only be partially explained and mirrored through human loving or partnership. Consider the transformative power of earthly love, which can and does evoke in us the divine response: unconditional acceptance and forgiveness, deep and unspoken communion and communication, the ecstasies of eros and the fires of union, a wave-tide of giving and receiving so abundant that it seems drawn from the very ocean of abundance itself, the living together of all life's dramas—tragedies, comedies, the theater of the absurd, and even mystery plays. This is the love that passes all understanding. And yet. . . . The breadth and depth of human loving both gives us the sense of what human-divine loving is about and instills in us the preparation, the *pothos*, for spiritual union.

What the Greek notion of *pothos* does, however, is to make a relationship deeply personal and emotionally potent as well as uniquely configured to each individual. Classical scholars conjecture that ancient mystery and initiation rites for wanderers, celebrated on the island of Samothrace, involved an unequal pair thought to be mortal and immortal, divine and human, or even old and young. It is my speculation that these rites spoke to the mystery of our twinned nature; indeed, it is known that the divine twins, the Dioskouri, played an important role in the rites.

In Plato's *Symposium*, Aristophanes says that human beings originally consisted of two persons in one body, with two heads and four arms and legs. These beings were shaped like a ball, and in their completeness and satisfaction, they rolled along in ecstasy, ready and able to do almost anything. The Titans, fearful of the enormous power available to these extraordinary double beings, forced Zeus to split them in half, thus diminishing both their powers and their happiness, and forcing them (us) to spend their lives yearning for the missing half. This little story offers a tragi-comic explanation for an essential, primary experience of the human race: we are twinned, but divided selves.

Both Plato and Freud, as well as existentialists down through the ages, have shown that in a state of isolation, we experience ourselves as strangers. What sacred psychology seeks to demonstrate is that apparent neurosis is also potential fulfillment. *Pothos* initially rises because I find that I am a stranger to myself and that I cannot discover myself except through finding the other. Thus I wander in search of this potential reunion.

The rites of *pothos* at Samothrace spoke to this reunion and addressed the truth that you are both yourself and your archetype, the extended, godded self residing in the archetypal world. Thus, part of us dwells in the archetypal realm that transcends time and space, and part of us dwells here in existential space and time. In the Mysteries, the initiates grew into an awareness of their double nature. They essentially learned to "dock with [their] angel." Ultimately then, *pothos* helps us to navigate in two realms. Our yearnings and seaborne wanderings carry us into the depths, into transpersonal images and a larger evolutionary destiny.

Sacred psychology asks, "Who is your double in the extended realm of the soul?" "For whom are you here as the asymmetrical partner, the exotype of the archetype?" "Who or what is it that is yearning for you, calling to you; who is the Beloved you are always trying to remember?" The remembrance, discovery, and development of this union is key to this work, for it enables the emergent creative forms of the depth world, the world of your archetypal Beloved, to enter into you and, by extension, to enter into time and space. Thus the critical importance of *pothos,* the yearning for the great communion that completes our reality and causes the patterns of essential and existential realms to connect.

The great desire for the Beloved of the soul, while always present, emerges from background to foreground when civilizations undergo whole-system transitions. As I mentioned earlier, this occurred in the ecumenical and cosmopolitan culture of the Hellenistic Roman Empire when, with the relative freedom to travel and enjoy cultural interchange, people could pursue the spiritual and psychological realities of other cultures. At the same time, the mystery religions, with their emphasis upon dramatic inward journeys of anguish, grief, loss, redemption, joy, and ecstasy of union with the archetypal Beloved, gave people a sense of deeper identity and belonging.

Today we are undergoing a profound transition, for we are moving from cosmopolitan to planetary culture, with a convergence of cultures, beliefs, and practices. We are also experiencing a revolution in the relationship between men and women, and a revisioning of forms of friendship and community. Perhaps there should be ritual vows of friendship and re-marriage that will allow mutually empowering partners to state the nature of their co-journeying commitment. We've experimented with these kinds of rituals in our training schools and seminars, and they seem to have a profound and deepening effect on marriages and friendships.

A new natural philosophy of love seems to be on the rise everywhere.

It belongs perhaps to a "geo-theology" of love as the creative force in evolution, the lure of becoming, which is finding renewed expression in the rising archetype of the Beloved of the soul. The world may be urging us to coalesce into a new and higher unity for which we feel unprepared, and the only force emotionally powerful enough to call us to educate ourselves for sacred stewardship is communion and partnership with the Beloved.

There is a delightful story about this partnership. A young man in Northern India went on retreat with a master of Bhakti yoga (the yoga of love and devotion). The master told the young man to go into a secluded room and just think about love for a while.

After a few minutes the young man came out and sheepishly told the master that he couldn't concentrate because he was worrying about the precious little bull he was raising and for whom he cared so much. The master told him that his concern was wonderful, for it had brought him an object of meditation.

"Go back into the room and meditate on how much you love your little bull," said the master.

The young man did as he was told. Hours went by, and the young man did not emerge from the room. A whole day and night passed, and still he stayed there. After another day and night had elapsed, the master peeked into the room and saw the young man sitting there, lost in meditation, a beatific smile on his face.

"Why don't you come out and have something to eat?" he inquired.

"Oh, I cannot, Master," said the young man, beaming with happiness. "My horns are too large to fit through the door."

As Western teachers of spirituality and Eastern masters of Bhakti yoga have shown time and again, a deepening relationship with the Divine Beloved can result in a transformation into the *Imago Amore,* the image of the Beloved. It is easier to identify with the *Imago Amore* than with the *Imago Dei* because the great strength of *pothos* attracts you to the Beloved. This identification with the Beloved is basic to the practice of sacred psychology.

For St. Francis of Assisi, the service of love was to Jesus, the prime *Imago Amore* of the Western world. For Buddhists it might be Buddha or Kwan Yin; for Hindus it is often Krishna. For you or me it may be an archetypal persona unique to us and not of the order of a cultural archetype. The warning must be given, however, that the Beloved of our spiritual reality determines our religious and our human practice. We identify with and in a very real sense incarnate the *Imago Amore.* As the Episcopalian priest and spiritual counselor Father Morton Kelsey reminds us, "The love and celebration of Wotan can produce Hitler and Nazism, the love and celebration of Christos, a St. Francis of Assisi."[6] Thus we must be careful in our choice of the Beloved of the soul. Trivial beloveds, like movie stars, sports figures, media masters, and the heroes and heroines of our inner fantasies, are as potentially soul-shrinking as are archaic and undeveloped icons of earlier traditions. (Such a disclaimer can go too far, however, for a fantasy Beloved of our childhood or adolescence can be an initial movement toward a deeper encounter with the Beloved of the soul.)

The existence of a Divine Beloved would seem to indicate that there is an opposite archetypal force, a Shadow Destroyer of love and union that would pull us downward, sometimes with an almost erotic, certainly seductive, force. It is interesting that Dr. M. Scott Peck, after his superb study of love in *The Road Less Traveled,*[7] has now written a study of evil, *People of the Lie.* Love and evil necessarily illumine each other; the principle of evil drags us away from meaning, communion, and love.

Evil can be seen as the jester in the court of chaos. Its sleight-of-hand, cruel jokes, ironic twists, keep us diverted from seeing the creative purpose in chaos. Chaos, which means the great shadow and the great dispersion, lives in a dialectical marriage with cosmos. Now cosmos, which means creation and order, always comes out of chaos. The Big Bang created the ultimate chaos, the dispersion that contained the seedings of the cosmos. A study of history indicates that times of chaos hold within themselves the codings for new cosmos, new culture, a new and deeper commitment to love. The cosmogonic or highly creative times in one's life do not usually emerge out of little steady growths, but out of chaotic shifts when everything is shaken up. It is then that you decide whether you will grow or die, whether you will love or perish.

If I were Evil Incarnate, I would not fight against chaos. I would undermine its energy so that it could neither bang, shake, shift, nor seed the order, the cosmos, that is trying to emerge. The power of evil is to divert and dissipate energy, intention, commitment; to lure people into self-indulgence and narcissism; to promise absolution while sanctifying sloth.

"And God blew upon the waters of the deep, and created cosmos." In Hebrew "the deep" is *Tehom,* which is etymologically linked to Tiamat, the ancient Middle Eastern dragon goddess of chaos. In order for your spirit to blow strong enough to create cosmos, you need a certain water level of chaos to blow upon. As we have seen, present civilization, as well as planetary necessity, is an extraordinary vehicle to engender chaos to provoke in you the desire for cosmogenesis and the search for the Divine Beloved. Thus, chaos is a movement toward consciousness, which is also a movement into conscious creation, conscious genesis, and conscious loving.

Having now the responsibility for evolutionary and biological governance of the planet, possessing the powers once thought to belong to gods, we stand in dread before the inner shadows of our being, knowing that the evil we do can destroy the world. Yet if we regard this shadow principle as resistance, similar to the currents of air that support the flight of the bird, perhaps we can see evil as a force that galvanizes our energy so that we may be lifted up beyond its temptations.

EVOKING THE BELOVED

Drawing from the work of Morton Kelsey as well as from the understanding that has grown from my own study and reflection, I offer some insights into the nature and practice of the relationship with the Beloved. Different cultural metaphors are revealed in the journeys of transformation presented in Part Four. A meditation and ritual designed to lead you on the search for the Beloved follows this discussion. I suggest that you practice this meditation several times as an initial exploration to evoke a stronger sense of your Beloved. Once you have done this, other practices will allow the connection to deepen.

It is important that you use rich imagery in your evocation. The way of the Beloved belongs to the abundance of the *via positiva* rather than to the asceticism of the *via negativa.* Thus, in meditation or active imagination you invite the Beloved, consciously evoking visual, auditory, tactile, olfactory, and other sensory images. At first these images may not come at all. This is especially true if the Beloved is not a traditional and familiar archetype like Jesus, Mary, Buddha, or Kwan Yin, but is personal and unique to you as Beatrice was for Dante or the inner teacher Philemon was for Carl Jung. Do not be discouraged. For a while you may have to "put images in" consciously or act "as if" they were there. Start with the kind of imagery that is natural for you. If you are a visualizer, begin there. For example, if the Beloved has a traditional form for you, you might begin by reflecting on a loved and well-known image or statue seen with the inner eye. If your sense of the Beloved is nontraditional and nothing specific rises to your inner eye, then actively imagine looking through the lens of human knowing. Does the Beloved have a body, a face, or is the Beloved a pattern of energy, of light? Whatever the image may be, play with it and soon you will find that the form will respond by taking on greater specificity. If you are more kinesthetic and auditory, then feel and listen for images of the Beloved. You may find yourself hearing words or music, or you may be drawn into a dance. We have found in our research that the dominant inner sense soon activates the nondominant ones, so that before long you will have most, if not all, of the previously dormant senses involved in your meditations. Then relationship with your Beloved will be increasingly concrete.

Remember, too, that the Beloved is probably yearning for you as much, if not a great deal more, than you are yearning for the Beloved. Believing and knowing this can have the effect of allowing your imagery to be engaged by the Beloved. A sweep of color, a cascade of images, a symphonic play of feeling, a knowing that is as deep as it is beyond the powers of speech to express—such experiences can be the forms the Beloved takes to awaken your awareness to its presence. Many of these images and experiences will take you more deeply into the imaginal realm where your relationship with the Beloved often unfolds in story form. Guided by the Beloved, you may find yourself in a larger story, often of mythic proportions, where journeys may be taken, challenges offered, and training in the depths made available. There may be initiations or important transitions that attend the gaining of inner learnings. At a certain point the active, volitional use of imagination will pass into imagery that seems much more autonomous and surprising. Here the images are spontaneous; they do not seem to be the product of your directed imagination. Witness the surprise and joy of the great Indian poet Rabindranath Tagore at the sudden "arrival" of the Beloved:

> One day in spring, a woman came
> In my lonely woods,
> In the lovely form of the Beloved.
> Came, to give to my songs, melodies,
> To give to my dreams, sweetness.
> Suddenly a wild wave
> Broke over my heart's shores
> And drowned all language.
> To my lips no name came,
> She stood beneath the tree, turned,
> Glanced at my face, made sad with pain,
> And with quick steps, came and sat by me.
> Taking my hands in hers, she said:
> "You do not know me, nor I you—
> I wonder how this could be?"
> I said:
> "We two shall build, a bridge for ever
> Between two beings, each to the other unknown,
> This eager wonder is at the heart of things."[8]

The exercises presented later in this chapter help to provide those skills that deepen your capacity for evoking the Beloved. If they are done on a regular basis, you will begin to discover that access to the imaginal realm, where the Beloved is home, is a natural aspect of your existential reality.

However valuable the discovery of and entrance into the imaginal realm may be, unless the illumination that it provides becomes an active force in your daily life, the full potential of this relationship will not be realized. A basic premise of sacred psychology, as I have indicated, is that the Beloved is yearning for us just as we are yearning for the Beloved. Furthermore, the Beloved needs us to act in this realm. Thus both partners in the relationship are grown, and each has a deep responsibility to the other. As Joseph Campbell has shown us so well in his study of the monomyth of the hero's journey, the mission of the individual is to travel in these realms and to meet and enter into relationship with a form of the archetype, whether it is the Beloved, the teacher, the god, or the goddess. From this relationship comes fertile and transforming energy. Then the spiritual journeyer must return to the world, greening the wasteland, redeeming the time, and bringing spiritual gnosis into concrete form and action.[9] Both of the journeys in Part Four illustrate this basic theme.

DAILY LIFE WITH THE BELOVED

To deepen the relationship with the Beloved, follow the same principles of relationship that you pursue in the human realm. Thus you live the relationship throughout the day, bringing the same sensitivity to nuance and fine tuning that you would bring to a human love relationship.

Some of the practices have a homey quality. For example, in the morning when you get up, you may greet the Beloved in some fashion, either with an ordinary or a ritual gesture. If you were a Hindu, a Buddhist, or my Sicilian Catholic grandmother, you would have a shrine or altar with an image of your Beloved. Every day you would offer fresh flowers or other gifts at this shrine. Many who have established a deep relationship with the Beloved create a sacred space in their home to serve as a constant reminder of the Beloved's continual presence. Just as you might carry with you pictures of your family and home when you travel, so you might carry some token or image that reminds you of your Beloved.

You live through the day with the Beloved in a sense of partnership and communion, solving problems, enjoying the pleasures of life, reflecting together on the difficulties. At least once a week you might set aside a special time for deep meditation on the mystery and meaning of this connection in which you and the archetype are joined. Here ritual or other sacred practice may be most appropriate. The Zikr of Communion presented in the chapter on Rumi, or the chanting of "I Am, We Are, This Is Me," described in the section of basic exercises, may be useful.

While the realm of the Beloved may still remain "other," the distance can be bridged by bringing the extraordinary into the ordinary. Consider, for example, the direct, "down-to-earth" conversations between Athena and Odysseus when Odysseus has just returned to Ithaca and met Athena, at first disguised as a young shepherd. He gives her a cock-and-bull story about who he is and what he has been up to.

> Athena smiled and her bright eyes flashed, and she stroked him with her hand. Now she looked like a tall and majestic woman, clever and intelligent, and she spoke to the point:
>
> "A cunning rogue he would be, master of craft, who would outwit you! Even a god couldn't do it. Irrepressible! everlasting schemer! indefatigable fabulist!
>
> "But no more of this. We are both clever enough; you are the paragon of mankind at planning and story-telling, and I have a name among the gods for cleverness and intelligence. And you didn't know Pallas Athena, the daughter of Zeus herself, your faithful standby and guardian in all your labours!"
>
> Odysseus was not taken aback, but he answered at once:
>
> "It is a difficult thing, goddess, for a mortal man to know you at sight, even a man of experience; you turn yourself into all sorts of shapes. . . . I think you are only making fun of me to bewilder my mind. Tell me if this is really Ithaca my home."
>
> Athena answered with flashing eyes:
>
> "Ah, you are always the same, no one can catch you napping; and that is why I cannot desert you in misfortune, because you are so charming and discreet and always ready for anything. . . ."[10]

The Christian tradition reflects a conversational hominess in many of the old hymms of human-divine friendship: "And He walks with me, and He talks with me, and He tells me I am His own. . . ." Or note the delightful example of St. Theresa of Avila, on such intimate terms with her spiritual Beloved that she can berate him, "Lord, it's a wonder that you have any friends at all, seeing how you treat them." However and wherever it happens, conversation with the Beloved must never be allowed to lapse for long.

Although being porous to the Beloved increases the capacity to live in two realms, the growth and maintenance of this capacity seems to depend upon the faithful practice of a discipline. Discipline has had a very bad press. We must recognize, however, that the high practice of a discipline gives enormous freedom, and with this freedom comes a greatly increased capacity to love. Often we do not love others, much less the Divine Beloved, because we are caught up by every whim, irritation, and distraction. "The center does not hold, mere anarchy is loosed upon the land . . ." and runs riot within oneself. Discipline, conscious and mindful orchestration of the pieces of our lives, gives us a capacity to live in the depths as well as on the surface. Ideally, a discipline has a physical, mental, and spiritual component and is practiced each day. If, however, your discipline becomes compulsive—"If I don't meditate at least an hour, run four miles while saying my mantra, and write a spiritual parable in my journal, then I'll fall through the cracks in the sidewalk today"—then it is time to consciously change it and do something funny or ironic. Run backward, perhaps, while solemnly chanting, "Dog" (God spelled backward).

Just as discipline enhances the quality of the relationship, so, too, does a commitment to creativity. Since you and your Beloved are partnering creation, it is essential that you have an expressive form, be it an art or craft or science or project, in which this mutual creation can unfold in the most concrete manner. This helps dismiss the sentimentality and vagueness that can sometimes accrue around the loving. Love thus becomes an active, creative force in the existential universe, which is always a critical intention of the Beloved. Indeed, as my studies of highly creative and productive people confirm, a strong relationship to the Beloved of the soul enhances and sustains their work in the world. The local self, in and for itself, is not sufficient.

Grounded in spiritual reality, we become godseeds, and our capacity for growth and deepening becomes virtually infinite. Since growth goes on in the infinite world, and the archetype of the Beloved is continuing to grow as well, you also must work to develop your potential in this depth world, to do what Jesus referred to as laying up "treasures in heaven." Discovery of these treasures is made possible through loving communion with the Beloved, who knows their nature and purpose. Although we are citizens of at least two worlds, we have forgotten the uses and the ecology of the inner world. As we are about to become citizens in a universe richer by far than any we have ever known, we deeply need our archetype, our Beloved in the depth world, to partner us in this larger citizenship. Our Beloved and godded guide knows the patterns, forms, and places where the vast latencies and psycho-spiritual knowings are coded. In this way love grows reality.

HUMAN LOVING EXTENDED THROUGH THE BELOVED

Father Kelsey emphasizes that contact with the Divine Lover is never complete until some other human being feels more loved and cherished as a result of that contact.[11] In 1975, I helped to organize and chaired a conference at the United Nations at which Mother Theresa of Calcutta was one of the guests. A tiny woman bristling with joyous energy, she seemed so open and available that I found myself asking her:

"Mother, how does it happen that you are able to do so much, and why are you in this state of joy?"

"My dear," she said, "it is because I am so deeply in love."

"But Mother, you're a nun!"

"Precisely," she said. "I am married to Jesus."

"Yes, I understand, you're married to Jesus. All nuns are."

"No, you don't understand," she countered. "I really am. I am so in a state of love that I see the face of my Beloved in the face of the dying man in the streets of Calcutta. I see my Beloved in the day-old child who's left outside our convent, and in the leper whose flesh is decaying; and I can't do enough for my Beloved! That is why I try to do something beautiful for God."

What is the nature of the conquest by love? The more deeply we encounter the Divine Beloved, the more sensitively we feel the agony of the world, the more we are called to creative action. In the light of the enhancement of your inner and outer sensibilities, you will necessarily feel more, care more, and think more deeply about the decay in the social and moral order. There is usually a tension between the joy felt in the presence of love and the agony felt in an enhanced awareness of suffering in the world. Finding yourself in union with the Beloved, you also find yourself woven into the fabric of the world; having partnered the depths, you are also extended over the breadth of creation. As long as there is illness, bloodshed, hunger, war, racial tension, discrimination, exploitation, prejudice, poverty, rejection, and disempowerment, you live with an undercurrent of sorrow, regardless of the quality of your joy. Evil and abreaction exist in both internal as well as external worlds, and the lover of God has to reach out to allay or redeem the suffering of both. Together with the Beloved, you reach out to do what you can in the light of the perspective of grace and the energy of spiritual partnership.

Every human being has a unique destiny, an entelechy; and in communion with the Beloved, you begin to have a profound respect and even awe for the other person's godded potential. Certainly one of the primary exemplars of this attitude was Jesus, who could say and do remarkable things for others and be in reverence before them. The Christos is always the "you" who is in reverence before the entelechy or godseed in the other. In the mystery of love, as you learn to love another truly, you find the Divine Lover revealed within that other human being. That Divine Lover mirrors your Beloved and is, in some sense, the same. Then, like Mother Theresa, you cannot do enough for the other, for you cannot do enough for the Beloved. You are looking at the other with the eyes of the Beloved when you are able to see him or her in wonder and astonishment, in the fullness of human glory, even amid the conditions of everyday life. This "double vision" empowers and releases the other to become who or what he or she truly is. This is the "look of love."

The esoteric commandment implied by the great commandment to love is that you must become a mediator of love to all you meet. Contact with the Beloved of the soul allows you to become midwife or evocateur of the possibilities, both human and divine, in others. In this role you render yourself diaphanous to the Beloved of both yourself and the other and try to be a genuinely humble example and instrument of the grace of love you have experienced in encountering the Divine Beloved. In this ministry of love you are always servant and never lord.

This ministry can take many forms, and requires a constant mindfulness. For some, you serve as companion on the way, like a friendly dog who walks a piece of the road with you, and for others you serve as the midwife of the Beloved. Just as realizing your own relationship with your Beloved is not easy, so helping another to realize his or hers is also fraught with difficulty. You must be careful to do what is appropriate and evolutionary for the other. Otherwise you become a compulsive cornucopia, burying someone under all the gifts you are pouring out. Your apparent generosity is not always appreciated, and indeed may be deeply resented, as we often see in the case of parents who do "everything" for their children and rob them of their own need for autonomy and identity. Teachers and therapists, indeed many who are in the helping professions, are caught in this conundrum.

You must be especially careful not to bestow upon a loved human the divine communion that more properly belongs to the Beloved, although you can mirror that Beloved to the other. If you make the mistake of investing in human beings the love that belongs to the Beloved, you run the risk of blowing them out by the intensity of feeling you project. Almost inevitably they must escape, and you are left with an immensity of loss and bereavement. You may feel like you have been abandoned by God.

Consider the Buddha, whose father sought to protect his beloved child from the misery of the world. When the son finally escaped from the prison of his father's palace and discovered illness, old age, poverty, and asceticism, he never returned home again. You, too, may have had to leave those who, in the name of love, have held you too tightly in their embrace.

What happens to human sexual desire when one is engaged in relationship with the Beloved? It doesn't go away, but it can be reorchestrated lest indulgence dissipate the relationship. In many cases the desire for the Beloved begins with human love, and human love can be the symbol that then leads to the Beloved. It is the nature of human love to provide the pattern through which divine love can flow. It provides the context for gracing. A deep human relationship that increases the beingness of the other will often lead to the Divine Beloved. And you cannot love the Beloved of the soul without increasing your capacity for loving another human being. We may be on the brink of a transformational sexuality in which our sexuality becomes, in the context of a depth relationship between two people, a godding exchange so that larger creative powers emerge to restore the body and the mind and to transform the spirit. The East has had versions of such practices, as evidenced in the Tantric tradition. I believe that the Western form of Tantrism would have to be sourced in the experience of a transforming eros that mirrors the Beloveds in the being of the lovers.

There are increasing numbers of people for whom traditional relationships no longer suffice. Today many people are entering into new and deeper styles of evolutionary loving and transformational partnership, with models drawn from, but not identified with, the relationship with the archetypal Beloved. At this point of recognition, you and another become copartners of the evolutionary process for each other and for the earth. You become creators together.

OF TIME AND ETERNITY

Those who live in relationship with the Beloved experience a strong sense of continuity with this Beloved, opening to the possibility of further growth, development, and service beyond the span of mortal life. Having communed with eternity, you may diminish or even lose the fear of or regret over your own inevitable physical death. This knowledge places in a wider and deeper context your bitterness and frustration over the injustices and evils that you see. Gradually you gain a far larger perspective as you move out of limited time and space into Great Time and Great Story. The transtemporal perspective of the archetypal world brings a sense of high play and the resolution of patterns of healing and justice into existential time and space.

In the relationship to the Beloved, you discover the circularity as well as the linearity of time. You act, therefore, both in history as well as in the depth world of timelessness. You enter into the eternal place of the great patterns of creation and there get your codings, your dancing orders, to carry back onto the grid of time and space.

Most of us live and make our way slowly upon the surface of the great workings of reality, remarkably innocent of the levels upon levels that are going on. A sustained partnering with the Beloved of the soul allows us, however briefly, to shift out of our limited consciousness and gain access to the great workings of the timeless world. Herein we are charged by eternal patterns, which through us can enter into existential time.

THE EVOLUTIONARY LURE OF THE BELOVED

No consideration of the Beloved is complete until it is related to the evolutionary qualities of love. What does it mean to really love?

Consider the prodigious physical and evolutionary studies of Teilhard de Chardin, which conclude that love is the underlying movement and pattern behind the universe: atoms calling each other in search of union so that they begin to constellate and form molecules; molecules in resonance yearning for the Beloved of the next stage so that they can form more complex systems; these systems yearning to form bodies; bodies attuning until they find their partner and produce more bodies with more complexities. We yearn for the gods and the gods yearn for us, so that as we are becoming enspirited, godded beings, the gods are becoming human. Likewise, earth and nature long for spirit, and spirit longs for nature; out of this longing emerges a deeply physicalized spirituality and a deeply spiritual embodiment. In Dante's *Divine Comedy,* this embodiment is "the love that moves the sun and the other stars." Teilhard talks about tangential or connective energy being the lure between beings that causes the complexity of evolution, so that new associations, genes, and forms are created. Then, when a certain level of complexity is reached, radial energy helps the emergent forms leap to a whole new stage of being. Thus we may speculate that we have arrived at a place of tangential complexity so that the Beloved, acting radiantly and radially, evokes in us a leap of being into our next evolutionary stage.

Consider, too, process philosopher Alfred North Whitehead's philosophy of God as the loving lure of becoming, the Divine Lover calling the world into becoming, as any great and true lover does with any beloved. Compare this philosophy with Plato's view of the relationship between the beloved and the loved as one of mutual evocation and growth. In the case of the self and the Beloved of the soul, the lure is such that the divine and creative patterns are brought into manifestation in space and time, and the self is extended into the universe.

The search for the Beloved is the lure of human becoming. As you allow the Beloved to grow within you, you will discover a steadfastness to the spiritual journey that comes your way in the most remarkable fashion. It will seem that you have been clearly put on a journey of transformation that provides for a deep maturation of the psyche and access to the potentials of your own being. Opportunities for learning and service come one after another. You may even find yourself asking, "Can I have a little rest, maybe? Just a few months of nothing going on?" After a while you may discover that your relationship to your previous self is such that the old self is the honored "Neanderthal." You are now celebrant and explorer, settler and guide for others in this new world of love.

At this great transition point in human history, when we are taking on staggering new responsibilities and leaping off to the stars, both inward and outward, the goddedness in us is yearning for us—and a good thing it is. For we probably will not have the passion for the possible until we experience the motivating power of the relationship with the Beloved:

> Why should we two ever want to part?
>
> Just as the leaf of the water rhubarb lives floating on
> the water,
> we live as the great one and little one.
>
> As the owl opens his eyes all night to the moon,
> we live as the great one and little one.
>
> This love between us goes back to the first humans;
> it cannot be annihilated.
>
> Here is Kabir's idea: as the river gives itself into
> the ocean,
> what is inside me moves inside you.[12]

The Rites of Pothos: The Search for the Beloved

This process allows you to experience, first through a guided meditation and then through a powerful ritual, the experience of the search for the Beloved and the union with that deep force within you. In different ways you will experience this in each of the journeys presented in the last part of this book, for all of sacred psychology ultimately speaks to this quest. Here we experience it in and of itself. While each part, the guided meditation and the ritual, may be done separately, they are most powerful when done together. Everyone participating in the experience should have read the preceding text, or one person should read it first to the group as a whole. Ample time must be allowed for the fullness of the experience. Preparation and reading might be done before dinner and the actual process begun in the evening. I have found doing this at night most effective.

In the guided meditation the initial imagery is drawn from archetypal forms which have haunted the Western imagination, helping to lead you into deeper levels of the journey. Then the imagery enters into the search for the Beloved using classical images and situations common to the Celtic mythos.

The ritual of crossing the threshold to the realm of the Beloved is derived from my speculations on the little we know of the rites of *pothos* at Samothrace.

TIME: A minimum of 2 hours.

MATERIALS NEEDED: Have a fresh votive candle in a glass container for each participant, and an extra eight to ten candles to mark the threshold and to light the edges of the room. Flowers, incense, and other materials that help to create sacred space are good additions, however, having done this on basketball courts, I find that the essential ingredient is the atmosphere created by the intention of those involved.

MUSIC: As with all statements about music, these are suggestions, not rules. I have always found live music the most evocative if there is a musician sufficiently sensitive and skilled to improvise from the depths. But do not use this as an opportunity to work with someone you have never worked with before!

If you are using taped music, prepare repeating loops or several tapes of the same piece so that you do not need to suddenly rewind at a critical point. For the Guided Meditation, select music from *Area 1,* like Georgia Kelly's *Seapeace;* for the Ritual, music from *Area 2,* like Vangelis's *Ignacio;* for the Final Celebration, music from *Area 3,* like Irene Pappas's and Vangelis's *Odes*.

INSTRUCTIONS FOR WORKING IN A GROUP: Before doing this process, familiarize yourself with the general instructions provided in the "How-To" section of this book. Assemble the music and candles needed, and prepare the room in which you will be working so that it is free of furniture and is peaceful and inviting. Participants may be invited to decorate the room as the Temple of the Beloved. The room should be long enough so that the walk to the Beloved is neither crowded nor too short.

INSTRUCTIONS FOR WORKING ALONE: If you are doing this alone, you will need to put the meditation on tape with appropriate music, such as the pieces suggested here, and thoroughly familiarize yourself with all aspects of the ritual so that you can move from one stage to another without any abrupt changes. Take time to create an atmosphere conducive to welcoming the Beloved into your life.

SCRIPT FOR THE GUIDE: (To be read in a gentle, trance-inducing voice throughout. The signal . . . indicates a brief pause.) Sit up in a comfortable position and follow your own breathing, all the way in and all the way out, and all the way in and all the way out, and all the way in and all the way out, and all the way in and all the way out. . . .

(When the participants are fully relaxed, begin the next stage.)

You are walking in the snow. . . in what seems to be a wasteland. The trees are few and sparse and bare. . . .

It is a light snow. . . . Your footprints etch themselves in high relief. . . .

And as you walk, you pass various strange scenes. On the left, you see a priestess with a golden lion standing between a black and a white marble column. . . .

And as you walk further, you see a dwarf juggling with golden triangles. . . .

And as you keep walking, you come upon a scene in which demons are tormenting a man on a tightrope. . . .

Continuing to walk, you see a woman crucified upside down. . . .

Continuing to walk, a naked androgyne discourses to you about the nature of love. . . .

Continuing to walk, a skeleton in armor riding a black horse comes up to you, bows to you with great dignity, and hands you a golden chalice. . . .

You continue to walk and you find yourself in a cosmic zoo with animals and creatures from all over the galaxy. . . .

Continuing to walk, a company of deaf mutes are performing the story of your life. . . .

You now find yourself at the edge of a marsh of quicksand. You walk along this marsh of quicksand, and somehow pulling your feet up, you manage to get across. . . .

Now you find yourself in a quiet forest where a bird in a tree says to you, "Your Beloved is in one of the towers of the white castle yonder."

And ahead you see a glorious medieval castle with two tall white towers from which are flying banners, and you run toward one of the circular towers. . . .

You don't know which one the Beloved is in, but you choose one, and you run up and around and up and around and up and around and. . . .

Doors slam behind you, and you know they are locked but you don't care, you are so in yearning for the Beloved. You continue to run up to the top of the topmost tower, and the Beloved is not there. . . .

And the doors are locked behind you. But over in the opposite tower you see or sense the Beloved of your soul, who is similarly caught there yearning for you.

You have *a minute or so of clock time,* equal subjectively to all the time you need, to find out what happens next. Begin. . . .

And down on the ground, somehow you find the Beloved, and your joy, in each other and with each other, is enormous. . . .

But then a wind begins to come up and play around you, a gentle wind. . . .

But gradually it becomes stronger and stronger and even more violent. . . .

And the wind picks you up and hurls you away from the Beloved. . . . And a great whirlwind hurls the Beloved in the opposite direction. . . .

And you are separated and lost, and you can't find the Beloved.

And there comes along a giant hundred-pound porcupine, limping, badly wounded, and the porcupine says to you, "If you would carry me on your back and help me get away from the hunters, I will try to help you find the Beloved." So you pick up this giant animal with its terrible pointed quills and you carry it on your back in search of the Beloved.

You have *a minute of clock time,* equal subjectively to all the time you need, to find out what happens next. Begin. . . .

And at the time that you are nearly at the place of the Beloved, a rain begins, a strange rain. . . .

And the rains pour down and become torrential. And the little rivulets become mighty streams which become rivers. . . . And the porcupine is washed away. . . .

And the rain becomes acid rain, and it eats away at your complexion, at your body, making you look horribly ravaged, ugly, looking much like a monster. And you wander through the world so very ugly, almost a monster, ravaged by the acid rains, and people fear you because of your terrible appearance.

You have *a minute or so of clock time* to experience the wandering through the world in this state of ugliness. Begin. . . .

You come finally to a great grove of trees with strange surrealistic shapes, exuding choking, noxious smells. The trees are known as the Trees of Madness, and you have to pass through this grove. But the trees scream at you all kinds of horrible things, as well as telling you to go in different directions. . . .

They reach out to grab you, to slap you, and to tell you things about yourself that you wish you hadn't heard. To go through this grove is to experience pain and madness.

You have *a minute of clock time* to go through these Trees of Madness. Begin. . . .

One day in your wanderings in search of the Beloved, you find yourself in a little mountain village where you set up a small shop. . . .

And people begin to come to you for advice . . . because out of your pain and sorrow you have grown deeply wise.

And people begin to come from the villages around and from the countryside to get your wisdom, your counsel. . . .

And you give it lovingly and freely, and you stay in this little mountain village, in your little shop, giving wisdom and counsel to all who come, for seven years.

You have *a minute and half of clock time,* equal to all the time you need, equal to the seven years spent there giving wisdom and counsel in your little shop. Begin . . .

One day an old woman comes to the shop and says, "Now it is time for you to seek the Beloved in the chapel that lies between the twin valleys. . . . The Beloved is there in the chapel waiting for you."

And you say, "Oh, but I am so ugly, I cannot face the Beloved." And the old woman says, "No, look in the mirror. Look what your gift of so much loving wisdom has restored to you."

And you look in the mirror and your skin is clean and pure again; your beauty is restored to more than it was. And the old woman says, "You must leave now, it is important, the time has come. Many will try to stop you on the way because of your reputation. . . .

"They will stop and ask you to give counsel. . . . People will desperately cry out, but it is the rule that you may not speak to them, regardless of how desperately they ask you. . . . You may not speak. You must stay silent on your journey to the chapel."

You have *a minute of clock time,* equal to all the time you need, to walk through the twin valleys with many people trying to get you to speak to them and help them, beginning now. . . .

You come to the chapel or little temple, and you are filled with excitement. . . . For you feel certain that the Beloved is there.

And you run in and you see the most beautiful bowers of flowers on the altar surrounding something. . . .

And you run up hoping to find the Beloved nearby, and you see that the flowers are covering a coffin, a casket . . . an open casket. . . .

And you look inside, your heart hammering in your chest. . . .

And it is the Beloved . . . lying dead in the casket . . . and your grief is enormous.

You have *a minute of clock time,* equal subjectively to all the time you need, to experience the fullness of your grief. Begin . . .

In your grief, your senses have become more keen and you notice that there is carved on the coffin the words, "You who would save the Beloved must sacrifice yourself so that the Beloved may live."

And your eye falls upon a very, very sharp, beautiful silver knife. . . .

And you know that the sacrifice must be total, it must be complete. . . .

And so you begin to cut yourself apart with the knife. . . . You rend yourself and cut yourself in many pieces.

You have *a minute or so of clock time,* equal to all the time you need, to do this, beginning now . . .

You are dead. . . . You are lying there dead. . . .

Your soul ascends and looks down at your body lying in pieces there dead. . . .

But you also note that some of your blood has fallen upon the face of the Beloved. Gradually you see the Beloved gaining color. . . .

The Beloved begins to breathe. . . . The blood, having fallen upon the Beloved, seems to be restoring the Beloved to life. . . .

And you observe as the Beloved comes fully back to life, sits up, gets out of the coffin, and sees you in all your separate parts lying there. And the Beloved picks up your parts and with love and reverence puts them back together again. . . .

And your soul descends into your body. . . .

And you are more complete than you have ever been, and your life is restored. . . .

And you and the Beloved have now the time of joyful meeting, recognition, and communion.

You have now *a minute and a half of clock time,* equal to all the time you need, for the meeting of communion with the Beloved . . .

(After this time has ended, let the music continue as the participants take 10 to 15 minutes to write or draw in their journals or to share their experience in pairs.)

The Walk to the Beloved: The Ritual of Samothrace

This ritual is best performed immediately after the meditation of the rites of pothos. It may be done in the same or in a different room which has been prepared with candles. Start the music quietly and light all of the candles. Place four candles to mark a threshold about two-thirds of the way across the length of the room. Use four to six candles to mark the edges of the room. Place the remaining candles where they are easily accessible to all. As guide and hierophant for this ritual, you and one or two who may be assisting you will stand at intervals along the threshold.

The walk to the realm of the Beloved and time spent in communion with the Beloved will take about thirty minutes to an hour. This is a very deep process and should be followed by a time of rest and solitude. It is preferable to perform this process at night prior to sleep, and to return to the group in the morning, perhaps to follow through with talk, dance, drawing, or whatever creative expression seems appropriate to express one's new sense of communion with his or her Beloved. If this is not possible, arrange for a gentle closing in which all have an opportunity to recognize and greet the Beloved in the other. An exchange of candles with accompanying music often serves beautifully here.

SCRIPT FOR THE GUIDE: (To be memorized or read in a clear, strong, and gentle voice.) And so begins the ritual of Samothrace, the crossing of the threshold to join the realm of communion with the Beloved.

And holding the Beloved in your heart . . . without saying anything to anyone . . . go and take a lighted candle and stand with your candle at the end of the room farthest from the threshold.

Now, it may well be that there are those here for whom this *pothos,* this yearning, this meeting and entering into communion with the Beloved is not appropriate at this time. It may very well be appropriate at some other time. . . .

This is a state of mind and of meeting which cannot be forced. If this action is not appropriate for you at this time, what we ask you to do is to stand at the sides, serving as high witnesses and empowerers of those who choose to walk across to the realm of the Beloved, knowing that your time will come and that with friends you can perform your own ritual.

(Allow time for this decision to be made and for those who will serve as high witnesses to move to the sides of the room. Then continue.)

We are about to perform a ritual based on the rites of pothos performed at Samothrace. This will be the enactment of the communion and the commitment to the Beloved . . . the Beloved who comes from the deeper realms of being, which contain the great evolutionary patterns of love, knowledge, and creation.

Thus when you are together with the Beloved, this union and partnership extends you into the depth world and helps bring the depth world into time.

(Pause until you are sure everyone is ready.)

For the Beloved, when known in this kind of communion, arises and enters into creative partnership with you. Does the Beloved of the soul exist? Yes, in the realm of the psyche. Can you prove it? Yes, by your actions you will find out. You discover that you are enlarged, enhanced, extended. But remember that the relationship must be nurtured in order to continue.

The walk to the Beloved is very, very slow, and each step is a yearning. As you move very slowly in space, you move very deeply within.

And then, at a certain point, as you pass over the line of fire, you know that you are passing into the realm of the Beloved. . . .

There you find yourself a place where you sit down and enter into communion with the Beloved. It is the place of the marriage of the self with the Beloved of the soul. It is the place of the great union.

Let the walk begin.

(There is no speaking during the walk at all. The volume of the music is increased, but it should not be overpowering in any way. During the walk, the guide stands as witness in the center of the room at the place of the line of fire. When all have crossed over, and after some minutes of communion have gone by, the guide continues.)

Know yourself now in communion with the Beloved. You have entered into a union that, if you choose, will sustain and support you all the days of your life. Never again will you ever really be alone, for now you are in union. You and your Beloved of the soul can grow together in partnership in so many ways to bring more light, more love, more knowledge, more creativity, more courage into this world. Renew the sense of this union whenever you can, but for now, feel the sweetness of the communion and know yourself so deeply loved.

(Stately but celebrational music can be played here, or there can be quiet, if that seems preferable. An atmosphere of celebrational meditation should be maintained in the room, and people leave, as it is appropriate, to their own timing.

Alternate Ending:

As the music continues, people perform a dance of honoring the Beloved in each other, bowing to each other and exchanging candles as they dance. At the end of this, the guide might speak):

Now blow the light of love into your hearts, that it may kindle a life in union with the Beloved.

(At this point, all blow out their candles.)

PART FOUR
The Stories

Overleaf: Lovers embracing, symbolizing the reunion of the person with his or her essence. Though pictured as two, the couple represents being one in spirit, the state of Mithuna, beyond separation. Haut relief wall sculpture, Surya Temple, Konaraka, India, ca. A.D. 1250.

INTRODUCTION TO THE STORIES

There is but the one history and that is the soul's.

—YEATS,

INTRODUCTION TO THE 1928 VERSION OF "A VISION"

This section provides the discussion of two great stories, the first mythic, the second historical, and describes the processes to make them your own. These stories, as we will see, provide the templates for transformation. However ancient, they carry the coded matrices of the next steps in human development and evolution. Each is a kind of narrative Asclepian, which provides a total environment for the "doing of the work of the gods."

When actively engaged, the Great Story leads you from the frustrations of the personal-particular to the fulfillment of the personal-universal with its broadening contexts and more universal formulations. You "become" Isis and Osiris; with Percival you take on the quest for the Grail; you adventure with Odysseus; you assume the passion and the pathos of Psyche; you search for the Beloved of the soul with Rumi. As you engage these mythic and symbolic dramas, you take the journey of transformation by identifying with a mythic character who enlarges some aspect of yourself. Symbolic happenings then appear in undisguised relevance to your personal story.

Gradually you discover that these stories are your own stories. They bear the amplified pattern of certain rhythms and cadences in your own life. After having been Psyche and Eros and Shams and Rumi, you come back to your own life enhanced and with the ability to say, "I have the strength, I have the depth, I have the capacity, I have the wisdom, I have the purpose. I will prevail." And often you do.

Since theatre and drama provide so fundamental and effective a context for human learning and growth, sacred psychology teaches mythic stories by using drama. When we live this larger story dramatically, we create the conditions and impetus for extraordinary growth.

The two stories chosen for this volume, the myth of Psyche and Eros, and the love story of the great thirteenth-century Sufi mystic and poet Jalaloddin Rumi, present different aspects of a theme critical to the study of sacred psychology—the search for the Beloved.[1] The story of Psyche and Eros gives us the travail of a younger, more unconscious love, and describes the labors the soul performs in its harrowing path to consciousness—the path of gaining inner allies and growing resources until one is ready for the union with the Divine Beloved within. The mystic passion of Rumi tells of the refinements of a love that is older and more complex by far, wherein the search for the Beloved illumines the whole world.

One should be cautioned against perceiving these two journeys sentimentally. Each contains the full spectrum of the *agon* of transformation explored earlier: wounding and betrayal, suffering and loss, pathos and *pothos.* Each offers scenarios and practices that have the effect of quite literally reweaving the tapestry of one's humanness. In agreeing to participate in these stories you initiate a quickening in your own journey, a deepening of your own path.

Finally, the reader will note that in the discussion of each story I have indicated the places where the experiential scenario of the journey belongs. The actual scenarios and their processes are placed after the full discussion is given. Thus individuals who gather to perform these processes may wish to review together the discussion given and perform the scenarios where and when they are designated. Or, they could choose to first inform themselves of the entire discussion and then do the scenarios, one after another. These processes are designed to be performed over the course of a number of days. In presenting these and other journeys of transformation in my seminars, I generally allow anywhere from a weekend to five days for each journey. Technically, of course, it is possible to perform each journey in a single day, but that scarcely gives one any time to reflect upon the power of each experience.

12

PSYCHE AND EROS

O Butterfly,
What are you dreaming there,
Fanning your wings?
—CHIYO-NI

In the wonderful story of Psyche and Eros, as told in the rollicking Roman tale of *The Golden Ass of Apuleius,*[1] we have a full-fledged journey of the soul, one that tells of a significant turning point in the history of human consciousness. Like all great myths, the story unfolds on many levels. Before starting the journey itself, we will consider some of those themes and levels embedded in what may appear, on the surface, to be a very simple and "romantic" story.

This myth really started to find its form somewhere between 500 and 600 B.C. This was also the time of Lao-Tse and Confucius in China, of Buddha and Mahavira in India, Pythagoras in Greece, and Zoroaster in Persia. This was the time, therefore, of the rise of God-realized humans, of "heaven dropping like dew" into the human psyche. It is the time of the great mything link (if you will excuse the pun) being discovered by the human soul saying, "I am filled with God." The salvational figure in this story is no longer Pharaoh, or Priest-King; it is a human being, and a woman at that.

The age-old myth of Psyche and Eros is thus the story of the awakening of the immortal soul into time, offering us clues to the necessary awakening and metamorphosis of ourselves. It is no coincidence that many depth psychologists are paying attention to this story right now as it becomes increasingly urgent that we hear the alarm and wake out of our sleep. Robet Johnson in *She,*[2] C. S. Lewis in *Till We Have Faces,*[3]

Erich Neumann in *Amor and Psyche,*[4] James Hillman in *The Myth of Analysis,*[5] and Maria-Louise von Franz in *A Psychological Interpretation of The Golden Ass of Apuleius*[6] have each explored the myth for its psychological richness and powerful relevance to the waking up and development of psyche in our time.

Many have recognized the power of this metaphor. Drawing on the teachings of Gurdjieff, Ouspensky summarized Gurdjieff's key motif in all of his teachings:

> Man's possibilities are very great. You cannot conceive even a shadow of what man is capable of attaining. But nothing can be attained in sleep. In the consciousness of a sleeping man his illusions, his "dreams" are mixed with reality. He lives in a subjective world and he can never escape from it. And this is the reason why he can never make use of all the powers he possesses and why he always lives in only a small part of himself.[7]

Gurdjieff's remarks remind us that it is not only young and innocent virgins like Psyche and Sleeping Beauty who sleep. It is a universal phenomenon. We sleep through nuclear threat, the desertification of the planet, and the mounting evidence of our violence to one another. So, too, do we sleep through the great beauty around us: the gratuitous generosity of the stranger, the delight of the playing child, the extraordinary patterns of the night sky.

Yet the myth does not speak to any rough and rude alarm, shattering the dreaming dawn, but rather speaks to our awakening through the gift of love. This awakening of the sleeping soul through love is a recurrent theme in myth, folk tales, and art, as well as in visions and dreams. In itself this theme is archetypal. We think not only of Sleeping Beauty, but also of Snow White, Brunhilde, the maidens whose souls are suspended in the veils of sleep. We think, too, of ourselves when we have been awakened by love and have seen the world new. The awakening can only occur through the coming of the Beloved, for the awakening of the soul through the lure of the Beloved is essential to myth, archetype, and sacred psychology.

This myth does more than call us to wake up. Through the story, it offers us a pathway and process for doing so which engages us fully enough to insure that we wake up with a deepened capacity for loving and a greater connection to our own courage, strength, and wisdom so that we may become conscious co-creators of our world.

The ancient Greek word *psyche* means "butterfly," a creature who undergoes a long period of metamorphosis in the chrysalis state before transformation or awakening is possible. So, too, must the young girl

Psyche prepare herself for those changes which will allow her the necessary transformation. Everything that Psyche must do during this period is apparently beyond any human capacity. The "impossible" can only be accomplished through a metamorphosis of her relationship to herself, to the world, and to the spiritual powers. And because the process of the metamorphosis of the soul is the story of the creation of the psyche, and this story is *par excellence* the story of the recreation of the butterfly-bride Psyche, we can see it as a fundamental myth of psychological creativity, giving us clues to the awakening and metamorphosis of ourselves.

The sleeping being is a child, full of untapped potential, unconscious in its innocence. This is the story of the emergence out of childhood dependency on archetypal powers—be they parents, gods or goddesses, institutions, or the nursery culture itself—and entry into the full maturity of the human psyche.

This tale has been depicted in art since the fifth century B.C. In virtually all of these portrayals, Psyche and Eros are seen as children or adolescents, a little younger than those classical lovers Romeo and Juliet. In the classical art forms, and in the tale itself, they are almost androgynous. Psyche describes her lover's breast as being as smooth as her own.

Thus the tale is also about children, particularly the wounded child. The wounded child in us is the part of us that becomes needy for love, for nourishment, for intimate caring in return for affection. As James Hillman has noted, "We regard childhood wounds less as the result of nutritive and sexual trauma than as wounds of love. We feel the wounds as abandonment."[8] Much of the deep suffering and sense of inadequacy that adults feel comes from the initial abandonment of love in early childhood. Hillman refers to "one's swollen reservoir of love unwanted, without adequate or permitted recipients."[9] This can take subtle and all too familiar forms: "Tell me later, dear." "Don't touch me; you're going to spoil my makeup." As parents of nuclear families are increasingly absent, for whatever reasons—some noble, some inevitable, and some apparently quite selfish—the situation is exacerbated. The television set is no substitute.

The wounds of neglect and abandonment stunt the development of the psyche. The violation of the natural weakness and simplicity of the young child not ready for autonomy can turn into a protective infantilism that lasts through one's life. These wounds may be redeemed through the natural simplicity of loving; indeed, they may offer the gateway through which love may enter. Yet there is another side to this story, and a critical one. As long as our psychology remains at the level of the personal-particular and the profane, we see the world polarized into "offenders" (for which read parents) and "victims" (for which read children) and we reinforce the devastating cycle of guilt and blame. As we have seen earlier, wounding prepares for the entrance of a larger story. This is not in any way to condone the abandonment or abuse of children; clearly it must stop. Yet it is possible that the pattern can only be broken when those of us who have experienced these woundings know them again at the deeper level of Great Story.

Many of the great myths of childhood, including this one, are not myths of incest or starvation; they are myths of abandonment. The child is thrust, unprepared, out of the nursery culture into impossible situations—into the middle of a river, onto the highway to the Wicked Ones, or alone in the forest. Consider the case of Moses, or that of Hansel and Gretel. In time they must exhibit prodigious skill and precocious cunning to save both themselves and the world at large. First they must be thrust out of dependency, "ready or not" as the childhood game reminds us, into the Larger Story and learn to trust.

So, too, as we shall see, is Psyche abandoned, and dramatically so. Psyche's childhood is lived from a basis of emotional attachment and desire. This makes Psyche, and us—for we are all Psyche—childlike in dealing with reality. Through the journey of suffering and love that then ensues, Psyche matures until she becomes a power in her own right, ready and able to act in both existential and archetypal worlds.

In Psyche's great search for the Beloved, we learn again how human love becomes the vehicle for the launching of vast creative powers. As a child, Psyche created nothing; she was cherished, even worshipped; yet the fire of her creativity had not been ignited.

On still another level, the story of Psyche is a unique myth of the development of the feminine principle in women and men alike. Most much-told myths are essentially variations on the hero's journey, myths of the development of the masculine principle in men. Women serve as allies, mentors, comforters, mediators, lovers, and inspirers, but they are essentially static and passive, in a state of being rather than of becoming.

In this story, however, the development of the feminine principle is fully played out. The feminine principle is a part of all of us, men as well as women. One aspect of this is that we learn to partner nature and listen deeply for the wisdom within, thus resolving impossible situations and bringing to fruition incredible tasks. This is radically different from the masculine capacity for controlling and shaping nature, and offers now a restoration of the balance needed at this time. Another aspect of the feminine principle that is played out here is the importance, indeed the centrality, of relationships. Her relationship to others, whether absent or present, forms the basis of Psyche's story. It is quintessentially a tale of relationship: relationship between the sexes, between the component opposites within each of us, and between the mortals and the gods. Thus it addresses some of the deep questions of our time.

THE JOURNEY

This myth begins with the birth of an extraordinarily beautiful daughter to a king and queen. She is born of "heaven's dew," and with her birth, the essence of all goodness falls on earth. Psyche's birth is a critical event in the story of human consciousness, for this is a tale of heaven (spirit) falling into residence in the human soul.

So great is her beauty that all who see her marvel at it, claiming that her beauty even surpasses that of Aphrodite, the goddess of beauty and love. As the citizens of Greece flock to admire the chaste and exquisite beauty of Psyche, the temples of the goddess are abandoned and her rites ignored.

Aphrodite, representative of the old order in which there was a great and rightful divide between the gods and humans, is, necessarily, enormously offended. She is a staunch defender of the status quo: mortals are to be mortals and serve the gods; they are certainly not to challenge or threaten their status. In this she reflects the tyranny of all old dependencies and unreflected archetypes.*

To avenge the threat from the human realm, Aphrodite entices her son-lover, Eros, to wreak vengeance on the beautiful mortal. She implores him by the bonds of a rather incestuous mother love, kissing him "with parted lips . . . long and fervently." Naturally, Eros, the enraptured, bonded child, cannot refuse, and is probably grateful to capture some of his mother's wandering attentions. (He is certainly a lively archetypal candidate for the abandoned child syndrome, what with his mother's many other interests.) She orders him to shoot Psyche with one of his arrows so that Psyche will be "consumed with passion for the vilest of men," one who causes enormous miseries. (This is, of course, prophetic, for Eros himself is peerless in provoking endless agonies.)

Back on earth, although everyone adores Psyche, no one will marry her because there is a quality of "too-muchness" about her. Her apparent perfection awes rather than attracts. She grows more and more lonely, coming to "hate the loveliness that charmed so many nations." In desperation, her father asks the oracle of Apollo to send her a husband, receiving back the awe-full message that his daughter was to be the bride of Death.

Despite the grief of her family at this irrevocable pronouncement, Psyche is prepared for her marriage in funeral robes and led in a procession of mourners to a high crag to await her fate.

*By "unreflected archetypes" I mean archetypes such as Aphrodite or the early Dionysius—who exist as unconscious dependencies *under* whom you serve, but *in* whom you cannot come to consciousness. People caught in the grip of a mania or an obsession are tyrannized by unreflected archetypes.

This question of too-muchness raises sad and poignant issues for many. You may wish to consider the place and sacrifice of too-muchness in your own life or in the life of others. Have you been seen and then been sacrificed for having too much energy, or enthusiasm or beauty or joy? Have you been accused of excessive intelligence or sensitivity, of too much insight, strength, or even grief? Have you felt too large for a too-small world? Are you all dressed up with all kinds of talents and qualities but with no place to go? To accommodate to the apparently shrunken reality of the "real world," many choose to shrink. The prevalent indulgence in drugs and alcohol, the squandering of one's powers and talents, and the sacrifice of one's essence speak to the great and widespread desire to forget who one is in the confinement of culture and consciousness. Then, too, there is the issue of our curtailment of the abundance of others—our children, loved ones, and professional associates—all in their "best interests."

The sacrifice of Psyche is, of course, the classical mystery of the marriage of doom, recounted in many myths and legends of the maiden sacrificed to the monster, the dragon, the wizard, or an evil spirit. Despite the terrifying external circumstances, it is a setup for a *hieros gamos,* a sacred marriage between the world of light and the realm of shadow.

It is also symbolic of a holy sacrifice, the sacred wounding that is essential to the development of feminine consciousness. In many cultures the initiation of the maiden into womanhood occurs through the sacrificial wedding—the sacrifice of the innocence of the maiden to the monster of man's desire. The sacrifice may be underlined by physical stigmata: in Orthodox Judaism the woman cuts her long hair; in some African tribes there is female circumcision, while in other tribes the woman is wounded and scarred for her wedding; and in Islam there is the veiling of woman at marriage. Each of these represents the death of the child beauty, the sacrificial offering that enables the girl to die as a simple wondering child in preparation for marriage and maturity.

At the command of his mother, Eros has been waiting for Psyche, hovering nearby until the wedding/funeral procession leaves. Seeing her thus for the first time, he is so enraptured by her beauty that he leans on one of his arrows, pricks himself, and falls deeply in love with Psyche. Instead of falling over the cliff as the bride of Death, Psyche is wafted by the Western Wind to an idyllic paradise and becomes the bride of Love, of Eros himself.

And so, as in many other classical tales—"Beauty and the Beast," "Sir Gawain and Dame Raglan," "The Princess and the Frog"—the marriage with death undergoes an *enantiadromia,* a big turnaround, and Psyche, fully expecting to die, is instead wafted into the paradise of Eros, an Arabian Nights–like palace with golden walls, jewelled floors, marvelous food, invisible servants, and the world's greatest lover coming into her bed each and every night.

From the chaste innocence of childhood she enters into the bliss of first love, an enraptured paradise in which she still remains unconscious. She "falls" in love, one of the great "descents" in the journey of the soul, yet she does so in a way that is archetypally feminine.

In the male myth of the descent, there is the fall of spirit into matter, recounted in many gnostic and scriptural myths. Examples would include the fall of Lucifer from the side of God, and the entering of the Holy Spirit into Mary. However, in the female myth of descent, there is the fall of a mattered being into the archetypal or spiritual realm. Thus we have the descent of Persephone into the Underworld, the fall of the feminine gnostic principle of Sophia from the highest realms of Being to the lowest, the adventures of Alice in Wonderland after she fell down the rabbit hole. Falling in love allows us to be transported magically into realms we never knew existed—yet it is still possible to remain totally unconscious; indeed, it is seductively easy to do so.

Psyche's lover-husband is Eros, and herein lies a considerable philosophical and psychological tale: Eros has a mission with the soul. Without Eros, the soul cannot grow; the psyche remains infantile. Eros gives psyche its yearning, its impetus, its desire for the fullness of life.

In his great dialogue on love, *The Symposium,*[10] Plato acknowledges the potent force of Eros, whom he represents as the son of Need and Plenty. Eros is the catalyst for the joining of the two into a deep erotic and transformational experience. While the beloved and the lover may fall initially in love because of the beauty of face and form (as Eros did with Psyche), they then fall in love with the beauty of soul and mind of each other. Then they discover the beauty of the many things around them, until they are drawn to contemplation of the archetypes of Beauty and Goodness themselves. Finally they are moved by Eros to create beautiful works together.

The lure of Eros may not necessarily be sexual, but it is often a lure of "muchness" (as we see in the glory of Eros' palace), a lure into the deep gestating patterns of reality where you see the great forms of things, the Patterns that Connect. This lure calls you to the places of re-creation in the soul where you are seeded, spiced, excited, stimulated, evoked, into becoming. You become much much more than you were, and you create much much more than you could have before.

Eros connects the personal to something beyond, and brings the beyond into personal experience. He is the *psychopomp* (in ancient Greece, the priest who leads the sacred procession) leading the soul to the gods, and brings the gods, the great patterns of creativity and possibility, into the human soul. Without Eros in some form, creativity suffocates;

the soul does not grow. Indeed, as we see in this story, Psyche will (apparently) die. Creativity is grounded in the longing for the beloved, the extended archetype of the self within the soul.

Eros belongs to the order of the entelechy. As we have seen, entelechy is that dynamic purposiveness coded in ourselves, longing for unfoldment and expression. It is the possibility of our next stage of growth and evolution entering into time. Without the lure of becoming, the entelechy remains unused, untapped, unerotic. Thus the entelechy and maturation of the soul unfolds through the lure of Eros.

Eros joined Psyche in a magic kingdom that really is no place. You can't really find it on any map, heavenly or human. C. S. Lewis sheds some light on this motif in the marvelous retelling of this tale in *Till We Have Faces.* The heroine is the sister of Psyche, a great-souled one herself, who looks everywhere to find her lost but much-beloved sister. She finally sees Psyche, dressed in rags, by the bank of a river, enraptured with a quite ordinary forest, insisting it is a majestic kingdom. For just a fraction of a second, the veils lift and the sister sees what Psyche sees, but then the vision disappears.

What is this magical place where Eros has taken Psyche? It is an unpeopled place, yet everything is attended to by invisible servants. Psyche is even forbidden to see her lover; she must know him only in the dark. The reason for this no-place atmosphere is that in the search of our own psyche for the god, for the agent of transformation, the two poles of heaven and earth, the realms of essence and existence are too extreme for the requirements of this mysterious conjunction. They are either too subtle or too strong. Thus Eros, as the intermediary between worlds, must create the world-in-between, providing sacred time and space to do the work of love and transformation. He has created a chrysalis from which the butterfly may emerge.

Without Psyche having been in this magical no-place for a while, she would never have had the erotic quickening by love to enable her to go out and do the impossible, awesome, and awful tasks to which she is later assigned. So, too, with ourselves. People may sometimes ask, "Why are you imagining things?" If you were to reply truly, you might say, "I am going to my imaginal place where I get nurtured, seeded, and fed so that I can then go out and do my work in the world." Yet this answer is forbidden, as it was for Psyche. Eros has warned her: "Do not speak of these things." This is the warning of the mystery—there is no language to carry it, and the language of everyday exchange will destroy it.

When you enter into this imaginal, creative world, there is often an ecstasy of darkness. Nobody would guess what is going on between you and the hidden regions of your soul, and you really cannot or should not tell them. How often have you destroyed the magic and creativity of your inner life by talking about it so much that its gestation was harmed?

When you do start to talk about it, your sisters and brothers out there get nosy or jealous or alarmed, and try to lure you away. As in the story, chances are you have been warned. The Beloved of your soul speaks through your conscience and says, "Don't let the right hand know what the left hand is doing." In more contemporary language, don't let the logical left brain know what the intuitive right brain is doing until the time is ripe. The closet of the corpus callosum keeps the secret.

There is, however, a time to move out of the darkness, to tear off the veil across the mystery, as Psyche reminds us. Her ecstasy in the darkness can only last for a limited period of time. Should she remain there too long she would not grow; indeed, she might even decay or go mad.

A taboo is placed upon Psyche which has in it the seeds of its own transgression, like every taboo. She is told by her lover that she must not look on him with lamplight, lest he be cast from her forever.

What does this mean? On one level it is certainly a warning that the unprepared soul must not look upon its creative matrix prematurely. On the everyday level it is the age-old tale of the male lover who says, "If you actually looked at me or knew me, you would not want me." In many relationships the female lover, or young wife, begins to awaken from the archetypal sexual role, with its bliss of unconscious rapture in the dark, with a lamp in one hand and a knife in the other. Also, when people are in love they don't look *at* each other but they look *through* each other, and the universe becomes a miraculous collaboration of their paradise. The initial impetus to the soul is to be felt deeply, experienced rapturously, but not analyzed and examined.

So, too, the sensual, sexual, and emotional swoon of first love is truly one of unconsciousness in which the archetypes of male and female are the givers and receptacles of the seed. This is a deep physical and biological meeting, and offers the initial physical and romantic means for awakening. While this is an initiatory love experience, it may happen again and again throughout a lifetime as you fall in love with other people, with ideas, with nature, and perhaps, ultimately, with God. Socrates once said that all his life he'd been in love with someone and that's what had given him his impetus and kept him going.

The snakes (and there is more than one, as you may have discovered in your life) in this garden of Eros's paradise are Psyche's sisters. Belonging to the "real world," they have made "wonderful" marriages with ancient patriarchal types. They see their lives as ones in which they spoon-feed their husbands and have little, if any, sex. One sister describes her husband as "balder than a pumpkin and feebler than any child." Although they may have apparently achieved a maturity that Psyche has not, their disillusionment has made them doubting and envious, classic representatives of the necessary doubts that arise when things are one-sided, childlike, "perfect," and essentially unconscious.

In fact, Psyche herself has sought them out because life in paradise is rather lonely. They succeed in convincing her of what, at some level, she already knows: an exclusive life of rapture in the dark leaves something to be desired. In fact, they suggest, she is being ravaged by a demon. In this case, of course, the demon is really a *daimon,* a god, but at this state of unconsciousness, one cannot yet tell the difference. Psyche's existence is a nonexistence, a being in the dark, a biological and somewhat impersonal rapture of sensual sexuality and impregnation which may fittingly be characterized as being devoured by a demon. And so Psyche is advised by her sisters to light a lamp when he is asleep and then to slay the monster with a knife.

Here we have two classical symbols. The *lamp* is the source of light in the darkness. Throughout history the presence of women has been a lamp of remembrance for men. In this illumination one perceives the transpersonal dimensions of the other, making it possible for them to remember where they really came from and to recognize their own innate and enormous beauty. Now, with the rise of the feminine and the changing roles between the sexes, we are finally in the time in which men and women can hold for each other the lamp of *mutual light* and *mutual remembrance.*

The lamp that Psyche uses is an oil lamp. Oil is feminine, essence of the plant world, the *ichor* of Mother Earth. The warrior is anointed by women with oil when he returns home; the Jewish woman lights the Sabbath oil on Friday night.

The myth is quite explicit about the fear and terror about being truly *seen.* Eros, ironically a god of fire, is burned by the oil of the lamp of feminine seeing. Unfortunately, in many relationships the knife of words is used before the light of the lamp has brought the full meaning of the relationship.

The *knife* is the instrument of either destruction or discrimination, depending on the intention of the user; and, of course, is a masculine symbol. Psyche is being invited, in fact urged, to use both parts of herself. Actually, as we shall see, she never uses the knife, for what the lamp reveals is beyond her greatest expectations.

As Eros lies beside her, sleeping, Psyche lights the lamp and beholds not a monster but a very young man whose exquisite beauty matches her own. Having broken the taboo of his invisibility, she is no longer infatuated and naive, but is now a consciously impassioned woman, a woman who yearns to know as much as possible about this wondrous being to whom she is wedded. So she picks up one of his arrows to examine it, pricks her own finger, and falls in love with the god of love, in love with Love itself. In her desire to see him very closely, inspecting with wonder and delight someone so beloved, she spills some of the oil onto his sleeping body and burns him. The protective veils are broken.

The myth tells us that Psyche suffers from love, and so the girl is to be tortured into womanhood. Eros is tortured by his principle, fire. Having been seen, he must leave, for gods may not be visible in their true form to mortals. So Eros regresses, in pain, to his mother's house. The impassioned and despairing Psyche holds onto his foot as he flies up to heaven, but inevitably she falls back to earth. Eros is agitated, tortured, burning—without the Psyche he loves. Eros without Psyche is empty; love without soul is vain. It is only when Eros gains his mate, Psyche, that he gains consciousness. And yet he is powerless to do anything further to remedy the situation—at least for a while. It is up to the mortal Psyche to redeem the situation.

*(Scenario 1: The Lamp and the Knife)**

In the creative life of the soul, it is the fire of responsive passion that provides the basis for illumination. But first there must be the torture and the training that attend awakening.

Before the divine and sanctified connection is possible, Psyche must go through the Dark Night of the Soul, alone, pregnant, loveless, and often suicidal. Still she goes about the tasks without Eros, and thus without hope or energy. She searches for Eros everywhere, imploring the gods for help. They, afraid of the wrath of Aphrodite and the devastating arrows of her son, refuse. When she attempts to drown herself, the stream will have none of it and casts her up on the shore where the nature god Pan gives her comfort and fatherly advice. Respectful of all the gods, she sorts the grain offerings in Demeter's temple, whereupon Demeter, the goddess of agriculture, gives her sympathy but sends her away. None of the gods dares to have anything to do with the girl who has so deeply offended Aphrodite.

Now comes the soul work of Psyche as, at this point in the story, Aphrodite herself actively enters the scene. Aphrodite may be seen as the ultimate mean mother-in-law who cannot release her son to a younger woman; she may, however, also be seen as the initiator of the younger woman, of the mortal, so that she may gain the consciousness, the strength, and the depth to transcend the limitation of unconscious mortality.

The four tasks that Aphrodite will set before the young woman serve as a series of initiations leading to deepening structures of consciousness. As such they are symbolic of the psychological and erotic ordeals through which all of us are put in our search for union and completion. The labors comprise almost the entire province of tests that we need to go through for our deepening and maturation. Let us look at them now, seeing Psyche's story as our own and utilizing the accompanying scenarios to engage our own memories and experiences of initiation.

*"Scenario" lines in parentheses refer to exercises at the end of the chapter.

THE FOUR LABORS

SORTING THE SEEDS

Aphrodite assigns Psyche the task of sorting a huge pile of seeds so that each is "in its own place" before evening. Psyche collapses and sits in silent stupefaction, overwhelmed by the vastness of the task. Neither rational, conscious sorting nor her own biological unconscious process can help her now. She has already done both of these, having sorted the sheaves of grain in Demeter's temple and, in her pregnancy, is herself already seeded. She has internally sorted the seeds, for out of the billions of seeds of Eros, she has unconsciously and biologically selected the one with which she is impregnated.

Having "given up," Psyche can "give over" to another possibility, another potential. This comes in the form of an army of ants, earth creatures, cthonic powers, who serve as an army of instincts to help her, and with the zeal of their instinctive powers, they "one by one separate the heap, grain by grain," within the allotted time.

Psyche is able to accomplish the apparently impossible with an instinctive ordering principle that comes from beyond her own known resources. This accomplishment reminds us of our own innate capacity to select, sift, correlate, and evaluate. At a deeper level, it shows how "heaven's dew," the spiritual principle within our soul, works for us on earth by putting pattern into matter and so allowing matter and nature to work for us.

(Scenario 2: The First Labor: Sorting the Seeds)

THE GATHERING OF THE GOLDEN FLEECE

Aphrodite is apparently furious with Psyche's success, and suspects that some other power has been helping her. She orders Psyche to perform a second labor, the gathering of some of the golden fleece of the sheep who graze across the river. The innocent Psyche does not know that she has been assigned by Aphrodite to certain death, for these sheep are frenzied and will kill anyone who approaches them.

The symbol of the rams, of the golden fleece, is a very ancient one and has to do with both the creative and the destructive power of the blazing sun. In Egypt the solar ram, Khnum, is also the potter who creates the forms of sentient life on his wheel. In the tale of Jason and the Argonauts, we see hyper-macho types facing grave danger in order to steal the fleece, the ultimate male symbol. Jason "rams" his way through and takes the golden fleece with the help of the priestess-magician Medea, who sacrifices all the things that she holds most tender to help Jason and is self-exiled by this act. Later, in Greece, having borne children to Jason, she feels grievously betrayed when he abandons her to take a younger woman as wife. The horrible consequences of her vengeance become the stuff of high tragedy and mythic drama.

With this background, we know that whenever we hear of golden rams and golden fleece in Greek stories and legend we are in for very powerful and dangerous masculine energies that must be redeemed in order to be reintegrated. In the world of women, masculine "battering rams" spell the collapse of women's hopes. The rams of the sun, symbols of the destructive power of the masculine, are present today in the ramming power of technological might, the destruction of the ecology, and in the belligerent giant superpowers squaring off like two rams ready to charge at each other with atomic horns and destroy the whole blooming world.

Again in despair over the impossibility of her task, Psyche plans to throw herself in the river. She is stopped by a singing reed, breathed through by some spirit in the wind who reveals to her the secret of getting the fleece. She is advised to avoid the sheep during the day when their power is great, but to wait until evening when they sleep and the masculine solar spirit returns to the feminine depths. Then she is to cross the river and take some of the golden wool clinging to the bushes that the sheep have brushed against during the day.

The reed rising from the waters of the depths represents the wisdom of growth, with its sense of appropriate timing. The wisdom of the oracular reed is a feminine wisdom, advising Psyche to get what is needed by moonlight and by indirection, advising also that it is only the fleece that is needed, not the entire ram. She may avoid the direct masculine approach and take just a few strands; she does not have to kill the sheep.

In feminine gnosis the part contains the whole. In ourselves the reed is the taproot channeling the depths of our psyches where we know so much. The reeded self of the moontime of alternate states of consciousness knows something that the existential self of suntime, of ordinary states of consciousness, does not know. The reeded self knows that everything is possible, but that it is possible by the practice of paradox, intuitive knowing, and indirection.

(Scenario 3: The Second Labor: Being Reeded and Gathering the Golden Fleece)

GETTING THE WATERS OF LIFE

When Psyche brings the wool back, Aphrodite is thoroughly frustrated. The unreflected archetype is being provoked and she is forced to reflect on "What is Psyche?"—something she has never had to do before. She is also forced to reexamine all of her assumptions about mortals, and she assigns Psyche yet another task.

Having gained the seeds of the earth and the fleece of the animals, Psyche must now acquire the Waters of Life. She is given a crystal vessel which she must fill with the waters that feed the streams of the Underworld. These waters flow from the highest crag of a huge mountain, virtually impossible to climb, and guarded by dangerous dragons.

These dragons represent the recurrent and universal mythic demand that the young girl has to face the dragon. They are keepers of the threshold, cthonic guardians of the secrets of life who stop you if you are unprepared. Dragons, perhaps the mythic representation of our own ancient reptilian brain with its insistence on repetition and ritual, may also be your professional superiors or the local keepers of the rule books. They don't give you much respect if you go to them through the proper channels and dutifully follow the known path. Then you just become one of the many assistant dragons with no access to the Waters of Life. The high dragons only truly appreciate you if you can fool them and creatively find your way through.

Again Psyche is overwhelmed by her task: even the stream has warned her, murmuring, "Hence! Beware!" In Apuleius's rendition of the story, "Though she was present in the body, her senses had flown far away from her, and quite overwhelmed by such vast, inevitable peril, she lacked even the last solace of tears."

And again help arrives. If this myth teaches us nothing else, it shows that help is always present. Zeus sends his eagle to help her, and we learn of the paternal god's initial sympathy for Psyche. It is this noble bird who now informs Psyche that the task of getting even one drop of the waters of life is even beyond the capacities of gods, much less mortals. Taking her crystal jar, he flies up among the crags, dodges the dragons, and goes with clarity and decisiveness to just the right spot to gather the waters.

The noted author Robert Johnson points out that the feminine way of taking the elixir from the treacherous and fast-moving river of life is to take one goblet at a time. A woman may take successive goblets, one at a time, but each one that is pursued with high consciousness leads to satisfaction in life. The "more is better" attitude of our society leads to a kind of cultural restlessness, for in the midst of a rich experience, we are always looking about for something even grander and better. The human ego is like the fragile and precious crystal goblet, a container for some of the vastness of life. But to acquire this life, as Psyche must, one must see like an eagle to have the right perspective, dipping into the stream of life in the right places and trying to contain only one goblet of water at a time lest the local self be shattered.

In all of these tasks Psyche is moving more and more toward the integration of masculine and feminine powers and understandings within her. In the first labor she uses the instinctual powers of nature in the left-brained task of ordering and sifting; in the second she manages to avoid the assault of the dangerous forces of the rams to gather enough of the golden fleece, the masculine force, to perform her tasks adequately. Now in the third labor, the eagle of the masculine spirit allows her to draw from its particular perspective and strength. In Jungian terms, she is engaging her *animus* in these labors, but not being overcome by it. These lessons are especially important for women in our time, when we need to come into true relationship with the masculine principle rather than becoming second-rate men. For men the lesson is to engage the *anima* with sufficient *animus* so that the *anima* is luminous and not effete and the psyche is deepened, not weakened.

(Scenario 4: The Third Labor: The Waters of Life)

THE JOURNEY TO THE UNDERWORLD

Psyche, now strengthened and integrated by the completion of the earlier tasks, is given the ultimate and final test—one that people rarely get to or are extremely hesitant about ever taking. Aphrodite tells her that she must journey to the Underworld and obtain from Persephone, the queen of the Underworld, a jar of her own beauty ointment. Again Psyche collapses into her depths, and again tries to commit suicide by climbing a tower from which she intends to hurl herself.

Yet this very tower is an ally, speaking to her and giving her very specific instructions about how to proceed safely with her mission:

She is to go to the outskirts of a nearby city where she will find the vent of Dis, which leads to the path of the Underworld;

She must not help the lame donkey driver pick up his sticks;

She is to take two coins in her mouth and two pieces of barley bread in her hands;

She will give one coin to Charon, the ferry man, as she goes in, and she will give the other coin to him on the way out;

She must refuse:

- the dead man with the rotting hand who wants her help;
- all others who wish her to stop and help;
- a man braiding a rope of the black and white threads of ambiguity;
- the entreaties of the old women who weave the web of fate.

She must feed a piece of bread to Cerberus, the three-headed canine guardian of the Underworld, as she enters and as she leaves. This will give her time to get through as the three heads argue over the bread.

She must refuse the feasts of Persephone and eat only coarse bread.

When she has the ointment, she must return promptly by the same route and *under no circumstances open the jar!*

In these instructions is coded an entire guide to initiation. The tower itself serves as symbolic of the given wisdom of a culture with its logic, rules, and disciplines—the masculine orderings of the knowledge of the "way things work." It may also symbolize the traditional wisdom of the ancestors, the tower of culture and of civilization. The tower urges Psyche to remain conscious, to stay aware, to stay awake, critical to any journey into the Underworld.

You might ask yourself, "What is the dominant tower in my life?" Is it your profession, your culture, your family? Is it a friendship or a network of associations and affiliations? Is it a spiritual or psychological discipline that you practice? All of us have towers which, if we can agree to leave them, will be immensely helpful in that they give us the wisdom of traditional knowledge.

The tower warns Psyche to curb her availability to others. What may appear to be generosity is often distractibility and a refusal to stay focused. Women, who from time immemorial have been totally interruptible, totally available, for whomever or whatever needs their attention, must now move from the automatic and mindless "giveaway" into mindful and conscious generosity. So Psyche must learn the creative "no" and store her energy for the critical task.

Many people lose both a sense of their task and their charge because they have been dissipated by responding to anything and anyone that calls. Thus she is advised to refuse the principle of ambiguity in the form of a man who is braiding rope of black and white threads, which will cause her to hesitate and stray from her task. So, too, must she also refuse the tempting invitation to weave the fates of others. This is an enormous seduction, especially for parents, therapists, and counselors of all varieties. The warning given Psyche here speaks to the need to avoid busybody attitudes and interference in others' lives. This meddlesome attitude all too often wastes our time and stops our own life initiative, causing us to become experts in others' lives and dunces in our own.

We must come to discipline our involvement with others. Psyche must not rescue the dead man, symbolized by the groping hand, for death will be with us always, and always is a prelude to birth. She must not eat any "serious" food down there, for in many cultures, to eat or banquet with others is to forge permanent ties. So, too, with ourselves, when we are in our Hades places, we should not set up housekeeping or rejoice masochistically in our station and predicament. When in Hades, eat only basic and simple foods.

Psyche is wonderfully successful in following these instructions.

Having suffered so much, she is now expert in the avoidance of suffering. She meets the glorious figure of Persephone-Isis, the goddess of the deeps, and she receives from her, the gift of eternal life and beauty. For whenever one approaches the deep world with mindfulness, the Beneficent Presence of the deep world will give you what you wish.

In spite of her mindfulness to this point, Psyche, on her return trip, is undone by vanity. We remember that she is the human being worshipped as the new Aphrodite, and so she necessarily has something of the vanity and preoccupation with surface beauty of Aphrodite.

Tempted beyond all of her good intentions, Psyche opens the jar. Upon opening the jar she falls back into the sleep of old consciousness, literally succumbing to a death-like swoon. She has sacrificed her erotic paradise for spiritual development, but now, at the end of her spiritual journey, she falls prey to ancient habits, as do we all, especially when we are close to the goal. How many times in your development do you find yourself having to deal again with old habituations that you thought you had gone beyond? You may have spent years of prayer or therapy or exercises to rid yourself of old patterns, yet they always seem to recur as either ego-grinders or lures to oblivion. That is the hallowed aspect of these habits—they are the tragic flaw that provides the opportunity to make the colossal mistake that will lure us at the optimal moment into the death of our little local self. Without this lure to local ego death, we would not gain the opportunity for grace, or love, or God to come and resurrect us.

Psyche falls prey to her old habit of being beautiful, and by virtue of her total, if adolescent, femininity she is willing to sacrifice everything to be again the beauty that Eros loves. This is her chance for death and resurrection, and indeed the myth recalls Christ, Jonah, Sleeping Beauty and the Savior who dies in order to be transformed into life lived on a higher level. She has gone about as far as she can go, and has by consequence gained much depth and wisdom and the use of parts of herself that she didn't know she had. The gods are not about to throw her away. That would be bad *psychic* ecology, and worse, a poor story.

If, in the middle of the dark descent into yourself, you return to old consciousness or neglect to follow the discipline of your personal tower, you will probably fall into one or another kind of deep, deep sleep. But this need not be pathology, but rather, as in the story, the entrance into a place of deep gestation, like Jonah in the belly of the whale. Here you undergo the fetal sleep that prepares you for life lived out of a fullness you never knew before. In this place and time of gestation you are tended by the deep Eros powers of nature, of goddedness, of patterns of evolutionary quickening. These powers can now help you, for they recognize you as having opened to your many latent capacities of psyche by virtue of being seeded with instinct. You have gained the golden strength, received the waters of life, become mindful, suffered deeply, and are now ready for transformation. Psyche's willingness to die and stop her tasks allows the restive and hitherto unemployed Eros to rescue her. He moves from wounded boy to manly savior. No goddess could ever have given him the depth, dimensionality, complexity, and consciousness he has gained from humanly loving Psyche.

Eros cannot rescue Psyche until the right moment. True, he suffers and burns until that moment, but takes no action until the time is right. That is why it is important to know when in our lives it is appropriate for the Eros figure to rescue us. Many people play the game of "Rescue! Rescue!" with each other all of the time, and so betray and lose the "kairotic" moment. A good many persons in the helping professions can learn from this myth about the power of timing.

Most of the myths of transformational friendship take place between humans and gods. The complexity and richness of the archetypal world engage the evolutionary depths of the human possibility, while the passion and liveliness of human necessity engage the creativity and deepening of the gods. This dynamic underlies our relationship to the Beloved of the soul. But it also addresses the possibilities in transformational marriage and transformational friendship. In these relationships partners agree to be mutually empowering, challenging, engaging, difficult, and persistent for each other in the great co-journey of becoming.

In the final stages of the story, after Eros has lifted the sleep of death from Psyche's eyes, they fly off to Olympus where he confers with his proud father, Zeus, who is very happy to have Psyche as a member of the family. Zeus knows what all the world suspects, that the marriage of Psyche and Eros is a historical event in consciousness; for it allows for a saving of the gods through their gaining a more humane experience and compassion, and a transformation and deepening of humanity, allowing the beauty of ordinary life to surpass anything that could be suspected at the beginning of the journey. At this point Aphrodite offers no objection or resistance. She, too, has grown by virtue of Psyche's success at her tasks, and is now willing to relinquish her son to deepened Soul as personified in Psyche. Psyche is now made a goddess and then is formally and sacramentally married to Eros. The crowning of the marriage occurs in the birth of their child, Voluptia (sometimes interpreted as Pleasure of Joy), whose ancient meaning is "plunging into life." Thus Psyche's search for the Beloved of her soul has plunged her into discovering the psychic source of instinct, wisdom, discrimination, and culture. She now rises on strong but gossamer wings as the vision of transformation and the call to the soul.

(Scenario 5: The Descent into Hades and the Sacred Marriage)

Scenarios for Psyche and Eros

SCENARIO 1
The Lamp and the Knife

In this scenario you explore the question of the use of the "lamp" and the "knife" in your life. You engage in dialogue with a partner concerning various kinds of experiences in your life in which, metaphorically at least, the burning lamp and the cutting knife were used at different times either *by* you or *on* you. During the process you try to remember times when you were loved or acknowledged deeply but then the knife or the burning lamp were cruelly used on you. You will also be asked to remember when you were the perpetrator of the injury. When was it? How did it happen? What do you remember?

TIME: 1 hour.

MUSIC: Quiet and evocative music from *Area 1* can be used as background here.

ROOM SETUP: A good-sized room is required for this and all of the following exercises. In this process, however, the lights should be dimmed and the floor cleared.

INSTRUCTIONS FOR WORKING ALONE: This process requires another person to be done effectively.

SCRIPT FOR THE GUIDE: As the light dims, I want you, with half-closed eyes, to begin to walk backward. I am going to ask you as you walk backward to try and remember that magical time before the knife and the lamp—the bliss, the joy, the unconscious state, the nature of the relationship (2 minutes).

Remember the experiences of the lamp and the knife in your life, recreating in yourself those experiences. Perhaps you might remember the first time this happened, when you were much younger. Try to recall how you felt at the time as well as recalling consequences of the event (2 minutes).

Remembering now also how you may have used the lamp and the knife, as well as how the lamp and the knife were used on you.

Just remembering, walking backward in the dark (2 minutes).

And now, find a partner and sit down. If you don't know each other, so much the better. At this point, each person is all persons. Each woman is all women and all men. Each man is all men and all women. The other person is not just who or what they are in this space and time. They are all the people that ever were and are and shall be.

Share your names should you not know them, touch each other's hands and begin breathing together.

The kinds of questions that are going to be asked may be personal, but you can disguise the answers. You don't have to be explicit. Furthermore, this is sacred space and time, so what you hear here is sacrosanct. You cannot speak about it in the outside world. What is about to be said here remains here.

Decide who will be the first questioner. The questioner will say: "Describe the time before the lamp and the knife. Tell me about the bliss, the joy, the unconscious state. Tell me about the relationship—with a person, with an organization, with a way of life, whatever it was."

The answerer has about *five minutes* to answer, and then I will give you the next question (5 minutes).

Now, coming to silence, switch roles. Let the person who was answering ask the same question. The question is: "Describe the time before the lamp and the knife. Tell me about the bliss, the joy, the unconscious state. Tell me about the relationship—with a person, with an organization, with a way of life, whatever it was." You have about *five minutes* to answer (5 minutes).

And coming to silence, now let the person who has been answering ask the next question: "In your role as Psyche, how did you use the lamp and the knife? In your role as Eros, how were the lamp and the knife used on you?" (5 minutes).

Come to silence and change roles. Let the person who was just answering ask the question: "In your role as Psyche, how did you use the lamp and the knife? In your role as Eros, how were the lamp and the knife used on you?" (5 minutes).

Once again, come to silence. Now would the person who has been answering ask this question: "What happened to you as a result of all this? What were its consequences as you moved from innocence and unconsciousness to lack of innocence and consciousness?" (5 minutes).

Come to silence and change roles. Let the person who was answering now ask the question: "What happened to you as a result of all this? What were its consequences in your move from innocence and unconsciousness to lack of innocence and consciousness?" (5 minutes).

Come to silence now. Begin to come back into yourself. And move back just slightly from your partner so that you are no longer touching.

Close your eyes and place both of your hands on your belly, just sitting, remembering, letting whatever feelings that come up just be there. This is the seat of sentiment, of tragedy, of rapturous bliss, and the fire from which awakening comes. What comes from here is a fundamental and basic part of all our stories, but it is not all that there is, even though many of us have been trapped here yearning for bliss and avoiding the awakening. So, appreciating the fullness of our nature and the vastness of our human journey, I would like you now to pay full respect to this part of your own journey and all that it has given you—the pain, the pleasure, the fire, the emotion, the movements of energy and of life.

Now, keeping your right hand on your belly, reach over and put the other hand on the center of the chest of your partner, and receive the hand of your partner on your own chest. . . . Then feel the energy in motion, moving from your belly to your heart. When you feel you have a real sense of that, lift the hand that is on your belly and place it over your partner's hand on your heart. Lift the hand from your belly when you're ready, when you have a full awareness of the difference in those energies. (Pause.)

Begin to breathe under that hand on your heart into that hand. Don't tighten your stomach; breathe all the way up into your chest. Do this as you begin to feel that inclusiveness, that expanding sense that you are not holding on to something, but you are expanding to make room for all there is—the forms of light, the forms of darkness. The movement from the belly to the heart is a movement from a space in which there is not room for everything to a space in the heart where there is room for all and everything.

And in this communion with your partner, breathing love directly, open your eyes and look in silence for a while on your partner's face. (3 minutes).

And so you have begun your journey, the great myth being played out in the memory of your own soul, this great starting point of the journey, the remembrance of the lamp and the knife. And with your soul stirred—stirred by its own creative forces, stirred by its own eros for creation, stirred by memory and emotion—thank your partner now for being with you.

(Allow time for dyads or the entire group to share their experience. Journal writing and dancing are also appropriate here.)

SCENARIO 2
The First Labor: Sorting the Seeds

TIME: 1 hour.

MATERIALS NEEDED: In preparation for this exercise, the guide needs to have ready a large quantity and assortment of different kinds of seeds and beans like rice, millet, barley, black-eyed peas, split yellow and green peas, kidney beans, lima beans, lentils. The more varied the assortment as to color, size, and shape, the better. The seeds should be mixed together before the exercise is begun. Participants can each be given a paper cup full of seeds at the appropriate point, or can scoop out the seeds themselves into small cups. Large sheets of paper onto which the seeds can be sorted are also needed for each participant.

MUSIC: Any soft background music from *Area 1* may be played, but this is optional.

INSTRUCTIONS FOR WORKING ALONE: There is no problem with working alone in this process. Just make sure you are thoroughly familiar with the instructions given below. Working alone, you can take much more time and work with many more seeds than you would with a group. Instead of the dialogue called for between the participants concerning the meaning of the seed sortings, you should plan instead to write in your journal.

SCRIPT FOR THE GUIDE: This is what we are going to do. We have here many, many different kinds of seeds. You are going to get paper, and for about *thirty to forty minutes* you will sort the seeds, allowing a kind of instinctual knowing to rise in you to do the actual sorting. Sit near a partner as you sort so that after a certain point you can share what the process has meant. But you will do the sorting itself alone and without conversation.

Many of you will start by sorting the seeds in separate piles. Then, after a while, some may begin to sort in different ways. Some may continue to sort in piles; some may sort in designs, some may create messages in seeds. The important thing is to let your instinctual self do the sorting while allowing some part of you to observe what goes on. This exercise can be quite a revelation. You may notice that some seeds carry a high charge or a pain. Some others may represent different relationships in your life. Some colors or seeds can stand for different aspects of your being. Some may symbolize how you deal with the ordinary "rice" of the world. You will find that you will be sorting your life.

Now get yourself some seeds and some paper on which to sort them. Give yourself plenty of room for your task, but remain in proximity to your partner. Spread out the paper in front of you and begin to sort the seeds in silence (30–40 minutes).

All right, the time for sorting is finished. Now, in silence, get up and walk around the room and see what others have done with these seeds. Get a sense of the enormous amount of emotional and psychic sorting that has gone on in these last thirty minutes, the thousands of seeds that have been handled, this group's collective activity. Walk through all this almost as an initiation, honoring what you see.

Now go back to your partner and share with each other, first one of you and then the other, what has been revealed to you in this process of the sorting of the essence of your life. What patterns of your life emerged as you applied your discrimination and your instinct to this task? (15 minutes).

(This process is then followed by a period of group sharing of general experiences about what happened during the process, the different kinds of meaning the seeds had, the patterns they evoked and their content, as well as their emotional charge.)

All right. Take several minutes now to decide what you are going to do with these seeds that you have labored over. For some of you it will be apropriate to keep them because they may be symbolic of much meaning. For others, you may want to throw them outside to feed the birds. Or you can put them back in this container.

Remember that each one of you is unique. For each one of you, the seeds have their own coding and reveal something of a kind of DNA unfolding of your psyche, of your past and present patterns and possibilities. The process is not just a diagnostic tool, but can also be an evocative and revelational one as well. Seeds are always expressive of revelation, of springtime, of the bursting forth, and reveal the patterns that are coded, lost in winter's long cold. The seeds can therefore reveal the unfolding of patterns and potentials in your life, and the roots from which they come.

You may want to repeat this process again, perhaps every season, because you may find that you will do something different each time. When you do it alone, however, plan to spend several hours at it, letting yourself go from focused concentration to a state in which you let your instincts take over. Your work here today has given you a sense of the possibilities of this process in bringing clarity to aspects of your life, just as the ants brought clarity to the first labor of Psyche.

SCENARIO 3
The Second Labor: Being Reeded and Gathering the Golden Fleece

This process uses the suggestion in the story that Psyche is taught by a reed how to gain the Golden Fleece by indirection. The reed, symbolic of both the knowledge that comes from deeper orders of being and the use of appropriate timing, becomes here a metaphor for the gaining of knowledge from the states of consciousness that are deeper than your ordinary state and that can avail you of more subtle and comprehensive knowledge.

The process involves the induction of an altered state of consciousness, one that can carry you into your own inner space, there to meet the images and knowings of your own depth reality. The importance of the guide in this process cannot be overemphasized, for he or she must maintain a steady, clear reading of the instructions, which themselves are trance-inductive. The instructions are repetitive and use a style of language that has been found to be especially effective in the evoking of these kinds of altered states.

TIME: 45–60 minutes.

MATERIALS: None.

MUSIC: None.

INSTRUCTIONS FOR WORKING ALONE: If you do this process alone, you will have to put it on tape, remembering to pause for the stated amounts of time. Since this can be a trance-inductive process, you should plan to repeat the instructions to wake up a number of times. Should you not immediately respond to the suggestions for awakening, rest assured that you will pass into a sleeping state and wake up shortly.

SCRIPT FOR THE GUIDE: I want to prepare you now to enter into inner realms that enable you to get some of the Golden Fleece of strength and power. Women need this solar energy, and men need to learn how to get it by being reeds instead of rams.

This process involves a training in modes of using altered states of consciousness to become reeds to your own deepest wisdom. Since this will take close to an hour, you need to be very comfortable, not lying down (for in that position you have greater likelihood of falling asleep) but rather, sitting up like a reed. You can sit back-to-back if you like, but be comfortable and sit with a lot of good support.

Now sit up tall and straight but with no tension, let your body become more and more relaxed. . . . You might even begin to move gently from side to side, the way a reed would move in the breeze. Allow your whole body to move like a reed that is flexible aboveground, with the wind whistling through, but is also tapped deep, deep into the wet loam, the streams of life.

And you can let your eyes remain open until they involuntarily close. For you are going to allow yourself to be reeded, so as you gently waft back and forth, allow yourself to begin to slip gently into an altered state, an altered state that is a state of receptivity to the depths to which you are connected. Your unconscious mind knows what the altered state is, and your unconscious mind will listen and respond.

And it does not really matter what your conscious mind is doing at all. The unconscious mind will listen and respond when it feels it is appropriate to do so. It may feel like a sleep or a dream, but it is a conscious dream in which, reedlike, you tap into depths and have access to different kinds of sensings and knowings, those that belong to you as a human being and those that belong to the reality of the reed. Thus you will receive wisdom in many ways and from many places. But know that in this state you will see and hear and taste and touch and smell and move in many remarkable ways, the ways of inward knowing. . . .

And now allow yourself to descend deeper into your reed consciousness. My voice will go with you, but you will hear it as if from deep in the reed and deep within you, my voice maintaining communication like a whisper in the dark.

Also be aware of your eyelids becoming heavier. And you can actually ask your eyelids just to become heavier and heavier, so that if your eyes are not already closed, they will close. Allow your eyes to feel heavy. Allow your eyelids to become heavy and your eyes, which are said to be the entrance to the soul, to have a sense of heaviness also. And your reed consciousness begins to deepen, deepen, deepen. And its roots go deeper and deeper into the waters, deeper into the waters.

And now I will begin to count you further down into the inward realms, because there is something about counting that allows this to happen. And as I count, you will feel the pull deeper and inward into the earth, into the depth of yourself. And you'll feel that there is a kind of sinking sensation, that you are descending in the reed and sinking deeper and deeper into the depths.

Continuing to go deeper, the reed sinking deeper and deeper, or growing deeper and deeper, deep into the ground as I count: 1 . . . 2 . . . 3 . . . 4 . . . 5 . . . 6 . . .7 . . . 8 . . . 9 . . . 10. The whole brain and nervous system going deeper. 11. The muscles and the bones going deeper. 12. The organs of the body, the skin, everything is deepening by the counting. 13 . . . 14 . . . 15 . . . 16 . . . 17 . . . 18 . . . 19 . . . 20 . . . 21. Deeper, deeper. 22. Deeper. 23. Deeper. 24 . . . 25. Going deeper and faster. 30 . . . 50 . . . 60 . . . 70 . . . 90 . . . 100 . . . 150 . . . 200 . . . 300 . . . 500 . . . 1,000 . . . 2,000. Going deeper and deeper. . . .

Move now in your imaginal body, for the reed world allows for the imaginal body to become active. Feel your imaginal body moving in this inward realm and then finding a circular pool. You may see it very clearly, or you may just know what it looks like. But this pool is a pool beneath the pool of the reed that you were in. A pool beneath the pool. And you look down and see your image reflected. The image may be your own face, or it may be a different face or even an image of something that symbolically reflects who and what you are. Notice now whether it is your own face that you see or some other face or image that symbolically reflects you. You may be surprised to find out what the reflection is . . . .

You are going deeper and deeper now, only to discover that there is another pool underneath that pool. But now you wear the face or image that you saw in the first pool. You look into that pool, into that deeper pool, and it reflects a deeper symbolic image of you, or perhaps still your own face. And you find, as you look in that pool, that you are carried to still deeper pools, always reflecting still deeper images of you. And it may seem that there is no end to looking, for your depth is infinite.

And keep looking at ever deeper pools reflecting ever deeper images of yourself for the *next minute of clock time,* which will be equal subjectively to all the time you need to be drawn deeper and deeper into these deeper symbolic forms of yourself (1 minute).

Now my hand will stir the water in the pool, and you will find yourself drawn down and down and down, going deeper and deeper and deeper. And as you go deeper, now you can assume other forms in your imaginal body. Sinking faster and deeper. You can choose to become almost anything. You could choose to become a piece of coral or a heavy sea turtle. You might want to be a heavy rock or a dolphin or a whale. Choose whatever allows you to go deeper and deeper. But as you go deeper, retain the human consciousness that allows you to observe what you are seeing in your descent: many kinds of sea creatures, coral formations, strangely wonderful underwater plants, perhaps the wrecks of ancient ships. . . .

Continue to go deeper, past ruins of ancient civilizations—stone columns, ancient buildings, statues, temples. Go deeper past stone tablets, reliefs carved on walls, hieroglyphs, and other figures and symbols you may not recognize. Deeper, deeper, deeper. And sense that as you go deeper you are also going farther and farther back in time to older parts of your psyche and of the cultural psyche where it is even easier to continue to go deeper into this altered state.

Just continue to sink and sink, now passing through three-dimensional color. So that you may sink for a long time through blue, through purple, through green, through yellow, whatever the color may be. Sink through colors which also have textures. You can feel, and you may be able to hear or taste or touch these colors as you pass through. Continue to go deeper through this succession of colors and textures.

Continue to go deeper until finally you come to the bottom of this place. You find yourself in a cylindrical room. And, looking out of the room, discover the fact that the circular room is the top floor of a reedlike structure that itself has four levels and a cellar below. Know that each of these levels is a level of your own psyche, your own self. You are Psyche descending through the reed of yourself.

Know that as you descend through this reedlike building you will go deeper and deeper inside yourself. The altered state will deepen, and more and more of your depth mind with its wisdom and knowing will participate. And by the time you reach the level below the ground, you will have achieved a deep altered state (if you choose to allow this state to happen).

Now lying there in this room at the top of the reed building, feel that the surface is soft beneath your body and that this room is like an elevator. It can descend and the floor of the fourth level of the building can move down into the third level. So the floor of the fourth level begins slowly to descend toward the third level of the building. You may look out of the window as you descend and see what is out there. You may observe what is in the room, or you may sleep very deeply and dream. If you dream, have dreams that will enable you to go further and further into this state. The dreams may also tell you something about your own psyche, your own capacities for mental, spiritual, and emotional life.

A great deal can happen during the descent from the fourth to the third level. You can see countless images, participating in as few or as many experiences as you choose while you continue to descend toward the third level. In an altered state you can accelerate internal processes; the amount of time within a subjective experience of clock time can be greatly extended. A minute of clock time can seem like an hour or day or even longer. I am now going to give you *sixty seconds of clock time*. During that sixty seconds you are going to have a very long experience. Continue to feel the descent as you experience whatever your deep mind provides for you in the minute you now have, beginning now (1 minute).

Finally you are approaching and reaching the third level. The movement of the floor beneath you stops for a moment. Looking around you, come to a sitting position in your internal imaginal body. Observe that there are set on tables in this room a number of large crystal balls. There are images inside these balls. One of them is that of an infant. One of them is the image of a young child. One of them is the image of an adolescent. One of them is the image of a young adult. There are also other crystals containing persons thirty years old, forty years old, fifty, sixty, seventy, and even older.

You can choose to observe or, if you don't see them, to sense in other ways what is occurring in one or several or even many of these crystals, however many your consciousness can experience. And so you can look from one to the other from time to time. Within each of these crystals a kind of drama will unfold as you observe that person living his or her life. You may recognize it as someone else's past or present or future time, or it may be your own.

The room begins to descend now, and you feel the physical sensation of the room descending. The figures in the crystals are moving. Your altered state is deepening, and I'm going to give you *a minute or so of clock-measured time* as you go deeper and deeper to the second level, deeper into your own psyche, into the reed of yourself, observing what you can see of the lives unfolding within these different crystal balls. You might observe a week, a month, a year, a lifetime, in each crystal. You have that time now as the room descends, sinking down, sinking down, sinking down. And the time to observe the crystal balls begins now (1 minute).

And now on the second level, focus your attention first on the right side of your brain, and then on the left side. . . . Let your consciousness begin to roam inside your brain, exploring the different parts of your brain and its convolutions. . . . Now let your consciousness come down to the level of your ears, your eyes. Let it roam around the cavity of your mouth, and then down to your lungs and down your ribs. Move around to the shoulders and the chest. Your consciousness roams around the abdomen, down your arms and your hands. It will wander through your body. It can be borne along through the blood passages, wandering through the nerve pathways, wandering and wandering, going deeper and deeper, but always moving around inside your own body. Your body is becoming more and more involved with this deepening state. Sensations are changing, and you feel changes in your body wherever you go.

You may find within yourself places that seem to need healing, places where you just want to focus awareness for a while. Breathe into these places. Make space wherever there seems to be constriction, expanding and sensing the release and the flowing movement of the energy that had been blocked. Become aware perhaps of radiant networks of energy connecting and sustaining the vast spaces between the molecules, between the electrons and the atoms and within the nucleus of the atoms. Move with your attention wherever in your body you feel the need for releasing a flow of healing energy. You have now a *minute of clock time,* equal subjectively to all the time you need, to give your body this release of radiant healing and sustaining energy wherever you need it, beginning now (1 minute).

Now you will begin to descend down to the first level, the ground level. Go deeper and deeper and deeper inside the reed of yourself, going deeper into your own depth mind, your own unconscious. You may find that you want to roam around in your brain for a while as a way of continuing this experience. Do it without the eyes straining. Just let attention focus on the brain area as you continue to descend into still deeper areas of yourself. But feel as you descend this time as if you are breathing in through your ears to your brain. . . . and then add an awareness of breathing in also through your eyes to the brain. . . . Then become aware that you are of course also breathing in through your nose. As you focus on three separate breathings into your brain you become aware that your brain is coming to be more and more clearly delineated and charged in your awareness.

And the body's altered state deepens greatly as your body and brain go deeper and deeper within the depths of this wise reed that is yourself. The possibility of going deeper and deeper into your own psyche increases. You can meet figures of importance to you. Perhaps you can deal with problems of importance. Or you can just allow yourself to observe whatever images or presences that are given to you from this deeper level, knowing as you descend to this first level that you are in the realm of your personal unconscious. You have now one minute of clock time equal to all the time you need, to descend to the first level while experiencing the images and presences of your personal unconscious (1 minute).

And now you will move beyond that realm into the transpersonal, collective unconscious realm, where a still deeper wisdom blows through you like a wind. The wind seems to carry in it myths, symbols, stories from every time and place, images and icons, the arts of all ages and the heritage of ways of knowing from everywhere. The wind carries with it the harvest that has accumulated from all human wisdom, all knowledge, all knowing. It blows from the depths of you and fills you with an awareness of increasingly universal experience. Feel the room sinking and sinking as you start to have an experience of this, of the wisdom of all cultures and all times passing through you. You have now a minute and a half of clock time equal to a much longer experience of subjective time, beginning now (1½ minutes).

And with this wisdom flowing through you, you have arrived at the ground level and are now ready to descend to the basement area. This is the area of your challenge in gathering whatever for you is the Golden Fleece. When you reach the basement area you will be in the deep night world, the moon world of yourself. Here you will take some of the Golden Fleece off the bushes and the branches. But as you do that, also be aware of what the Golden Fleece symbolizes in your life. Know what the metaphor of Golden Fleece is, what it stands for in your life.

You are free to experience whatever you want or need to experience here. This is a magical world where much is available to you of what you need in your life. Your senses will become keener here. Awareness and mindfulness will also be more acute. Descend now into this depth realm symbolized as the basement level. Know, too, that what you are doing down here in this magical world can also affect the way you live when you come back up. You have a *minute and a half of clock time,* equal to all the time you need, to gather the Golden Fleece from the bushes, beginning now (1½ minutes).

And now having the strands of the Golden Fleece, you will have a final minute of clock time in this magical realm. Strengthened by the Golden Fleece, try to explore what for you is the most mysterious and most challenging thing that you need to do. Remember that you are now in the strengthened form of the imaginal body, and you can protect yourself down here deliberately by virtue of the consciousness of that body. It has the freedom of choice. It can be protected as if it had magical powers. It can do the things that normally you would not be able to do. So it can transform its shape. It can fly. It can move through fire and ice, through all spaces and all times. It can have any experience it likes. Going deeper and deeper, but with the Golden Fleece in your hand strengthening you, explore that thing which for you may be most mysterious and challenging. You have *a minute of clock time,* equal to all the time you need, beginning now (1 minute).

And now, strengthened and deepened, having gained access to so much wisdom and strength from the moon side of yourself, know yourself to be reeded. Know yourself to be reeded. Know yourself to be reeded. So that whenever you need the wisdom and strength of your own deep psyche, know yourself to be reeded and listen and act accordingly. From this moment on, you have access to the reededness of yourself.

I am going to bring you up now, bring you up to full waking consciousness. Bringing you up through colors and textures, bringing you up through ancient cultures and civilizations. Swim upward in the bodies of sea creatures. Coming up and up and up and up.

Come up as I count back from 2000 to 1. 2000 . . . 1500. Coming up. 1000. Deepened, keeping all that you have gained. 900 . . . 800 . . . 700 . . . 600 . . . 500 . . . 400 . . . 300 . . . 200 . . . 100 . . . 90 . . . 80 . . . 70. Coming up. 60 . . . 50 . . . 40 . . . 30 . . . 29 . . . 28 . . . 27. Coming up, coming up. 26. Higher. 25. Refreshed and revitalized by the deeps. 24 . . . 23. Coming up, refreshed and revitalized. 22 . . . 21 . . . 20. Energized, refreshed, revitalized. 19 . . . 18 . . . 17. Coming up. 16. Fully vital into awakening. 15 . . . 14. Having full body awareness. 13 . . . 12 . . . 11 . . . 10 . . . 9. Becoming more and more alert. 8. More vital. 7. Refreshed. 6 . . . 5 . . . 4 . . . 3 . . . 2 . . . 1. Fully awake. Stretch yourself and take a deep breath of air.

For the next few minutes, reflect silently and write in your journals any images or knowings that may seem appropriate to remember and record so that you do not lose them (10 minutes).

(Now allow for discussion of what has occurred, either in groups of two or three, or with the whole group. Relevance to the process of initiation could be stressed.)

SCENARIO 4
The Third Labor: Fetching the Waters of Life

(Some of this process uses movement taught by my husband, Robert Masters.) In this scenario you will engage the imaginal body to first gain the eagle's perspective over the Torrent of Life. Then, performing a simple psychophysical exercise, you will fill the goblet of yourself with the breath of living waters. Let us begin.

TIME: 30 minutes.

MATERIALS NEEDED: A feather.

MUSIC: None

INSTRUCTIONS FOR WORKING ALONE: This process can be done alone if the instructions are previously taped.

NOTE TO THE GUIDE: Timing is very important. Err on the side of going too slowly, and observe closely what is actually happening.

SCRIPT FOR THE GUIDE: You need to be very relaxed, but not lying down. Sit so that you have room enough to move in place. Sitting back-to-back with a partner is not appropriate for this exercise.

Start settling in, and begin to use your breath as you would use the keel of a boat to steady you. Just become aware of your breath. . . . And as you breathe slowly and deeply, begin to feel some part of yourself becoming a goblet, a very precious, strong but also fragile goblet which is the container for life. And take this goblet which you are and which you will now hold as you begin to assume the eagle's perspective.

Now in your imaginal body feel yourself to have wings. You might begin just physically to make the movement of wings. But as you feel these wings, become aware that you have eagle eyes and that with each movement of your arms-wings your eyes are becoming more and more acute. You are the eagle.

Actually physically engage your arms as wings, as behind your closed eyes you gain imaginal eagle's eyes. And you are able now to soar higher and higher and higher. Your imaginal eagle's body is carrying you over the mountain, up–up–up–up–up, higher and higher, circling higher and higher, to observe the rushing Torrent of Life.

What you view down below is something of the history of the twentieth century. You may see reflected through the sun, reflected in the waters, the sun that was brighter than a thousand suns, the atomic mushroom cloud and blast over Hiroshima in 1945. You may see the wars of the twentieth century—the First World War, the Second World War, the Korean War, the Vietnam War, all the different wars. You see the rise of superpowers, the extension of the Industrial Revolution all over the world. You see the rise of great technological states and corporations, the webbing of the world with media and satellites in the sky, and the spread of an electronic communication system like a planetary nervous system. There are places where people are well-fed and nourished as they have never been before in human history. And there are whole areas in the world of starvation and hunger and suffering as there has virtually never been before in human history. There is the growth of knowledge and the rising of despair. There is connection to all the different peoples of this earth, as well as an extension of responsibility and awareness such as humanity has not had before.

You are now at the place of the river which is the torrent of your own life. You don't have to worry about flying low; with your eagle eyes you can see it. Look down along the banks of the river at different parts of your life. See yourself being born and growing up. See yourself as an adult. I will give you *two minutes or so of clock time,* equal subjectively to all the time you need, to view the banks and the river of your own life. See your life from your birth to the present in this minute or so of clock time. Begin to fly over the incidents of your own life now (2 minutes).

And know that you are both the eagle and the goblet. As eagle, being the eagle, fly to the appropriate place in the stream. The snakes and the dragons crawl away, for they know that the eagle brings the goblet.

And you are also the goblet to be filled with the vitalizing substance of the life force. And as this happens, you will feel the eagle's feather brush against you. You will be blessed by the eagle of clarity and discrimination as the goblet, which is you, is filled with the crystalline Waters of Life.

(If possible, the guide will have an assistant circle the room, brushing each participant with a feather.)

See the place, sense the right place at which you dip in and fill yourself. And as you do this, you are going to make a slight movement to the right. Just bend to the right slightly. And as you bend over your right knee, exhale fully. Then bend around toward your left knee and inhale as you come up. Slowly fill your lungs, fill your goblet, until you reach the center position. Then start to exhale again as you come down. Move slowly over your right knee, exhaling until you reach the midpoint. And slowly, as you move toward your left knee, begin to inhale, filling your goblet as you come up to the midpoint. Exhale, and repeat this circle of breath.

Exhale as you go down, circling and inhaling as you come up. Filling yourself with the Breath of Serenity, continue to make this circling breath. Exhale over the right knee, inhale as you come up to the midpoint. Truly bend as you take the breath, allowing your whole body to participate in the circle of the Breath of Serenity. Feel the freshness of exhaling fully and slowly before you inhale. Fill up fully before you exhale. For breathing, taking breath, is like drinking in the Waters of Life. Continue to do this a number of times. (The Guide will observe the participants, allowing them to make this circling Breath of Serenity about a dozen more times.)

And now, when you have fully inhaled and reached a midpoint, you will then want to reverse the direction. Exhale in the other direction—that is, over the left knee, and inhale as you come up over the right. Very slowly, fully inhaling, fully exhaling, draw in full and deep the waters of your life. Know that the clarity of your goblet is always there for you, that it is always available. Continue to breathe in, drawing in the water, the clear water, the clear energy of your life, as you are blessed by the eagle feather. Do this about a dozen times in this direction.

Now, to conclude, make a long inhalation and then pause for about eight seconds. Then make a long exhalation and pause about eight seconds before the next inhalation. Do this breathing and pausing a number of times. For it is in the stillness of the pause that you gain the eagle's knowledge and clarity. . . . Know that this simple practice, to be repeated whenever you need it in your life, is the completion of the third task.

Now take a few rapid breaths with the diaphragm, and then open your eyes. In full alertness, know that you can do this anywhere at any time. When the frenzy seems to be creeping up and the waters seem to be flooding the river, simply stop. Allow yourself to fill with the breath of serenity and the clarifying energies of your own Waters of Life.

(Allow time for people to write in their journals and then share their experience. What do they now know? What can they now do? How are they the eagle? How the goblet?)

SCENARIO 5
The Fourth Labor: Descent into Hades Followed by the Sacred Marriage

This scenario will be taking place on two levels: enacting and dramatizing the story of Psyche, and enacting symbolic correlates of that story in terms of the happenings of your own life.

In enacting this process of descent into Hades we engage in a very ancient initiation rite, receiving the gift from the immortal realms. Then, at a certain point, you allow yourself to die and to be rescued, and to enter into a variation of the process given earlier as "The Walk to the Beloved." This initiatory process and its conclusion invites union with the Divine Beloved.

TIME: 90 minutes.

MATERIALS NEEDED: A drum, votive candles and holders, at least a dozen candles for illuminating the room plus one for each person.

MUSIC: The music requirements are complex for this scenario and are indicated throughout the text. Also, rather than selecting music from the different areas, it is advisable to use the music indicated since this scenario needs more specific kinds of music than the other processes in this book. Appropriate and effective music for the first part of this scenario is Vangelis's *Odes*, especially the parts where Irene Pappas is chanting.

INSTRUCTIONS FOR WORKING ALONE: It is not recommended that one attempt this process alone, since it tends to need witnesses to be effective. With this caveat, however, it should be stated that the process could technically be done alone with suitably taped recorded instructions and sufficient time allowed for the instructions to be carried out.

SCRIPT FOR THE GUIDE:* To begin, clear the room and the floor so that you have unimpeded space in which to move.

Find a place in the room where you feel centered and balanced. Then with your eyes fully closed or half closed, begin to walk backward to the "towers" of your own life. You are walking backward to the realms of your ancestors, to all those towers and different cultures that have gone into giving you the substance of who and what you are. You are walking backward now, harvesting the essence of your ancestors—and not just your ancestors, but you are walking back harvesting culture, the ancestors giving you their wisdom, the cultures giving you their essence. Move back and back now through time: 100 years . . . 200 years . . . 300 years . . . 400 years . . . 500 years . . . 600 years . . . 700 years . . . 800 years . . . 900 years . . . 1000 years . . . 2000 years . . . 3000 years, or more. Walk backward harvesting the ancestors, gaining the knowledge of the many, towers of culture that inform your being (Pause for 5 minutes with "Odes" and drumbeat continuing. Then start the "Hell" section of Vangelis's *Heaven and Hell*.)

Stop now and be instructed. Begin walking forward in a circling path now for the descent into Hades (2 minutes).

Now you are entering Hades. Be very mindful as you walk. Be aware that your name is Psyche, Soul, that you are soul in body, embodied soul. Be aware of your physicality, of your feet on the ground, of the movement in the joints

*The guide should work with someone who will keep up a slow and steady drumbeat until the collapse of Psyche. Use of a second reader and even of a third reader, which allows for a contrast of voices during the "Descent into the Underworld" section, will heighten the drama. An appropriate woman should also be asked to act as Persephone when Psyche asks for the Box of Deathless Beauty.

of your hips. Maintain as much body awareness as you can. . . . Know, too, that as Psyche, as Soul, you are carrying, growing new life within you. Be aware of your task, of everything you must do in the life of Psyche in descent into the Underworld, and of what you must do in your own life in your descent into places of transformation, of obligation, of challenge and demand. Be fully mindful of your body and deeply aware of everything that is going on in your life of demands, rules, challenges. . . .

Stay mindful, even though people are groping for your attention. Stay mindful.

(Note to Guide: The accusations and entreaties throughout this scenario are meant to be suggestive of the kinds of statements that are made to us in our lives. Feel free to use these statements as written or to make up your own. No matter how it is done, it should have a quality of spontaneity and real-life drama.)

"I want you to stop everything and come over right now!"
"You must go to these committee meetings."
"I need you to work with me only fifteen minutes a day, that's all."
"You're selfish, always running off when I really need you."

Hear them in your mind, stay mindful, and keep going.

And now there is *Charon the Ferryman,* here to take you to the other shore. Remember to open your mouth and give only one coin. Don't give it all away. Don't be tricked. Give only what is appropriate.

Stay mindful of your task, your destination. Even with all the people asking you to give it all away, stay focused.

A dying one floats by and says, "Come down with me. Come and die with me. Come suffer with me. Here are my hands out of the water. Please! Just grab my hand and let me pull you down so that you can help me."

Consider those in your life who are going by and drowning and saying, "Help me! Stop! Stop! Stop! Please help me!" Stay mindful. Awful as it is, stay mindful. Stay on your path.

You reach the shore, climb out of Charon's boat, and soon meet the *Daimon of Ambiguity* who says, "Stop! Hesitate. It's all ambiguity anyhow. It doesn't really mean anything. It's black and it's white. It's male and female. It's yin and yang. It's this and it's that. I'd like you to help me braid together the "this" and the "that," the male and the female, the yin and the yang. Help people to see the ambiguity of things. This will give you more ideas. This will really give you a sense of what it's all about. Just hesitate here. Just hesitate for one minute and help me braid the polarities."

Stay mindful. Be aware of all the seductions toward diversion in your life. All the people who say to you:

"Stop, hesitate, hesitate and let's have a nice long chat about all the ins and outs of everything."

"How about a cup of coffee and we can really chew the fat."

"Come on, you can help me see all the different ways that I can change my life."

Here now are the *Weavers of Fate*:

"Oh, there's so much you can do to redesign other people's lives. Be on this committee. Help determine the fate of the whole community."

"Don't be selfish! Come on, please help. Help me!"

"Do you want to hear some really interesting gossip? Only you can help straighten things out."

"You don't want to hear secrets? You're getting so stuck up! You don't want to hear secrets and weave?"

"You really don't want to have a two-hour phone discussion with your friends so that you can weave everything together?"

"Choose your son's college! Choose his career!"

"What should I do with my life, Mother, Dad?

"Please help me! Help me change my life! Help me find someone to marry."

"You do such special healing. You can help me with the pain I have."

"Only you really understand. Tell me what to do and I'll do it!

"Please weave my life."

There is *the Dog, the Guardian,* the three-headed dog who wants to stop you from ever getting on with it. You've got to throw him what he wants: a piece of barley bread, a college degree, a certificate of merit, your credentials. Throw him the bread. Good! Now you can get by.

(Music changes to *Carmina Burana* of Carl Orff. The woman who is going to be Persephone needs to be prepared and in the center of the room.)

In the center of it all is *Persephone*. And she says to you, "Welcome! Welcome to the Underworld! Come and enjoy. Feast with us. We've the finest of wines and beers; duck stuffed with pistachios and truffles; exquisite vegetarian food from China; grilled shish kebab; minted chocolate mousse piled high on angel food cake and topped with gobs of whipped cream; homemade peach ice cream." (The guides should enticingly describe some of their own favorite foods.) "We can really make you comfortable down here. All the tasty things of life! Stay a while and enjoy!—What! *You only want white bread with margarine!* What a fool!"

Don't weaken now. Eat only the white bread with margarine. Drink only water.

(Discontinue the tape. Let only the drumbeat be heard now.)

And having refused the delicacies and enticements, actually go to Persephone now for *the Box*. (Persephone will hand something, actually or imaginally to each participant and say the words, "Receive now Deathless Beauty.")

And quickly, without dwelling on it, receive from her Deathless Beauty. Feel the fire and the beauty in that ointment. Move very quickly. You are eager to return from the Underworld. Just come and receive from Persephone the small box of Deathless Beauty. Receiving quickly and moving on. Receiving quickly and moving on. Receive the ointment of Deathless Beauty.

And begin to find your way up through the Underworld. It is easier this time. You know the rules. Be very mindful. Avoid all the beings who try to lure you into helping, into weaving, into saving them. Remember to give the bread to the Dog. Remember to pay the Ferryman.

Stay mindful on your journey back. Stay mindful, but all the time you are feeling the lure of Deathless Beauty which you hold in your hand. As you go back, review all the stages of your tasks: Psyche's labors and your own tasks that have brought you here so worn out and tired. Burnout they call it. And the sense of Deathless Beauty just glows in your hands, for you know that it will reverse all the weariness and exhaustion that you have experienced from being too long on life's journey.

But still you are mindful. You do remember to throw the bread to the Dog. You do remember to pay the Ferryman. You listen not to the Weavers, nor to the Daimon of Ambiguity. But your ears are still filled with cries for help.

"Please help me! Please help me!"
"With my homework."
"Through school."
"Feed the dog tonight."
"I'm dying, and only you can help me."
"Help me find someone. If you don't. . . ."
"You know so much. You've been everywhere."
"You used to be such a kind and generous person."
"What happened to you all of a sudden?"
"Please help me! I need you!"
"I'm your own mother. I've given you everything."
"I'm pregnant with your first grandchild."
"If you loved me, you'd stay with me."
"I used to think you loved me. Now nobody does."
"Daddy, I want you to be someone I can admire."
"Why can't you be the wife you used to be?"
"Why can't you be the husband you used to be?"
"But I'm your family! I'm your best friend!"
"I've never needed you so much!"

Stay mindful. With so many people asking you to give away all that you have, stay focused.

Remember the blessed gift of Persephone that you hold now in your hands unopened. And feel the longing and the need for beauty, and know, somehow know, that this ointment you are carrying will restore and make you more beautiful than before. You have been so long on the journey. And your Beloved, Eros, is so near. Maybe he—she—won't look at you. Maybe Love will find you too ugly, too uninteresting. So go ahead. Who knows? You've come so far, done so much, found helpers everywhere. Risk it. Go ahead now. Risk it. *Open the jar of ointment.*

And allow yourself to fall to the ground and die. Everyone. Allow yourself to die. Allow yourself to die into the deep silence (3 minutes of silence).

(All sound stops and the guide allows for a period of deep silence before the enactment continues.)

And now Eros, deeply moved by your sacrifice, your journey, your labors, comes. Eros comes, the Beloved of your soul, Love Incarnate within you; Eros, who is longing for you, Psyche, as you are longing for Eros. This is the Deep Beloved, with whom you are complete, the Beloved of your soul, who contains the goddedness of the depths. Eros, who has been yearning for you, comes now and wipes the sleep of death from your eyes.

And now we will perform the rite of the divine marriage of Psyche and Eros. To begin, reach out to anyone who is nearby. Since you are acting as noble surrogates and high witnesses for the Beloved of the soul, it doesn't matter whether you choose a male or a female partner. As partners, come and get a candle and then stand in the back of the room. You need only *one candle for each couple.*

(The guide and those assisting will have placed candles about two yards apart across the center of the room. The guide, accompanied by Persephone and the drummer, without the drum, will stand at intervals along the line of fire holding candles.)

As you gaze across the line of fire, feel the longing for the bonding, for the union with the Beloved rising. Zeus finds favor with you. Aphrodite has been touched by your struggle and your victory. Your life is now ready, both mythically and existentially, to be deepened.

Stand quietly together at the back of the room. Feel the longing for the Beloved, who actually exists in your soul, who is the Eros, the lure of your becoming, who is as real as you are. Understand that your tremendous longing for union prepares you to be godded in the sacrament of union with the Beloved. We not only join with the Beloved but, as in the story, our psyche is honored and godded. With your partner you symbolically become Eros and Psyche for each other. Together you represent the call of the Beloved, the yearning for union, which is growing in your hearts.

(Play Vangelis's *Ignacio,* Part 1.) *Now begin walking forward together very, very slowly.* This is your walk of longing for the Beloved, with your partner playing Psyche to your Eros, Eros to your Psyche. This walk is the sacrament of goddedness, of marriage in goddedness.

When you cross the line of fire, you are in the realm of the gods. You are on the peaks of Olympus. When you cross this line, you are in the place of the mysterious conjunction in your own heart. Your partner is with you as symbolic and representative up to this point. Once you have crossed the line of fire, release your partner and allow the union to occur within you. Your own inner Psyche marries your inner Eros. Walk very, very slowly now, each step being a step of yearning for the Beloved of your soul.

(After everyone has crossed the line of fire and has had a few moments to reflect, the guide will continue. The music to be played is "Eric's Theme" from Vangelis's *Chariots of Fire*.)

GUIDE: This is the moment of the marrying, the bonding, the communing, the partnering with the Beloved. Know yourself now as being godded in this union.

Know that you are always, every day, renewing the sacrament of this union. You are always marrying the Beloved of the soul.

Now blow out the light of your candle so that you may ignite the fire of the inner sacred marriage in your heart, where it will burn for time out of mind. . . .

So ends the story of Psyche and Eros. And so this story, with its labors, its despairs, its lostness, its foundness, its learnings, its quickenings, its deepening, its goddedness, its humanness, is in you forever. *So be it.*

(Now allow a time for dance and celebration.)

13

THE ECSTATIC JOURNEY OF JALALODDIN RUMI

I am a sculptor, a molder of form.
In every moment I shape an idol.
But then, in front of you, I melt them down.
I can rouse a hundred forms and mix them with spirit,
But when I look into your face,
I want to throw them in the fire.
Do you merely fill this drunkard's glass?
Or do you really oppose the sober?
Is it you who brings to ruin every house I build?
My soul spills into yours and is blended.
Because my soul has absorbed your fragrance, I cherish it.
Every drop of blood I spill says to the earth:
I blend with my Beloved when I participate in love.
In this house of mud and water
My heart has fallen into ruins.
Enter this house, my Love, or let me leave.[1]

We turn now to a journey of transformation that engages the story of one who is neither mythic nor divinized—Jalaloddin Rumi, a teacher who spent most of his life in thirteenth-century Anatolia. With Rumi we see how a richly human man of great passion and passionate complexity is transmuted through the most intense and ecstatic of love experiences to open the door to the next stage of human possibility. Rumi's life provides us with abundant documentation of the intoxication of spiritual love, as well as some of the most sublime expression of human experience ever recorded in history, literature, or biography. In knowing Rumi we are meeting ourselves writ large, in completely human form.

THE LIFE OF RUMI

It is December of the year 1273. The inhabitants of Konya in Anatolia are filled quite literally with fear and trembling. For days and nights, the earth has been quaking and trembling, and the most beloved man in Konya, the great Sufi Master and poet Jalaloddin Rumi is dying. Lying on his bed, surrounded by friends and students, he says, "The earth is hungry. Soon, it will get a fat morsel and then give rest." As he becomes weaker melting away in the eternal sweetness of God, he begins to sing with joy:

> The lovers who die well-informed,
> Die before the Beloved like sugar. . .
>
> O birds which are at present separated from their cage,
> Show again your face, and say, "Where are you?"
> O you who were born when you arrived at death—
> This is a second birth—be born, be born![2]

What a great way to die!

On December 17th, at sunset, Jalaloddin Rumi passed away to be united with the eternal Beloved. His funeral was extraordinary, for it was attended by people of all beliefs and religions. The Christians were there in great numbers, as were Jews, as were Sufis, as were members of the various Islamic sects. A Christian was asked why he cried so bitterly at the death of the Moslem teacher. He replied, "We esteem him as the Moses, the David, the Jesus of the age. We are all his followers and his disciples."

To explore the life of Rumi is to explore a path of illumination through love.[3] To discover Rumi is to see in one life how yearning can be met so completely that the walls of the local self dissolve into a continuously living intoxication of the spirit. The world is illumined with unquenchable cadenzas of meaning; the mouth is split with poetry and music; the body is danced to a dance that moves without restriction through mortal and immortal worlds.

It is an ancient saying that "giants come forth from Afghanistan and influence the world." Rumi was born in Balkh in Afghanistan sometime between 1203 and 1207, the son of a noted mystic theologian Baha'oddin. At that time Balkh was one of the main centers of Islamic learning and had formerly been a center of Buddhism, and so it probably served as a place of mediation between Buddhist ideas and Sufi thought. When Rumi was just a small child the king of Balkh turned against the Sufis and especially against Rumi's father. The family was forced to leave, and for sixteen years wandered through Mecca, Damascus, Armenia, and Turkey, studying and teaching and learning the vital Islamic and Sufi teachings which were undergoing a renaissance. As it turned out, leaving there was a hidden blessing, for a few years later Balkh was sacked by the Mongols of central Asia, led by Ghengis Khan, and many of its inhabitants were killed.

The way of Sufi training was to be sent from person to person and from city to city to apprentice with different teachers. After a teacher had given you what he could, he might tell you, "Now you go to Damascus and see Ali the Cobbler who has a shop in the souk." You would seek out Ali and chances were he would keep you waiting for some time before working with you, feigning ignorance of any Sufi teaching. Then, if he was convinced of your serious intention, you would be allowed to help out, as well as learn the art of making the pointed-toed camel slippers. He would gradually convey his teaching, and then send you on to study with Baba, the rug weaver in Medina. You would learn weaving for a while and struggle with Baba's whimsical teaching by indirection before being sent to Al-Akhbar, a Sufi and master of sword tempering with quarters near the Alhambra in Spain, and whose teaching would consist of the telling of Sufi stories. Important in all these journeys was the Sufi understanding that each soul's path back to God is individual, so that each pilgrim's "curriculum" of teachers and experiences was different and unique.

In the course of their journey, the family paid a visit to the great mystic poet Faridoddin Attar, who blessed the child Rumi with the Sufi *baraka* (or spiritual power charge). He presented the boy with a copy of his *Book of Mysteries* and said, "This boy will spark a fire of divine exaltation for the world. This boy will spark the lovers." In most mythic or legendary lives we encounter this phenomenon of the child being recognized as "special" by a wise one, and his or her future greatness foretold.

In the mid 1220's, Baha'oddin and his family reached central Anatolia, Rum, meaning "the place of the Romans;" hence Jalaloddin's surname, Rumi. Here the young scholar was married to a girl from Samarkand, and two sons and three daughters were born to them. They finally moved to the capital, Konya, where the father became a professor. In 1228, the learned old man died and his son Rumi was appointed his successor.

Up to that time, the young scholar seems to have been interested mainly in the outward sciences as well as Arabic poetry, but he was certainly no mystic. Shortly after his father's death, however, a close friend of his father's, Burhand al-Din Muhaqqiq, a dervish who had lived in solitude in the mountains in a state of mystical ecstasy, came to Konya. Rumi's serious training began when the dervish began to introduce him into the *Ilm Ladoni,* the deep mysteries of inner life, as well as how to live in a state of inspiration. He put Rumi through many series of mystical exercises, as well as requiring him to keep many *chillas*—that is, forty-day periods of seclusion and meditation, until he reached deeper stages of illumination. He also sent him, Sufi style, to Syria and Damascus to meet and study with the various spiritual teachers of the time.

*(Scenario 1: Zikr of the Ultimate Communion of Love)**

Returning to Konya, Rumi became a well-known teacher, a rather orthodox professor of religious science. The results of his Sufi training seem to have remained largely dormant as he pursued a path of respectability, continuing for years as a fine but not extraordinary professor, getting more and more involved in his didactic studies and yearning for something that apparently was not happening.

And then, suddenly, his world blew up. He was somewhere between the ages of thirty-nine and forty-three when a wild-looking dervish climbed over the wall in the court where Rumi was teaching, took his valuable books and threw them in a pool of water saying, "Now you must live what you know." (How is that for an introduction?) When Rumi leaped up to save his treasured books, the wild man, Shamsoddin Tabriz, said, "Why don't you speak what you know? That theoretical knowledge in your books is meaningless. But, if they mean so much to you, here, I'll help you get them out so they can dry." Rumi looked at him in shock . . . and fell into love. The two men embraced and Rumi said, "The God which I have worshipped all my life appeared to me today in human form."

There is a fable that Rumi told of a man who knocked at the Beloved Friend's door. The Beloved Friend asks, "Who is there?" The man replies, "It is I." The Friend tells him to go away—"it is not the time yet; at such a feast as mine there is no place for the unprepared. . . ." And so the unprepared one wanders for a year suffering the wasteland of separation. Then he returns, very nervous this time, afraid that he might say the wrong thing, and knocks once more at the Beloved Friend's door. When the Beloved calls, "Who is that at the door?" the man replies, "It is you, O

*Throughout this chapter, "Scenario" lines in parentheses refer to the exercises at the end of the chapter.

Beloved." The Friend then says, "Now since you are I, enter, O Myself; there is no room in this mansion for two I's."

This was the extraordinary experience of the respectable Professor Rumi with Shams-i Tabriz—a dervish and wanderer with no particular affiliation, who hung out in caravans—the ultimate theological hippie. They merged in goddedness and found in each other a perfect example of the reflection of God. In each other's presence they were able to experience the unity of Love, the Lover and the Beloved. Rumi was the teacher, the prophet, while Shams was the perfected man, the catalyst of God who knows and knows that he knows. They became, as they said, their own planet. Rumi, the earth, his function to evoke and evolve human consciousness, revolving around and finally merging with Shams, the sun, the lure of becoming.

They were utterly lost in the ecstasy of each other. The inhabitants of Konya were deeply shocked when they saw the respectable teacher neglecting all of his social, professorial, and religious duties, and giving himself over entirely to the company of this wandering dervish ecstatic who didn't fit into any category they knew as respectable or even nameable. (It's one thing not to be respectable, but not to be nameable—that's a real problem!)

For a hundred and one consecutive days the two God-intoxicated men were lost in each other in a state of mystic unity. The jealousy of Rumi's students rose to a dangerous pitch. There was nothing in their experience that could explain this phenomenon—the sheer ecstasy of reflected goddedness that evoked such intensity in the two men.

One day Shams departed suddenly, leaving Rumi in a state of overwhelming heartbreak. The extreme pain of their separation turned the pedant and scholar into a passionate poet and singer, and he who had reckoned poetry as a waste of time began to sing his passionate longing and his pain in verse:

> What place for patience?
> For if patience were the world encircling
> Mount Quaf
> It would become annihilated like snow by the sun of
> separation.[4]

Rumi took to music and mystical dance, whirling in his search for Shams. The whirling itself was thought to bring all space and all time into the eternal center of God and his being, where Shams Tabriz would surely be found. He wrote many many letters which perhaps never reached Shams.

> I wrote a hundred letters, I showed a hundred ways,
> Perhaps you do not know the way, or do not read a letter.[5]

Several years later, news came from Syria that Shams was there in Damascus. Rumi began to sing of his joy: Damascus, the place where the beloved was found, became the center of his world.

> We are enamored and bewildered and enraptured of
> Damascus,
> We have given our souls and bound our heart to the
> passion of Damascus . . .[6]

Rumi sent his son, Soltan Walad, who brought Shams back to Konya with great honor. Their meeting so astonished onlookers that the story has become legendary. They evidently clung to each other for hours. Nobody knew who was the lover, who the beloved. The deep soul engagement was mutual. Rumi saw his Beloved of the soul in Shams, and Shams found in Rumi the Friend in God for whom he had been searching. Rumi writes of this:

> Not only the thirsty seeks the water,
> but the water seeks the thirsty as well.[7]

These lines hold the essence of Rumi's philosophy of love and longing as the way of spiritual transformation. The seeking of the Beloved of the soul who is the reflection of God as the Friend burns away one's circuits of pedantry, of traditional, respectable ways of being. One is burned, shocked, seized by the breadth and depth of the reflection of the God in each other. One does not know where one begins and the other leaves off, so that literally all of one's being is rendered available. This religious experience of the beloved is perhaps the single experience in the world in which one is literally reconstituted. One is fired in an alembic of new being, and all of one's habits and strengths and weaknesses are transformed.

Let us not forget the issue of Rumi's great lines that the water seeks the thirsty as well. Shams, knowing that he contained the fullness of God, wandered the world looking for someone to whom he could give this. And the vessel was prepared in Rumi. The two men at the time of their meeting were prepared to incarnate archetypal forms: the Beloved, the Loving, and the Lover.

Fortunately, they lived at a time in the world of Islamic and Persian mysticism when there was a high tradition of finding in the other the reflection and totality of God. In the present Western world we look at this with a pathologizing eye. Because we have labels, we cannot see something that exceeds all our naming, and so we fall into reductionism and the syndrome of "nothing but." But "nothing but" is never true. The relationship of the men was a both/and: they saw each other as the reflection of God, and they loved each other as human beings with a depth and intensity that became legendary. The kind of rare experience that happened between Rumi and Shams is one in which there occurs a flooding of reality so intense that every level of existence is touched and deepened. One is literally rewoven on the loom of love.

In trying to keep his friend with him, Rumi married him to Kimiya, a girl who had been brought up in his house. Shams became deeply devoted to the young woman.

Again months passed in ecstatic conversation between the two beloveds, and this time the jealousy of the disciples knew no bounds. They plotted to murder Shams. On the night of December 5th, 1248, something approximately like this happened: Rumi and Shams were in their usual ecstatic discourse until a very late hour when someone knocked on the door and asked Shams to come out for some purpose. He went out and stepped into the garden, and the disciples of Rumi circled him and stabbed him. His last words were the prayer of Islam, "La ilah illah Allah," there is no other God but God. His words shattered the consciousness of his slayers and they all fell into a trance. When they awoke, all they found were a few drops of blood on the ground, but the body of Shams had disappeared.

The followers tried to keep news of the death from Rumi for a long while, but one can sense in some of Rumi's verses at the time a presentiment of this knowledge:

> This earth is not dust, it is a vessel full of blood.
> From the blood of the lovers, from the wound of
> checkmate.[8]

People kept telling him that they heard that Shams's had been here or there. Rumi cried:

> Someone said; "I have seen Shamsoddin!"
> Ask him; "where is the way to heaven?"[9]

Forty days after the murder, Rumi ordered mourning robes, a white shirt opened at the chest and a honey-colored wool fez. On his feet he wore rough sandals. Totally given to thought of his beloved, he would whirl around one of the columns of his garden. At this point, it is said, he formalized the dance of the whirling dervishes, a practice he had evidently begun after Shams's first departure. He would turn and turn until he reached the place of disassociation of body and thought, and his heart opened into ecstasy.

His poems which come from this experience show all the stages of mystical passion, yearning, searching, and—again and again—hope for union, love never-ending. Many of his ghazals, his lyric poems, are born out of the dancing rhythm with which Rumi began to be filled more and more often. Hear one of these songs in Persian to get some sense of the power of the meter of yearning:

> *Bahar amad, bahar amad, bahar-e muskhbar amad;*
> *Negar amad negar amad, negar-e burdbar amad.*

> The spring has come, the spring has come, the spring with loads of musk has come. The Friend has come, the Friend has come, the burden-bearing Friend has come.[10]

Rumi began to see Shams in everything—in the glories of nature, the jewels in the hills, the sea, the religious figures of other cultures, cooking pots, sweetmeats. "All my love is like halva!" he exclaims. The following lines are typical of his Shams-filled perception:

> Not alone I keep on singing Shamsoddin and Shamsoddin—
> But the nightingale in the gardens sings, the partridge in the hills,
> Day full of splendor; Shamsoddin, and turning heaven; Shamsoddin
> Mine of jewels; Shamsoddin and Shamsoddin is day and night.
> Shamsoddin is Jesus—breathed, Shamsoddin is Joseph—cheeked.[11]

His whole being is now transformed into poetry and music in his yearning for the beloved. He describes what Shams has done to him:

> I was a devout man. You made me a singer of songs.
> You made me a wine-bibber, a drunkard, a fool.
> I was a grave man, of formal praying.
> You made me the sport of the children in the street.[12]

Indeed, he started to talk to everybody. He began to bow to everybody. A little boy came up to him and said, "Wait for me, I've got to go away for a little while. Then I want you to bow to me." Rumi waited on the street till the boy came back and they bowed to each other. Everybody was surprised, wondering why he waited so long, and Rumi said, "Well, he wanted to bow to me and I wanted to bow to him. It seemed very natural."

He even began to take women for his students!

There is no question that Shams was to Rumi as Socrates was to

Plato—the master who, without leaving anything written, was the inspiration of his chief disciple's greatest writing. Shams was the spark that kindled the fire in the lamp that was Rumi. As one Islamic scholar writes,

> Mowlana [Rumi] was ready for the enthusiastic experience. He was, so to speak, a purified, cleaned lamp in which oil had been poured, the wick had been placed. To make this lamp burn, the fire, a spark was needed, and there was Shams to do this. But when the light of this candle, the oil of which does not end, became so strong that it could not even show Shams, he turned into a moth and he went into the light, giving up his life.[13]

The fiery spiritual light of intense mystic communion had this effect. In Rumi's words:

> The result is not more than these three words:
> I got burnt and burnt and burnt.[14]

Needless to say, Rumi gave up his position as professor of religious science and became instead a teacher of sufis, an initiator of states of mind and heart that would lead men and women to the Beloved of the soul.

And so the human beloved is seen as noble surrogate for divine love, and the power of the love serves as the bridge from the phenomenal world to the spiritual realm. The human beloved becomes the *way through which* one can engender that ecstasy of engagement to fall in love with God and live in the world of God.

In the years following Shams's death, Rumi would discover the noble surrogate of the divine Beloved in several other people. After Shams it was Salahoddin, an illiterate goldsmith of great sweetness and saintlike bearing in whom he found the mirror of God. This was a quieter spiritual union, one which provided Rumi with great serenity.

When the disciples began their usual complaints against Salahoddin, he scolded them by saying, "Men have left their own country, their fathers and mothers, their households and kinsmen and families and have journeyed from Hind to Sind, making boots of iron till they were cut to shreds, happily to encounter a man having the fragrance of the other world . . . as for you, you have encountered such a man here in your own house, and you turn your back on him. This is surely a great calamity in recklessness."[15]

In order to affirm the relationship, Rumi married Salahoddin's daughter, Fatima, to his own favorite son and successor, Soltan Walad, so that the families could be one. When Salahoddin died, instead of the usual funeral, Rumi created for him, a glorious *sama,* a mystical dance accompanied by drums and flute—for death is not a separation but, as the dervishes say, a spiritual wedding. Needless to say, this shocked the orthodox circles of the population.

Ater this death, Rumi found the Friend in his student Hosamoddin, who inspired Rumi to commit to paper his thoughts, ideas, teaching stories—his whole wisdom for the benefit of his students. As the great Rumi scholar Annemarie Schimmel has written, "After the ascent in the love of Shams and the calmness of his friendship with the goldsmith, he now showed himself as the inspired teacher, entering into what the mystics call, 'the arch of descent,' returning to the world as guide and master."

Rumi agreed to follow the wish of his beloved disciple and began to write with him what has become known as the Mathmavi-ye Ma'navi, the spiritual couplets. For years Hosamoddin followed his master around writing down every verse that flowed spontaneously from his lips, be it on the street, in the bath, during the *sama,* or in the house—some 22,000 verses comprising a vast tapestry into which have been woven fables, folk tales, historical events, theoretical discussions about free will and predestination, love and prayer, Koranic revelation, scenes from everyday life, history, and even neo-platonic metaphysics. It is a work that has been called "The Koran in the Persian Tongue," and in his lifetime he was named the second Muhammad because of it. Through it all, however, the meeting with and love of Shamsoddin runs as an undercurrent of poetic and spiritual transubstantiation. He says:

> I read the story of the lovers day and night—Now
> I have become a story in my love for you.[16]

And

> Every hair of mine has become due to Thy love, verse
> and ghazal,
> Every limb of mine has become, due to Thy relish, a
> barrel of honey.[17]

He says he cannot help himself. He is merely a pawn of his inspiration, deprived of his own will. "When I do not recite a ghazal, He splits my mouth."[18]

He even complains about poetry in another book, *Fihi Ma Fihi,* "What have I to do with poetry? By Allah, I care nothing for poetry and there is nothing worse in my eyes than that. It has become encumbent upon me, as when a man plunges his hands into tripe and washes it out for the sake of a guest's appetite because the appetite of the guest is for tripe."[19] Rumi protests further that poetry is a most unfortunate profession in the lands of the eastern caliphs:

> I have studied many sciences and taken much pain so that I may be able to offer fine and rare and precious things to the scholars and researchers, the clever ones and the deep thinkers who come to me. God Most High Himself willed this. He gathered here all those sciences, and assembled here all those pains so that I might be occupied with this work. What can I do? In my own country and amongst my own people there is no occupation more shameful than poetry. If I had remained in my own country, I would have remained in harmony with their temperament and would have practiced what they desired, such as lecturing and composing books, preaching and admonishing, observing abstinence and doing all the outward acts.[20]

Yet after meeting the Beloved, it was all over for proper behavior.

> We've given up making a living.
> It's all this crazy love poetry now.
> It's everywhere. Our eyes and our feelings
> focus together, with our words.[21]

Rumi's poetry deals with absolutely everything. It is a cosmic, encyclopedic outpouring of an ecstasy of knowledge that overflows into words, sounds, images. It is a knowledge of the whole as well as the parts. His path of spiritual love has brought him in consonance with all possible Patterns that Connect. Thus he deals with everything, and everything quite literally finds illumination in his poetic alchemy.

Also, remember, as a Sufi poet he is a resident of many simultaneous worlds. The immensity of his exploration of the outer world serves as but a metaphor for the immensity of his awareness of the inner world. The inner world of the Sufis, the *alam al-mithal,* has as many gardens, as many flavors, as many different realities as do all the outer worlds in all the universe. These worlds, as we have seen, are felt to be real, and provide the source world for the patterns of creative form and innovation that try to enter into this world. Islamic mysticism held that the Koran itself existed in essence in the inner world before it was revealed by the angel to Muhammad in the outer world.

The Sufis had a most sophisticated, complex psychological science of getting to and living in the inner world. Some of these practices were not unlike what we have offered earlier in this book as methods for extending the senses, training in activating imagery, and in developing an imaginal body with which to travel in inner and imaginal worlds.

Rumi, as a highly trained Sufi, certainly studied the science and practice of entering the *alam al-mithal* or imaginal world, so that when love came he could be blown through to this realm and so filled with patterns of creative energy that every nightingale and garden and mountain there reminded him of its complement here. Being seized with the creative impetus of the depth world, he had to write, talk, sing, and dance the metaphor of the great connection. Analogies and associations flowed from him as from the unending well of someone whose life is a bridge between all possible realities. He himself said that, after Shams, he lived in at least seven worlds all of the time. And so the immensity of his exploration in seeking the Beloved in the outer world found its companion awareness in the immensity of his exploration in the inner world.

Remember, too, that this is the time in which the knowledge of the ecology of the inner and outer worlds reached its peak in human consciousness. Consider the Islamic Sufi mystics of the time—Avicenna, Ibn Arabi, Attar, Al Gahazzali, Suhrawardi, Sana'i—all within about a century of each other were expressing with the most exquisite spiritual and poetic metaphors the relationship between inner and outer realities. This was not just an Islamic phenomenon. It was happening all over Europe as well.

The thirteenth century was perhaps the most intensive of all times for breakdown and breakthrough, for decadence and rebirth. As Ghengis Khan was ravaging the Eastern lands, Europe was torn by religious and secular marauders and the breakdown of all of the old orders. But there was also occurring amid the highly charged alembic of medieval culture in the West an enormous cross-fertilization of cultures encouraged by the Crusades. There were new leagues of cities and the growth of trade guilds; there was a considerable influence from the sophisticated scientific, philosophical, and aesthetic knowledge of the Islamic worlds together with a rise and spread of universities. And as a result of this phantasmagoria there was an unleashing of interior images, with new combinations of beliefs, doctrines, and gnosis. What resulted was a rising of the depths such as has been seen only a few times in Western history. Psychological energy, no longer bonded to the destructive and demythologized social forms of church and state, turned inward and was accompanied by a longing for a green world within that would reseed the wasteland without. This was the time of the spread of the courts of love and the reverencing of women to balance and heal the holocaust of deranged masculinity. This was the time of the writing and telling of epics having to do with the quest for the Grail and the quest for a new and higher vision of humanity seen in the noble band of secular angels depicted in the Arthurian stories. And above all this was the time in the West of the rise of many spiritual movements of inwardness, as well as the time when the greatest spiritual teachers were working and planting seeds that would be harvested for centuries to come. Thomas Aquinas was introducing many neo-platonic ideas into Christianity, ideas having to do with the relationship between physical and spiritual realities; St. Francis was teaching his doctrine of love; Meister Eckhart and Johannes Tauler, both Dominicans, were developing a Celtic-Germanic mysticism that considered the exploration of the inner world in consonance with the earthy metaphors affirming the inspirited realities of the outer world. It was as if this period of historical breakdown served to blow open the doors between inner and outer reality, causing consciousness to quake into new growth and extended being.

And so, in the full seizure of this temporal quake, Rumi poured out his longing for the union of these two worlds in more than 30,000 verses of lyrical poetry and more than 20,000 verses of didactic poetry, as well as in his lectures and thousands of letters. It is Rumi, perhaps more so than all of the spiritual giants who lived in his time, who expressed in the most exacting and exquisite and powerful images what was trying to break through into time. In the pages to follow we will see many examples of Rumi's imagery of breakthrough, drawn from images of everyday life. In these images you may experience in yourself the seizure and quickening of consciousness that occurred so powerfully in the thirteenth century and is occurring again in our time. Here are a few more of them that astonish and delight:

> There's a strange frenzy in my head,
> of birds flying
> each particle circulating in its own.
> Is the one I love everywhere?[22]

> God's joy moves from unmarked box to unmarked box,
> from cell to cell. As rainwater, down into flowerbed.
> As roses, up from the ground.
> Now it looks like a plate of rice and fish,
> now a cliff covered with vines,
> now a horse being saddled.
> It hides within these,
> til one day it cracks them open.[23]

> Turn me like a waterwheel turning a millstone.
> Plenty of water, Living Water.
> Keep me in one place and scatter the love.
> Leaves move in a wind, straw drawn toward amber,
> all parts of the world are in love,
> but they do not tell their secrets: Cows grazing
> on a sacramental table, ants whispering in Solomon's ear.

Mountains mumbling an echo. Sky, calm.
If the sun were not in love, he would have no brightness,
the side of the hill no grass on it.
The ocean would come to rest somewhere.[24]

So that was the mind and soul of Rumi. When he died and the funeral prayers were over, music and dance and whirling into ecstasy and union with the Beloved went on for hours and hours, for he had taught:

When you come visiting my grave,
My roofed tomb will appear to you dancing.
Do not come without tambourine to my tomb, brother!
For a grieved person does not fit in God's banquet![25]

A stream of visitors to his tomb never ceases to this day. Even today, even this morning, visitors to his tomb come singing and dancing and seeking the Beloved.

(Scenario 2: Spiralling in Search of the Beloved)

RUMI AND THE SACRIFICE OF THE HEART

Rumi wrote a marvelous story about a bunch of chick-peas that, when put in a pot of boiling water, yell bloody murder over their fate and try to leap out. But the housewife consoles them by telling them that she is to them as Abraham was to Isaac, reminding them that Isaac was quite ready and willing to be sacrificed by his father, since only by sacrifice can one acquire a higher status. She even goes so far as to quote the martyred Sufi mystic Hallaj (died A.D. 922), who so lost his identity in God that he could proclaim, "I am God." Condemned to death for this heresy, he is reputed to have said, "Kill me, O my trustworthy friends, for in my being killed, there is my life." She then admonishes them that being cooked and eaten is the only way for chick-peas to reach a higher level of development, for then they will be integrated into human form.[26]

Rumi loved to use the imagery of the kitchen, constantly referring to concepts like raw and cooked to symbolize the transformational process in life. How raw are you? How cooked? Do you have freezer burn? Have you been cut into precise and equal pieces and then packaged? (Rumi would have had a field day with modern food preparation.)

"Die before ye die," said Muhammad. Rumi would agree: "As the hard shell of the walnut has to be broken in order to free the sweet kernel which in turn must be crushed to release the fragrant oil which is the innermost heart of the nut, so the human has to be stripped of the hard shell of his lower or conditioned qualities in order to develop the deeper and nobler ones."

Rumi sees that everything follows the rule of sacrifice to reach essence. The word "sacrifice" is from the Latin *sacer-ficere* which means to make sacred, and even to refine.

The field must be plowed in order to receive the seed; the seed grows and is harvested and the grains are crushed under the millstone; the flour then has to endure the heat of breaking in order to become bread which then will be crushed by a person's teeth; and in digestion is the deluge of destruction and reconstitution. Similarly, raw hide has to undergo the painful process of tanning before it becomes smooth and beautiful leather—and how could grape juice develop into tasty wine unless it ferment for a while? An ordinary stone, during long periods of contraction, matures into a ruby. At a certain level, to be broken, to be sacrificed, is the prerequisite for new life. Once the vessel of ordinary human existence is broken, the God-wave can enter in. Rumi lived the Sufi promise of God, "I am with those whose hearts are broken for my sake."

Now this puts a very different light on the significance of suffering. It is too often missing in modern psychologies, and it has been distorted in the practice and preachment of traditional religion. In the course of this study of sacred psychology I have emphasized the sacrality of suffering and the recurrence of the themes of wounding and pathos found in all great myths and mythic journeys. With Rumi, however, we have the fullest expression of the transformational nature of suffering when understood from the perspective of the evolutionary change that is implicit in the suffering. With Rumi, suffering is both remythologized and ennobled. It was not all for vain, even though at the time it may have seemed like a huge conspiracy of meaninglessness. Rumi's gift was to see how one's suffering can be redeemed and how one can become nobler and deeper by consequence.

What are you being broken for over and over again? This question is generally followed by the whine of "Why me?" We take this attitude because we do not have the depth of insight to see ourselves in the extraordinary metabiological process of becoming more and more refined, more and more sacred, transparent to transcendence. If we could see this, our suffering would not turn into pathology. *We pathologize because we cannot mythologize.* We see ourselves as being overcooked by suffering and turning into sludge at the bottom of the pot. Also, many tend to keep on suffering to no purpose because the culture puts no purpose in its evaluation of suffering.

Think of all the times in your life that could have been opportunities for refinement and higher development, for the sacred to enter into time, that instead became times of despair and regression, of whining and of inauthentic suffering. What would your life be like if from this moment forth you regarded your sufferings as refinements? Then the image of sacrifice and refinement would work deep in your mind and soul. The suffering, which is inevitable, would be the vehicle for the recasting of your nature. Then pathos might becomes mythos, and instead of suffering in the school of hard knocks, you would find yourself whipped into consecrated shape, becoming a Grail instead of a crushed plastic cup.

Rumi wrote, "Wherever there is a ruin there is hope for a treasure; why do you not seek the treasure of God in the devastated heart?"[27] Rumi's heart was devastated when his beloved was killed; he had not known there could be so much pain. But from the rending of that pain, he was filled with constant inspiration and became the great mystic poet, teacher, saint and friend.

Rumi, the source of endless images, tells us that the house has to be destroyed so that we can find the great treasure hidden underneath, a treasure which is worth many, many houses. In Oriental folklore a treasure is always buried under ruins; it is the house of the heart, crushed and sacrificed, under which the treasure, God can be found.

It is interesting to discover in the world's religions how constant is this image of the sacrificed heart, the tender heart, the wounded heart. Consider the sacred heart of Jesus, the bleeding heart; the sacrifice of the heart among the Aztecs; and the far more complex sacrifice of the heart in Rumi's theology. Why the recurrence of this image?

As we learn in the literature and the liturgy of the world's sacred psychology, the heart is clearly the single organ that needs woundings and sacrifices in order for higher development to occur. You never hear about the collapsed lung, the bilious liver, or the stomach ache as the path to God. It is the closing of the heart far more than the closing of the mind that keeps folk from transformation and deepening.

We tend in our age to dread the closed mind more than the closed heart, not realizing that a closed heart can wreak infinitely more destruction than a closed mind. It is almost as if, for many people, a membrane forms around the heart as a protection against more life, more feelings, more spirit. One can almost hear them saying, "I want my heart closed because if it's not, I will go into overload. Ideas can come and go; these I can deal with; but, please, no more being vulnerable, no more love."

As to the question whether there can ever be a path of transformation without suffering, I would doubt it. I have never seen a flower grow without bursting its pod. I have never met anyone anywhere whose path of growth and deepening was not attended by the shattering of the membrane of the heart.

So we learn from Rumi that the heart must be sacrificed, must be broken open, for us to find the hidden treasure within. The lover whose goal is to become one with the Beloved agrees to the crushing and rending and devastation and ruin of everything in the local self that prevents, subtly and otherwise, the experience of union. Remember again the story of the lover who knocked at the Beloved's door and was sent away when he said, "I am here." And it was only upon returning after maturing for a year in the flames of separation that he answered the question by saying, "It is you, O Beloved." Then he was admitted. He had sacrificed his "I" in order that the Beloved might be all. For who else but the Divine Beloved has the right to say "I"?

In the path of love and spiritual realization, the lover undergoes two fundamental experiences: union with the Beloved and the terrible pain of separation. Now if union with God is self-annihilation, then separation from Him is self-existence. As long as you continue to live under the illusion of the cultural existence of your own ego, then you are far from God, and the gate of the heart is hardened. Only through the sacrifice of the heart and the surrender to the Beloved does the union occur.

During the spiritual journey, there are many consecutive experiences of separation and union or death and life. Life is filled with little deaths: the death of loved ones, of pets, illness, loss of faith, of money, of reputation, leaving a church, divorce, letting go of children, of ego, of who and what you think you are, betrayal, losing one's words, humiliation. What Rumi has done, which most of us have not, is to make a conscious use of his dyings so that they lead toward reunion. So Rumi speaks of having died many times, but each time he dies he is reborn and moves closer to that ultimate state of the I AM-ness with God. Since the dyings are inevitable, how much more valuable if you met them consciously as opportunities to allow the loss in some sense to provide the emptiness that can be filled by the Beloved.

In this experience of the sacrifice of the heart, which may seem very strange and perhaps alien to less robust modern spirits, you are urged to welcome the suffering in the knowledge that it increases the love for its opposite, the joy and ecstasy of union. For the only way to flee from suffering is to seek refuge from your own local self in God. If you consider how much the local ego with its "issues" and "vulnerabilities," its sensitivity to being hurt, causes you to be in a state of chronic pain, then you see the wisdom of the longing for union and why suffering persists in spite of all of our attempts to banish it.

The mystery of human suffering may be the mystery of human transformation, for ultimately the pull up the ladder into unitive being can probably only come from the impetus beneath, from the pain that tortures our lower being. So listen to Rumi when he says:

> In order to pull us up and help us travel, messenger after messenger comes from that Source of existence:
>
> Every heartache and suffering that enters your body and heart pulls you by the ear to the promised Abode.[28]

> He has afflicted you from every direction in order to pull you back to the directionless.[29]

> Between God and his servant are just two veils; all other veils become manifest from these two: health and wealth.
>
> He who is healthy says, "Where is God? I don't know and I don't see." As soon as he begins to suffer he says, "Oh God! Oh God!" He begins sharing his secrets with Him and talking to Him. So you see that health was his veil and God was hidden under his pain.
>
> So long as man has riches, he gathers together all the means of achieving his desires. Night and day he busies himself with them. But as soon as he loses his wealth his ego weakens and he turns round about God.[30]

The imagery is intense and the metaphors range far and wide as Rumi describes the suffering that leads to union.

> When someone beats a rug with a stick, he is not beating the rug—his aim is to get rid of the dust.
>
> Your inward is full of dust from the veil of I-ness and that dust will not leave all at once.
>
> With every cruelty and every blow, it departs little by little, from the heart's face, sometimes in sleep and sometimes in wakefulness.[31]

> The grapes of my body will become wine only after the Vintner stomps upon me with His feet.
>
> I surrender my spirit, like grapes, to His stomping, so that my inmost consciousness may revel in joy.[32]

> Fire flees from water because water puts it out.
>
> When the water of His light drips upon your fire, it sizzles and jumps up.
>
> As it sizzles and splatters, call it "death" and "pain"—until this hell of your ego becomes cold.[33]

Thus are we called to become winter so that we may see the coming of spring. Out of the sacrifice, creation appears; to be given up and to be given over, almost, it seems, to be nothing, is the condition of God's creative work. This is one of the highest mysteries of all: that God needs our local "dyings" to restore life. The sacrifice is the bridge toward higher stations of being. There is no backsliding or regression in this journey. No ripe grape ever again becomes green, and no cooked food ever again becomes raw. Nothing can return to its previous lesser state. No mirror can become iron again, no bread again wheat. There is no return to being a little green apple after you have gotten the blush of the Beloved on you.

The movement caused by dying through love carries us to resurrection on a higher plane. Whereas our era has extolled regression in the service of the ego, the perennial movement of sacred psychology is toward dying in the service of the Self.

And so we ask what is it in you that keeps the membrane of the heart tight and enclosed? What is it in you that needs to be crushed, shattered, rent, torn, ruined? How do you enter consciously into the "tavern of ruin" so that the Beloved may come to turn your ruin into resurrection, and you find intoxication of union within the tavern?

Our Western-derived psychologies and cultural styles of self-presentation have given us perhaps the most structured and strictured egos in the history of consciousness. Modern psychologies abound with ways with which you can protect and embellish these structures and strictures; how we can "look out for number one," becoming "one-minute managers," celebrating the illusion of "I'm okay you're okay," affirming against the sea of suffering the "power of positive thinking," asserting finally your self-sufficiency and independence from the divine Beloved as you militantly and masterfully "become your own best friend."

What would Rumi say to this pathological avoidance of man's true nature? He would probably laugh and laugh and say,

> A basket full of bread sits on your head but you beg for crusts from door to door. Up to your knees in the stream's water and you seek a drink from this person and that.
>
> Would that you could know yourself for a time! Would that you could see a sign of your own beautiful face.
>
> Wretched human! Not knowing his own self, man has come from a high estate and fallen into lowliness. He has sold himself cheaply; he was satin yet he has sown himself onto a tattered cloak.
>
> If you could only see your own beauty—for you are greater than the sun! Why are you withered and shriveled in this prison of dust?
>
> Why not become fresh from the gentleness of the heart's spring? Why not laugh like a rose? Why not spread perfume?
>
> Why is your Jacob deprived of the lightning of your beautiful face? Hey, O lovely Joseph! Why remain at the bottom of the well?[34]

Now let us try to get out of the bottom of the well.
(Scenario 3: The Sacrifice of the Heart)

THE LADDER OF BECOMING IN THE THOUGHT OF RUMI

Each form you see has its unseen archetype;
if the form should pass, its essence is eternal.
If you have known beauty in a face or wisdom in a word,
let this counsel your heart: what perishes is not real.
Since the springhead is timeless, its branches refresh.
Since neither can cease, what is the cause of your sorrow?
Think of your soul as the source and created things as
springs.
While the source exists, the springs continually flow.
Empty your head of grief and drink from the stream.
Don't think of it failing—this water is endless.
From the moment you came into the manifest world
a ladder was given that you might escape.
From mineral substance you were transformed to plant,
and later to animal. How could this be hidden?
Afterwards, as man, you developed knowledge,
consciousness, faith.
See how this body has risen from the dust like a rose?
When you have walked on from man you will be an angel,
and done with this earth your place will be beyond.
Pass, then, from the angelic and enter the Sea.
Your drop will merge with a hundred Seas of Oman.
Leave him you called "Son," and say "One" with your
life.
Although your body has aged, your soul has become
younger.[35]

In this great poem of Rumi are contained the joining of two of the most fascinating aspects of his thought—the ladder of evolution and the existence of the archetypal imaginal world. The opening lines, with its neoplatonic message of every form having its deep, essential prototype in the source level of existence, then becomes an invitation to enter the imaginal world and climb the ladder of becoming into the future of human possibility under the guidance of the archetypal forms of the next rungs of evolution.

We have seen how the imaginal world in the Sufi and other traditions is key to the understanding of how creative possibilities enter into time from the springhead of all patterns and forms, and how what we call ordinary imagination is to the imaginal as grotesque shadows. The example that Rumi uses is the imagination of the architect who can conceive of a building in his heart with such precision and realism that it can become manifest. The architect's conception of that house is like the patterns stored in the imaginal world. By comparison, an untrained mind imaging the same house produces not a building but collapsing ephemera, shadows of walls that dissolve within themselves.

Now a trained imagination can access images that are both seen, heard, touched, tasted, felt, and known with such inner acuity that they seem to have as much reality as the same images perceived in the outer realm.[36] It is thought by many esoteric schools that this quality and intensity of focused imagination can help bring the object of the focus into manifestation. This is more the province of active imagination. Deeper training such as the Sufis offered had to do with knowing how to get in touch with the passive imaginal realms, where one can access autonomous archetypal realities. For to get beyond local active imagination to archetypal imagination is the way of the saint and the Sufi. To get there may involve priming the pump of active imagination, but there is a threshold beyond which the "waters of the well" begin to prime you. This is when the creative ideas and forms begin to rise in you.

According to Rumi, one of the most powerful and consistently accurate ways of doing this is through the way of love, wherein one's heart and mind are so extended by the Beloved that instead of perceiving the images of one's own mental and emotional faculties, one perceives images that exist independently of oneself. In other words, to all practical purposes you are perceiving in this state through the inward senses of the psychospiritual organs. As an extension of this, another way of entering the imaginal world is by so joining with the Beloved that you are perceiving through the psychospiritual senses of the Beloved—whatever those senses may be. Then you are much closer to the perception of the very forms of things. You perceive, as it were, the primal constructs, the original architecture, the very plans of creation. Primed with the power of these images from which flow the re-creation of the world, you become an instrument through which evolution enters into time.

Such an instrument, according to Rumi, is one who says continuously, "Be! Be! Be!" bringing new creation into the world.

> Sit at the image-house of the heart, behold each
> painting We draw!
> One by One we send new paintings, so that the
> first may become the second's morsel. . . .
>
> The beauty of the Unseen form is beyond
> description—borrow a thousand illuminated eyes,
> borrow!

I said to my heart, "How are you?" It said,
"Increasing, for, by God, I am His Image's House.

Like Jesus, Thy Image goes into the heart to
bestow a new spirit-like Divine revelation, it descends
upon
Moses at the mountain.

Such a form that were its radiance to reach a
painting on the wall, the painting would gain a spirit and
begin to talk and see.[37]

But then there is the place of union with the Beloved, the *fana* or annihilation of self and images in God.

All paintings have gone, the whole ocean has
become blue! All pride has gone, all Glory has
come![38]

The creative images exist in the heart of the Beloved—the dwelling place perhaps of the archetypal forms of the next steps of evolution. Witness the famed and controversial poem by Rumi:

I died as mineral and became a plant,
I died as plant and rose to animal,
I died as animal and I was a Man.
Why should I fear? When was I less by dying?
Yet once more I shall die as man, to soar
With angels blest; but even from angelhood
I must pass on: all except God doth perish.
When I have sacrificed my angel-soul,
I shall become what no mind e'er conceived.
O let me not exist! For Non-Existence
Proclaims in organ tones "To Him we shall
return."[39]

Every interpreter of Rumi has offered theories on what these remarkable lines mean. Some feel it is the earliest expression of a theory of evolution. Others see it as God pulling consciousness up the ladder of being through the magnetic power of love (an idea consonant with Teilhard's notion of the power of love of the Omega, the spiritual emotive force, luring evolution through time). Some see it as demonstrating that human existence is nothing but the evolutionary unfoldment of God's existence (a good Hegelian idea). Then there is the idea that implicit in these lines is the gnostic notion of a "Fall," with the proviso that after having been separated from God the Beloved, man has to pass through all stages of being until he reaches once more the only source and only reality, God. In so doing, however, he grows God, by being the occasion for the coming of complexity and creative innovation.

All of these interpretations may have some truth to them, but I am constantly brought back to the story of the chick-peas which are cooked so that they might become part of something more evolved. The chick-peas in Rumi's verse, after realizing what alchemy, what transubstantiation they are undergoing say, "Since this is the case, O lady, let me boil happily—aid me well! In this boiling, you are like my architect. Strike me with the spoon, for you strike delightfully. I am like an elephant: beat me upon the head with blows, so that I will not dream of India and gardens, so that I will give myself to the boiling and be delivered into the embrace of the Beloved." And so this evolution is not "a cold magnetic force which produces the attraction and the upward movement in creation, but the free grace of God's creative love which enables the lower potencies to grow to higher levels, provided they follow the law of love which is, to sacrifice their small egos for the sake of something higher, i.e., finally, for the Beloved."[40] Or, in the great lines of Rumi:

> Only love produces this change: otherwise how would
> minerals be naughted in plants?[41]
>
> Love makes dead bread into soul,
> Love makes the soul which was perishable, eternal.[42]

The lure of becoming along the ladder of development and transformation, the next architectural images of human perfectability (in the Sufi sense of the "perfected man") are in the *mundus imaginalis,* waiting to be tapped through the yearning of the journeying mind and heart. The way to this gnosis of the next stage can be attained through entry into the imaginal realm of the heart, there to see or sense directly the pattern, the plan, and in so doing to be seized with the creative means and the transformational information and desire to become the friend of the Friend and help the Beloved in all his manifold patterns and forms enter into time. However, unless there is sufficient *pothos* or yearning, it is unlikely that this will ever happen. That is why for most people there has to be the tension of otherness to ignite the ongoingness of the yearning. That is why, too, in many religions there is a rich archetypal tradition in which the archetype can become incarnate in human form, be it Jesus, or Buddha, or even Shams, so as to set one up for the polarity, the distancing, which then creates the yearning. It is our yearning that will take us to our edges so that we will fall into the imaginal world where our destiny as co-creators lies. We are tricked into the imaginal realm through the trick of the heart, for the heart will trick most people faster and deeper than will the games of the mind. That is why through the vast collection of Rumi's poems and sayings there runs the undercurrent which proclaims: Blessed are the lovers, for they are willing to be such fools that they will be tricked—tricked into evolution, tricked into angelhood, tricked into bringing the transformational information into the world of space and time.

Thus the ladder of existence and the archetypal world meet in the crossroads of the heart to bring the archetypal patterns into time, and to raise the human being higher in his journey up the ladder toward the One.

(Scenario 4: Seeking the One Through the Ladder of Evolution)

Scenarios for the Ecstatic Journey of Jalaloddin Rumi

SCENARIO 1
Zikr of the Ultimate Communion of Love

We begin our scenario with one of the oldest of Islamic practices for establishing a natural communion of the heart with the Beloved Friend, the Beloved being God, the Divine Lover who is the source of all loving.

The practice we are about to perform is what is called a *zikr* (pronounced zicker), or spiritual practice of remembrance. This particular zikr is so old that it may go back to ancient Egypt or even to prehistoric times. But it was taken up by the Sufis as central to the practice of the communion of the heart with the Divine Beloved. This is the kind of practice that the young Rumi would have been taught by his dervish teacher, Burhand al-Din Muhaqqiq, which helped prepare his heart for the passionate search for and profound discovery of the Beloved of his soul. It remains one of the most powerful zikrs of love and communion that exists.

TIME: 20 minutes.

MATERIALS NEEDED: A bell.

INSTRUCTIONS FOR WORKING ALONE: This practice is readily done alone. One should, however, have a string or "rosary" of thirty-three beads to help in keeping count of the zikr sounds.

SCRIPT FOR THE GUIDE: To begin, sit in any position that will keep your spine straight. Close your eyes and breathe very deeply, following your breath all the way in and all the way out.

This zikr is a zikr of heartfelt communion with God, with the Beloved. As such it is a practice of the heart. It is a sound that you make deep in your throat and deep down in your heart. It is the sound of communion and it goes: Hmmm . . . hmmm . . . hmm. Hmmm . . . hmmm . . . hmm. There are three hmmms on each exhalation: Hmmm . . . hmmm . . . hmmm. From deep in your heart. Be aware of the vibration in your chest as you make this sound.

Keep on doing this, and as you do, be aware of communing with that which you understand as the Beloved—God, the Beloved of your soul, whatever and whomever that may be. Know that this is the ultimate sound. It is the sound of babies at the breast. It is the sound of yum-yum-yum in all kinds of enjoyable situations and circumstances. It is the sound of union. It is a sound that is deep and ancient in the brain. It is the baby cooing, the waves meeting the shore after their long journeys across the ocean. It is the cat purring, the dog humming happily. It is the infinite wag of the tail.

And it is the deep connection. For those of you who are deeply Christian, it is union with Christ. For those of you who are Buddhist, it is communion with the Buddhic Nature. For all it is the union with the deep Beloved of the soul, with the angel of the Self, with God-Not-In-Hiding.

And the communion is done remembering that the Beloved yearns for you, is yearning back toward you as you are yearning for the Beloved.

Stay very focused as you make three hmmms on each breath. We will now start the practice formally with a cycle of thirty-three breaths (99 hmmms). Do not try to keep the count; I will do it for you.

After thirty-three breaths I will sound a bell, and when I do that you will hold your breath—it will be for about twenty seconds—until I sound the bell again. While holding your breath let yourself be filled with the deep sweetness of communion. You are opening your heart to the fullness of the zikr coming back to you from the Beloved. You will let the sweetness of communion—"like sugar melting," says Rumi—move through you.

Then we will do ten more sets of the zikr, after which I will sound the bell again. And again you will hold your breath and let the sweetness of the communion fill you.

All right. Preparing for this practice of communion, centering our attention in your heart, begin feeling the connection with the Divine Beloved. And beginning: Hmmm . . . hmmm . . . hmmm. Hmmm . . . hmmm . . . hmmm. Hmmm . . . hmmm . . . hmmm.

(At the end of the cycles of 33 and 10, the guide will bring the zikr to completion by saying:)

In the tradition it is appropriate to acknowledge and give reverence. If you wish, sitting in place you will bow slowly and deeply now to the Beloved who is within you. (After this is done the guide says:) You now bow to the Beloved in others. (This being done the Guide says:) And finally you bow to the Beloved That Is.

And now sit quietly for a while meditating on your experience.

(After the group has performed this zikr several times on different occasions, the guide may choose—although it is not essential—to read aloud to the participants some of the spiritual love poetry of Rumi during the practice. If the guide decides to do this, he or she will say:)

And throughout this zikr of communion I will read in the background some of the ecstatic love poetry of Rumi to the Beloved of the soul. The poetry is actually to a real person, Shams of Tabriz, but it is also to Shams as the earthly counterpart of the Divine Beloved, the noble surrogate of God.

(Here the guide may want to use a good collection of Rumi's lyric poetry to read in the background, although this is not necessary. *Open Secrets: Versions of Rumi* by John Moyne and Coleman Barks, or *The Ruins of the Heart: Selected Lyric Poetry of Jelaluddin Rumi* by Edmund Helminski, are appropriate.)

SCENARIO 2
Spiralling to the Beloved

Why has this whirling been going on for 800 years? Because it works. It is at once a spinning into the core and a flinging away of that which needs to be released. The dross, the conditionings, the old habits are flung away and the inner centricity, where the Beloved can enter, is found.

In spinning, you transgress your boundaries; they become blurred. You can no longer say, "I extend only so far and no farther." You release your hold on your boundaries and allow them to disappear.

When we whirl, we want to hang with our eyes to something "out there." Hanging on makes us dizzy; it reflects our desire to grasp, to hold, to keep our reality in check.

In this exercise when you spiral in search of the Beloved, you will not be abandoned. You will be whirling with a partner who will witness and care for you. Should you go off balance, you will be caught. Should you begin to fall, you will be helped.

Do not forget that the whirling is only an enabler in the search for the Beloved of the soul. It is not an end in itself.

The Beloved is known in several ways; as the Beloved of Beloveds—God, Allah, the One, the Creative Force, the Friend, the Great Lover of the soul.

Then there is the Beloved of the soul of inner realms. For many practicing Christians, it may be Christ, Mary, or one of the Saints. For Mother Theresa it is Jesus, and she sees the face of her Beloved everywhere and cannot do enough for him. For Buddhists it may be Gautama Buddha or a Bodhisattva like Kwan Yin. For Hindus it may be Krishna. For many who cannot respond to a traditional cultural archetyepe it would be the Shams within. This union with the internal beloved as archetype, as your extended being in the inner world, then renders you available to God, the Beloved of Beloveds.

In our culture, this encounter and union usually comes when you are well into your prime—when you are mature enough, yearning enough, and have done enough "human homework" to be available for the mystery of this kind of experience.

The image of the Beloved in the other as experienced by Rumi and Shams is a pure, unpredictable gift of Grace, a gift that cannot be requisitioned. Nevertheless, the spinning that you are about to do is both physical and spiritual preparation for receiving the Beloved of the soul. "I am ready, O Thirsty One," the Beloved says. "I am ready to quench your thirst." And thereupon the Beloved of the soul, the Beloved that is God, begins to enter.

TIME: 60–90 minutes.

MATERIALS NEEDED: Each couple or group should have writing materials available and kept at the side of the room.

MUSIC: Any kind of music that has a circular, repetitive melody would be appropriate. However we have found Sufi dervish music to be effective, especially *The Sufi Song and Dance Album,* Side Two/Selection 1: "Universal Worship Dance and Round." Another excellent piece for this process is found in the album "Tom Bozigian Presents Songs and Dances of the Armenian People," Vol. III, side 2, selections 5 and 6.

ROOM SETUP: Be sure the floor space is absolutely clear so that there is nothing to trip on. The room must be large enough to allow all participants freedom of movement.

INSTRUCTIONS FOR WORKING ALONE: This process must be done with at least one other person.

SCRIPT FOR THE GUIDE: You are going to whirl in place. You will start very slowly and find how your own feet want to move as you go around. They have their own knowledge. Just stay on your own axis. Many people find it helpful to watch the left hand and let everything else blur. You will begin slowly, and then when you're comfortable with the slow movement, you'll speed up, but only to the extent that is comfortable for you. You want to stay conscious. Find a partner who is more or less your size, who can support you if need be, and then disperse yourselves around the room. (The whirling may also be done in groups of three of four.)

In Sufism the legendary guide is known as Khidir. It is said that he comes to help you reach the Beloved. Your partner, your Khidir, will be holding the field for you and really focusing on you as you turn. As guide and guardian angel, your partner will also be saying, "Welcome, O Beloved," inviting the One who will fill your thirst.

Like Hosamoddin with Rumi, your partner will also be there with pen and paper when you finish spinning to take down whatever thoughts or sayings or poems emerge from you.

In your spinning, you may find the name of your Beloved. You may find a song to sing to your Beloved, or you may hear the song your Beloved is singing to you. Images, phrases, whole poems may rise up in you as they did for Rumi. Or there may be only a feeling, a wordless intimation of the Beloved. Whatever there is to share, your Hosamoddin will be there to write it down for you when you are done whirling. Remember, should you fall, your partner will catch you and lay you on the ground until you are ready to resume spinning.

Before you begin spinning, we will do a little body work so that you are grounded. Start by loosening up and springing up and down on your feet. Just spring, and feel that in your ankles. Be aware of your feet on the floor. Be aware of the feeling in your calves as you're springing up and down. And as you spring up and down, open your eyes and look straight ahead.

Now turn your head slowly to the left, looking at everything that you see. When your head is as far as it will go to the left, begin turning it back to the right, gently pivoting. Continue the springing movement at the same time. . . .

And looking ahead of you as your head pivots, let your springing slow down but continue to turn your head. As you turn your head, see if you can allow your eyes to let everything blur. Not focusing on anything now, just allow the blurring.

As you are turning your head, raise your left hand up to the ceiling. You are still gently springing. Give yourself a good stretch and continue to let your eyes blur as you turn your head. . . .

And now put your right hand up, and let your left hand point downward. As your head continues to turn, be aware of your heart space, the inner heart. This awareness of the heart space is critical, for in a sense all the spinning in search of the Beloved is ultimately happening in the heart.

Come to quiet and now decide which one of you is going to be the Spinner, and which one is going to be the guide, the Khidir. (If there are three in each group, one whirls, one is the Khidir, one is Hosamoddin.)

Salute your partner or partners by bowing to each other. And now the one who is going to whirl, put your weight on your left foot. Put your left hand out, palm down to give to the earth. Put your right hand out, palm up to receive from heaven. And just begin to move slowly, in small circles, counterclockwise, experimenting to see how it feels and then going at the speed that seems appropriate. . . .

You who are spinning, remember that you are protected. You who are standing as Khidir, remember that you are there to keep the field and protect the one who is spinning to the Beloved.

(Music appropriate for spinning, such as dervish or Sufi dance music, now begins and continues for about 15 to 20 minutes.)

Begin to slow down. Begin to come to to stillness. And let your partner greet you and bless you and sit you down on the floor. And you who have been Khidir and witness, quickly get notebook and pen and return to your partner.

You who have been spinning, allow yourself to speak to your partner whatever comes out, be it an image, a poem, a song, a feeling of love, or the Divine No-Thing. And as you speak, make sure you maintain contact with the Beloved, with the opening and the connection that may have happened. (3–5 minutes).

All right. Put the notebooks away and change places. The one who did the spinning last time will now be the witness, the Khidir.

Once again, before the spinning begins, we will do some movement to ground you in your bodies. Be aware of your feet, your knees. Be aware of your pelvis; move it back and forth a little. Spring up and down a little, moving your head from left to right as you do so, not allowing your eyes to focus on anything. . . . Now, slowing down, keep on turning your head. . . . Now stop and move your attention to your heart. And be aware now that your eyes are going to see the world outside differently as you access the inner world.

(The guide should now repeat the instruction for the spinning, beginning with "Salute your partner . . ." and continuing through the reminder about speaking of the Beloved. Again, music appropriate for spinning continues for about 15 to 20 minutes. At the end of this sequence the guide will repeat the instructions should there be more than two partners in a group, until everyone has had a turn to spin. When the last participant has finished spinning and speaking his or her knowledge of the Beloved, the guide will say:)

Come to an end now and put the writing materials away to the side. Then quickly come back and all of you stand together. What we are going to do briefly is to spin together. Hold each other's hands and begin spinning gently. Let the Beloved of the Beloved meet and join with the Beloved of the Beloved.

(Let the spinning music play for about 3 minutes. At the end of this time the guide will say:)

Come to stillness now. Now move toward one another keeping the Beloved in your heart, letting your Beloveds greet and honor and hold each other, if holding is appropriate. Know yourself to be both the Beloved, the one who quenches the thirst, as well as the thirsty one, whose thirst will be quenched by the unending love of the Beloved. Now bow to the other, thanking each other for having been Khidir to you in your search for the Beloved.

SCENARIO 3
The Releasing of the Attributes and the Sacrifice of the Heart

The Releasing of the Attributes

We are now going to do a process called "The Releasing of the Attributes." You will sacrifice your attributes, the ones that allow you to function effectively and efficiently in the world. If you are a teacher, you give it up. If you are a good counselor, or a good mother, or a good lawyer or doctor or salesman, you give it up. You are giving up attachment to the way you are seen in the world, to the way in which you are "respectable." You will be like Rumi, sacrificing his honorable status as a respectable professor and becoming the mad, ecstatic teacher. You will sacrifice your attributes in order to be rendered sacred and take on new ability.

TIME: 90 minutes.

MATERIALS NEEDED: Before this scenario begins, the guide will ask each participant to gather five leaves from trees in the vicinity of the meeting place and to bring them to where the scenario is to be performed.

MUSIC: Music from *Area 2* should be played during the "Meditation on the Sacrifice of the Heart." The second half of Kitaro's *Cosmos* has proved effective, especially the part labeled "Solaris" and followed by "Heartbeat."

INSTRUCTIONS FOR WORKING ALONE: Although this process is best done with others, it can be done alone. The person doing so can follow the instructions of the guide given below and speak for and then sacrifice each attribute in front of a mirror. The meditation on the sacrifice of the heart can be put on tape and followed at the appropriate time.

SCRIPT FOR THE GUIDE: Gather now in groups of three. And when you have formed your triad, each of you will spend a few minutes writing your attributes on the leaves you have brought. Take your five major attributes and write them on these living leaves, one attribute to each leaf.

Select the five things that most "name" you in the world, so that if you dropped these attributes, you would be devastated, a ruin in your own terms.

They may be "good" qualities such as "I am a very responsible person," "I am a good provider," "I am a good parent." Some attributes may have such complexity and interrelationship that in giving up one, you're giving up many. Now begin writing these attributes on the leaves (7 minutes).

Now you will get up, one person at a time, and stand before your partners, holding your five leaves. Stand in the center and, one leaf at a time, speak for each attribute. Become that attribute and speak for it.

For example, you might say, as I would, "I am teacher. Oh, such pride I take in reading all those books and doing all that research and writing my lectures on my computer and then seeing the response in the eyes of my students. This is my identity." Go on and on about the attribute until it represents the totality of your persona. Then, when you have become the attribute, take that leaf and say, "I sacrifice it," and let the leaf fall to the ground.

And those of you who are serving as high witness, respond to the letting go with, "You are no longer that."

Go through each of your five attributes, taking a few minutes for each. Really become the attribute you are speaking for, and then release it as you drop its leaf. Feel the weight of release as you let go.

When you have finished, gather up your discarded leaves and hold them once again. Very soon they are going to be given back to the natural world as manure, given back to create new life.

When the first person has finished, allow a minute of silence, of respect for what has been sacrificed. The process is then repeated for each of you, pausing for a minute after each person has finished to honor the sacrifice. Do not do the exercise as a satire. Really be the attribute. Feel the fullness and glory of it before you let the leaf of the attribute float down and fall, sacrificed. When your triad is finished, sit in silence until the entire group is finished. Then we will do a meditation on the Beloved in the heart, after which we will finish this process out of doors.

Now let the first speaker of attributes stand up and begin. You will have a total of thirty minutes for this part of the exercise, about ten minutes apiece. I will indicate the time every ten minutes. (The guide will do so and can even advise the speaker when he or she has two minutes left to complete the time allotment.)

When you are done, come to quiet and begin to meditate on your own heart. Focus on your heartbeat.

Meditation on the Sacrifice of the Heart

(The music begins and is played through the entire process.)

Imagine now that you are traveling in a very small boat up a red river. On either side of the shore of this river are the scenes or the feelings of your sufferings throughout your life.

Perhaps the first one is being born itself, for agreeing as spirit to enter into a contained and bounded form, to be contracted into flesh, the suffering of being born. Then there is the suffering of knowing the mother and being separated from her for protracted periods, or the pain of not knowing why your mother and father seem to exclude you, or the knowledge that another little child is coming into the family.

You are passing by scenes of your sufferings all the way through your life. But as you pass these places and times of suffering, you will say to them, "You happened, and I know that you happened that I might be opened, rent, made available for new life."

You will say these words to each scene on the shore, so that each scene that may have been the cause of resentment, both known and unknown, remembered and unremembered, offers the crushed essence of its suffering and adds it to the River of Blood upon which you float.

In each place where there was resentment, now there will be acceptance, and a welcoming of the crushed kernel of that part of your life, the oil, or, if you will, the crushed grape of the vine of that part of your life—all going to help carry you on in this journey to the heart, where the Beloved resides.

If you do not see images along the shore of the River of Blood upon which you are traveling, then sense them. Sense them as scenes, or feelings, or shifts in energy; but this time, make yourself available to them. Witness to the holiness, the sacrifice, the making sacred of those times of suffering so that the essence of this suffering can carry you further on your journey to the place of the Beloved.

In this way you can redeem these wounded times of your life so that they are made holy, they are more open to God and the Beloved, and they are no longer just times of pain and distortion to be forgotten or endured. Now witness and see differently. Make sacred the sufferings of your life. I will give you four minutes of clock time which will be equal to all the subjective time you need to travel along the river of your life. Begin now (4 minutes).

And now be carried by the blood and the suffering made sacred into the deep heart, the great chambered heart, its luminous red-muscled walls contracting and pulsing. It is as if you were in the center of a strong turbulence, as if all of the suffering of your life were collected here in this center. And yet you have released your attributes, so you are released into a new possibility. (Pause.)

In the midst of this turbulence, with all of your sufferings made sacred, suddenly this heart itself seems to deepen, expand, become luminous. And lo, you are in your heart, but you are also in the Heart of Hearts. You are in the imaginal archetypal world as well. You are in the Archetypal Heart, the heart of the *mundus imaginalis,* the heart of the inner world where the Beloved of your soul resides. Here in your Heart of Hearts. (Pause.)

And you say, in your heart, "Live and be, my Beloved." (Pause.)

Then you sit and you wait for the Beloved, who sits encoded in your Heart's Heart, in your Archetypal heart, able to call to you because you have released so much. You have sacrificed and are now willing to be called forth. (Pause.) The Beloved of the soul, the Beloved who reflects the Beloved which is God, which is ultimately all that is. It is truly the God calling the God, the God in the state of the longing for the God. (Pause.)

And you, your suffering made sacred and redeemed, your suffering made holy, you are now available to receive the Beloved. Come, O Beloved!

As you sit there, experience in your heart the presence of the heart of your soul's Beloved, whether as an image or an inner knowing.

Now receive what is, for the Beloved is with you regardless of your awareness. That is what Rumi tells us. The Beloved is present even when we are unaware.

Begin to have a sense of the Beloved filling you, so that you cannot say, "It is I!" You have to say, "It is You, O Beloved, it is You in here."

All those journeyings and the sufferings and the diversions and the longings and the lostness and the meanderings were the separation. And you think of the pain of separation that has been so great and so long. And you discover that part of the pain of separation was caused by clinging to your attributes, to those things that defined you and limited you.

You need not lose your attributes. You lose your attachment to them that kept you so separated, so distant, so divorced from the Beloved.

Knock now on the walls of the Inner Heart, and say, "Beloved, it is You."

And feel yourself as the Beloved, filling the local body, filling the Archetypal Heart, filling and expanding it. The two of you so enormous together as one, filling the human heart, filling the lungs and the chest cavity, filling and playing through the flutes of the bones, filling the body itself, filling it fully. And then let this love of the Beloved flow and flood out beyond you.

Now, very quietly, take your leaves, the attributes of your local self, and give them back to the natural world. Feeling the image or the beingness of the Beloved filling you, see the Beloved in every tree and every stone, brook, face, bug.

(Note to guide: if this process is done in a city, have the participants go to a local park as soon afterward as they can to complete this part of the exercise.)

Drop the leaves by places of nature. And as you drop them, know that you are giving of yourself so that a Larger Nature may live. They become holy manure, or, if you will, the nutriments for the renewal of nature.

Then face the tree, the stone, the brook, that is being filled with your Beloved, and say, "Live and be, My Beloved." And wait for a response. And the response is the consecration, by the tree, or stone, or brook, of you and the Beloved.

Then go on to another place in nature. Feel the image of the Beloved in that, as Rumi did, and say, "Live and be, My Beloved." And wait for a response, the response that is your consecration of your Beloved in you in the stone.

You might go to a living stream or a lake, feeling the abundance of the overflow and the reflection of the water itself mirroring the Beloved. And you will say, "Live, My Beloved," and receive the consecration of the Beloved.

Whether you see the image in your heart is of no consequence. It is in you. It fills you like the two friends in the house that Rumi speaks of. And you will now see aspects of your Beloved everywhere. You will learn a great deal about your Beloved in the flow of water or the shadings in a rock or the pattern of the trees and the leaves. And you will say, "Live and be, My Beloved," and then wait for the response.

You will have half an hour to complete this exercise. Leave quietly, holding the fullness of the Beloved, the fullness of the Archetypal Heart pressing through you, filling everything.

Go now O Beloveds, O Lovers. Go now.

SCENARIO 4
Seeking the One Through the Ladder of Evolution

We are now going to take Rumi very literally and do a very different version of the evolutionary process known as *prolepsis*. (For the original process the participants may wish to review *The Possible Human,* pp. 95–113). We will explore your own cosmic and earthly evolution and your personal historical evolution. At the same time, we will build internally the imaginal ladder of archetypal and spiritual evolution in the imaginal body. In other words, the evolutionary journey will be taken in the light of the archetypal journey. This process needs to be centered in divine love yearning to be manifested in its wondrous particularity—whether as chick-peas, as roses, as grains of sand, as thunderstorms, as ice cubes melting, as you, as me, as God-knows-what.

Many of you have played many parts and traveled many paths in the course of your life. In order to find the deep path you have to bring together all these paths. At a certain point on your life's journey you discover that although the deep path may have many meanderings it is profoundly coherent—partly because the search for the Beloved provides a unifying direction. The Beloved is at once the way in and the way up, the way through and the way out.

TIME: 90 minutes.

MATERIALS NEEDED: A drum.

MUSIC: Music will be used during the spinning part of this process and should be the same music played during the earlier spinning.

ROOM SETUP: The process requires a spacious room with a floor covering suitable for crawling. Additionally, all participants should take off all watches, shoes, belt buckles, jewelry, and other similar items.

INSTRUCTIONS FOR WORKING ALONE: This process can be put on tape, allowing sufficient time between each stage of evolution to enact that stage.

SCRIPT FOR THE THE GUIDE: Now gather together in one big group, clustered closely in the center of the room. (Pause until this is done.)

You are the very elements of creation. It is ten seconds before the Big Bang. It is nine seconds. Eight. Seven. Six. Five. Four. Three. Two. Everything is there. The Beloved is ready and yearning. *One!*

(Note to guide: You may wish to mark the countdown with a drumbeat. Throughout this process you will decide how much time belongs to the performance of each stage of evolution, generally not more than several minutes apiece. Maintaining a certain momentum is critical, so be careful not to let the process lag.)

Spin out now. Spinning out. Spinning out. Spin as fiery light, gaining substance, gaining form. Spin out in the ultimate and initial dervish dance of creation. Spinning out. Spin out through creation in yearning for the Beloved. Spin, yearning for the Beloved, which is perhaps the unity you remember.

And in your inner world, sense the archetypal spin of the Patterns of Creation in the inner realm. Sense those at the beginning of the ladder in the inner, imaginal, archetypal world as you spin. Sense the great spinning, turning, throbbing of the Eternal Patterns yearning for creation in time.

And as you spin past one another, feel the magnetic fields charged with remembrance of the One. Become the stars entering into orbit, charged magnetic fields in relationship to each other because they remember the charge of being One. And in the field of love between the stars, planets are spun out—hot, fiery gaseous forms.

And in the inner world, there is the seeded coding of the possibility of planets. And you sense in yourself in the inner archetypal realm the seeded coding of the possibility of planets, all possible life already coded there in the DNA spiritual coding of the inner-planetary realm.

And the planet cools. And you begin to slow down and become water, and fire, and air, and earth. You are elemental. The fire causes the waters to rise as steam, to become rain and the rain pours down on the earth. The waters build and you become oceans, seething oceans.

And the oceans are teeming with new forms, protoplasmic globules, and you find yourself there at the instant of a great strike of lightning and life is born! The great, coded, seeded patterns in you rise as chains of amino acids join with other little chains, becoming primordial protoplasmic globules. Everything is teeming with life. And now become a protoplasmic globule.

You reach out, and as you reach out, you draw together more protoplasmic globules. Twos become fours, and fours become eights, and you become beds of early sea creatures.

And in the inner world, the creative substance of early forms of life are flowing into time. The creative forms are now flowing into time.

And gradually you become a bedded form in the body of the ocean, developing protective coverings like shells. And you die, you sink down, shells congregating and adding to the rock.

And the seas flow away and you all become rock. You are rock, enduring for ages upon ages upon ages in your rockness. Sometimes the rocks erode and suffer as the earth undergoes tremendous changes. It rises. It falls. It heats up. It melts.

Some of you become rubies in this suffering change; some of you become emeralds or diamonds or coal. Some of you remain just ordinary rocks. And the weather washes you away for millennia after millennia. You are battered by the rains and warmed by the sun.

Gradually you disintegrate until you become soil. And now you are soil—granulated, full of richness because other forms have enriched you with their substance.

And seeds have formed and you add your nutriment to the seed. And again the rains come and the sun warms you, and you are in the seed. And you split your pod. And the part of you that was stone, that was earth, that was sea creature, that was ocean, that was planet, that was sun, that was the One, adds its substance to the seed.

And you begin to grow, to become a plant. You feel yourself reaching up to the sun as a plant, with the full genius of the plant.

And in the inner realm you have climbed up the ladder to the realm of plants, having known stones and sea creatures and oceans and earths and suns and the One. Being fed by these, you are plant.

And as plant, you grow strong from the sun and the air and the plentiful rain and the richness of the soil from which you came. And you blossom. Flowering, you put forth rich fruits, seeds, blossoms.

And you fall to the ground and wither and die as plant. But some part of you is picked up and eaten by a crawling creature, a worm. In your death you're eaten and you become worm.

But you are a worm that is fed by the plant that has been earth, that has been stone, that has been sea creature, that has been sea, that has been planet, that has been sun, that has been the One.

And in the inner life of the ladder of evolution, another rung is reached. And in the archetypal life more complexities are entering into time as worm.

And you go near the streams to refresh yourself in your wormness and a fish grabs you. And you die as worm and you become a fish, moving in this stream into the ocean. And you now roll from side to side. Rolling from side to side. You are fish, with the flexibility and the fluidity of fish. You are fish that is fed by wormness, by plantness, by stoneness, by earthness, by sea creature, by primordial globule, by water, by planet, by sun, by the One. You are fish, rolling from side to side.

And at the same time, you have moved up another rung inside the imaginal world. Love is calling you up to another stage in evolution. And you feel this yearning, this call. Your inner life is more complex now, and you begin to move toward that call.

Your fins begin to take on the form of webbed feet and you begin to pull yourself along. You are being called by the sun. The sun! The sun! I remember the sun! I remember when I was called by the sun! And you begin to crawl up on the shore, dragging your tail behind you. And you have become an amphibian.

And in the inner life, on the ladder, you are in the place of the amphibian world, an important place, for it enables you to live in two worlds at the same time.

Crawling along, pulling yourself along, you are amphibian. And now certain human brain structures begin to be activated. If you get tired, just stop and do the movement in the kinesthetic imaginal body until you have more strength, and then pull yourself along again. Remember, you are able to go back and forth between the imaginal, archetypal, amphibian and the amphibian you are expressing with your physical body. You are making cross-lateral, purposeful survival movements.

And in the inner realm you've climbed up another rung of the ladder, and more potency, more complexity are entering into time.

You are still on your stomach, crawling over other creatures. You don't stop and say "Excuse me" because you don't have language. You move with a tremendous sense of purpose, knowing the intenseness of a path, perhaps not unlike some of the psychological and spiritual paths that you've been on.

And now you are reptile. Every so often, when you're tired, stop and have the archetypal reptile, the reptile in the realm of forms, move imaginally, kinesthetically. And when you're ready, then move on with the physical reptile.

Keep on moving, moving, moving. Stay in the reptile position, not changing it. Keep on moving toward the One, drawn by the lure of becoming.

And the blood of the reptile gradually becomes warmer. The reptile bears children and becomes a mammal. Now you become a mammal, perhaps a lemur. You become a mammal on all fours.

And in the archetypal realm you have moved up another rung on the ladder. More potency, more complexity, are entering into time.

You've become a mammal, moving on all fours. You discover sound and sociability.

And as mammal you begin to stand upright, and you have become the little monkey.

And in the inner world you have moved up another rung.

You are the little monkey, leaping and climbing, filled with playfulness and curiosity.

And the awareness of the little monkey grows, and you climb the ladder of consciousness. You become the higher monkey, like the great ape or gorilla. You are now the higher monkey.

And the higher monkey becomes the early human being, like the Neanderthal, who was crafty and inventive. And you are the early human being.

And in the inner life, in the imaginal realm, you've moved up another rung on the ladder of consciousness to the next stage of evolution. Greater complexity is entering into time.

As the early human being you grow immensely in consciousness. You learn to survive in a world you don't understand.

In the imaginal world, now experience all this craft, cunning, and wisdom coming through.

And at the height of this growth you fall down to the ground, dying as the early human. And you wander between the worlds for millennia. You enter into the imaginal world, the world of the soul where you, the unique human you, is in the womb ready to be born. But in this womb world, as fetus, you receive the great soul consciousness that contains the accumulated wisdom of the ages.

From this soul consciousness you can perceive all the patterns of possibility for the human being that you could become.

Inside this soul world in the womb, the Beloved of the soul says to you, "Good-bye, my Beloved, for a while. For when you come to full maturity you will seek me again, and I will try to come to you. But now go, live out our promise in the world. Good-bye, my Beloved."

And so the little fetus remembers, faintly, but the memory is there. And you are born.

And in the next *five minutes of clock time* you have all the time you need to live through incidents of your life from being born to where you are in the present.

Going through your infancy, your childhood, your adolescence, your adulthood, live through it now as intensely as you can.

Live through your life, feeling the fullness of evolution behind you. Reseed your life as you remember. Feel the fullness of evolution bringing pattern and meaning to the suffering and change and yearning and growing of your life, greening the story of your life as you live through it.

Feel the fullness of the sun, the potency of the planet, the rhythm of the oceans, the solidity of the stone, the flexibility of the fish, the adaptability of the amphibian, the purposiveness of the reptile, the gregariousness of the mammal, the curiosity of the monkey, the strength of the ape, the craft and wisdom of the early human. All of this is seeding you, moving in you, filling your bones and blood, giving your life multiple patterns and purpose.

You are the cutting edge of evolution. You are the one moving up the ladder with the understanding that human life is the most difficult of all because it is the highest rung on the ladder and has been attained only through all the dyings of the earlier forms of life. And in your present lifetime still more dying has been required.

Experience as fully as you can the little deaths that you have known throughout your life. Experience the sufferings, the rendings, the throwing away of parts of yourself, but this time be aided by all those stages of the ladder of evolution (5 minutes).

Take several more moments to come up to the present moment in time. And when you come up to the present moment, reach out to someone else who has also come up to the present moment. Stand up and, facing each other, place your hand on each other's hearts. So standing say to each other "Be!" And gaze upon each other in wonder and astonishment, seeing in each other the fullness of all of human history, all of animal history, all of reptile and fish and ocean history, all of earth history, all of sun history, all of cosmic history, until finally you perceive in each other the One from which has come the Many.

Say to each other, "Be!" And then in silence just look at the other and watch all of history, seeing all that has happened both in the outer and inner worlds, to bring you to this point. See the miracle of the worlds that your partner is and the millions of lives and deaths that have gone into this full stage of becoming.

Now with your partner you will enter into the next stage of the ladder, the evolutionary stage. Some call it the extended state; Rumi called it the stage of the angel. In this stage you can bridge the worlds, just as angels do, able to live fully in the imaginal, archetypal realm of Creative Pattern as well as in the world of manifestation in space and time. As angel, in Rumi's sense, you are the bringer of good news; you bring the new godded forms into time; you carry the path toward the One in this life.

We will experience this stage through consecrated spinning. This time one of you will hold the field, the field of the Beloved and the field of the ladder. Each of you in turn will stand there as guardian angel to the other.

One of you will now spin, spinning and spinning into the place inside you that is the next rung of the ladder, the top rung, there to be pulled up to meet the Beloved. And the Beloved will be reaching down to meet you. And it is there that you will know and be the next stage.

You who are holding the field of love, of the ladder, feel the love and the ladder increasing in you as you hold the field. Decide now who will be the first one to spin to the next stage of evolution, and who will be the Khidir, the one to hold the field of the Beloved of the heart and of the ladder of being. You who are spinning to the next stage are spinning to the Beloved.

And then you who are spinning, begin turning counterclockwise, turning to the left. Know this to be the door between the inner and outer worlds within you, the door between the imaginal creative realms and this realm. You become angel, the one who traverses both realms. I will keep the time for you. Begin.

(The spinning music will start. The guide will allow about twenty minutes for the spinning.)

Begin gradually to slow down now. Slowly. And when you have stopped, your partner will hold you, your partner as the representative of the Beloved.

And you who are holding your partner, feel that flow and say, "Welcome, O Beloved of the Beloved, to the next stage of the ladder. Welcome, O Beloved of the Beloved, to the next stage of the ladder."

Then you who have been spinning, share with your partner for the next couple of minutes the images, poems, feelings you have just known in your spiralling to the Beloved (3 minutes).

Stand up now and reverse roles. And the one who has been Khidir now becomes the one who spins.

And the one who is Khidir holds the ladder, holds the field, holds the sacrality and holiness of this moment as the other now spins to the next stage of the ladder, to the stage of the angel who can bridge the worlds.

You who are spinning, spin up to the next stage of the ladder, to the place of the Beloved of the heart, the Beloved of the soul, the Beloved of the mind, the great Archetypal Beloved of the imaginal realm.

When you reach that stage, subtle seedings and codings may begin to affect you, so that you notice them for days, weeks, months to come. Begin now this seeding, the entry into the next stage of evolution. Begin the spinning.

And those of you who are witness, know that in the witnessing you are also continuing to climb the ladder, to merge with your Beloved as you hold the field of the Beloved.

(Once again the music for spinning plays, and the guide allows about twenty minutes for the spinning.)

You who are witnesses now move to hold your partner as he/she slows down. Slowing down now. And as you hold your partner say, "Welcome, O Beloved of the Beloveds, to the next stage of the ladder. Welcome, O Beloved of the Beloveds, to the next stage of the ladder."

And when it becomes possible, you who have been spinning tell what you heard, felt, knew; but only if the words come to you. And, noble surrogate for the Beloved, be witness to that.

Now I'm going to ask everyone to get up, and this time everyone will spin. Begin to spin now, this time protected by everyone. You are spinning the Beloved of the Beloved. You are spinning not just yourself; you are spinning God like the original circling fires that came from the Big Bang of primordial creation. Everyone now spinning counterclockwise. Begin the spinning.

(Appropriate spinning music is again played here. As the spinning continues the guide says:)

You are like the original sparks of light, the original planets, the original suns. You are a roomful of spinning Beloveds—know that is what you are. You are like the suns that were spun out from the One. And you have taken evolution through the mattering of suns into living hearts.

Now begin to spin toward the center until you can spin no more. You started from the One; you are moving toward the One. Now begin to move toward the center until you are just beings turning together.

Feel the One, being back in the One, back home in the One. All the Beloveds are now spinning in the One. And no longer spin in the body, for your soul is spinning. It is all in the One, and you are the One. And the Beloved is loving you in the One. Let yourself be loved, O Beloved, in the One.

(The Guide will allow several minutes for the participants to gather together in the oneness of the center. This enactment mirrors the initial coming together for the Big Bang of creation. If the group spontaneously begins to hum or make the sound of "OM," this should be encouraged. Let the group discover for itself what it wants to do.)

And from this One, which contains the inward and outward worlds, so many patterns, so many forms desiring expression through you, move out into the world when we leave each other. Carrying within you the great potent energies of life which left the One to create the universes, you will leave this oneness to green your world, to create planets, suns, stars, stones, waves, oceans. You will leave to create new forms of life and expression—whether a friendship, a feeling, or a new form of vocation.

From this place of Oneness you will move out, as once before you moved out fifteen billion years ago to create a universe. You will move out to create and be instruments through which the new creation enters into time. As it was in the beginning, is now, and ever shall be, love without end.

And now bow to the Beloved in others, to the Beloved in yourself, and to the Beloved That Is.

Notes

PROLOGUE

1. Friedrich Nietzsche, *The Joyful Wisdom* (New York: Frederick Ungar Publishing Co., 1960), Aphorism 125, pp. 167–169.

2. Ibid., Aphorism 343, pp. 275–276.

CHAPTER 1

1. Quoted in Theodore Papadakis, *Epidauros: The Sanctuary of Asclepios* (Athens: Meletziz & Papadakis, 1978), p. 51.

2. A good description of the cult and practice of Asclepian healing is found in E. J. Edelstein and L. Edelstein, *Asclepius*, 2 vols. (Baltimore: Johns Hopkins University Press, 1945).

3. Quoted in Papadakis, pp. 14–15.

4. An interesting discussion of the incubation practices at the Abaton in Epidaurus and other ancient centers is to be found in C. A. Meir, *Ancient Incubation and Modern Psychotherapy*, translated by Monica Curtis (Evanston: Northwestern University Press, 1967).

5. Stan Gooch, *The Neanderthal Question* (London: Wildwood House, 1977).

6. Mary Renault, *The Bull from the Sea* (New York: Pantheon, 1970).

CHAPTER 2

1. Thomas Berry, "The New Story," *Dromenon* I (1978), p. 11.

2. *Brain/Mind Bulletin*, May 21, 1979.

3. William James, *The Varieties of Religious Experience* (New York: Modern Library, 1936), pp. 210–211.

4. Edward C. Whitmont, *Return of the Goddess* (New York: Crossroad, 1982), p. viii.

5. For example, Luis Marchado's work as Minister of Intelligence in Venezuela; Ruben Feurstein's work with children of below-normal intelligence in Israel; Paolo Friere's work in literacy in Latin America.

6. Many of these issues are addressed in my earlier books (see bibliography) and especially in *The Possible Human*.

CHAPTER 3

1. Evelyn Underhill, *Mysticism* (New York and Scarborough, Ontario: New American Library, 1974), p. 264.

CHAPTER 5

1. Jean Auel, *The Valley of the Horses* (New York: Simon & Schuster, 1982), pp. 44–45.

CHAPTER 7

1. A good general reference for exploring further these kinds of archetypes is Carl Jung's, *Archetypes of the Collective Unconscious*, Bollingen Series XX (New York: Pantheon Books, 1959).

CHAPTER 9

1. Harold Goddard, *The Meaning of Shakespeare,* vol. 2 (Chicago: University of Chicago Press, 1965), p. 208.

2. Gregory Bateson, *Mind and Nature* (New York: E. P. Dutton, 1979), p. 13.

3. William Irwin Thompson, *Darkness and Scattered Light* (Garden City, N.Y.: Anchor Books, 1978), p. 14.

4. The original research on these four levels is reported in our book *The Varieties of Psychedelic Experience.*

5. Helen Luke, *The Inner Story* (New York: Crossroad, 1982), p. 5.

6. This point is well made by David Miller in "Fairy Tale or Myth," *Spring,* 1976.

7. Joseph Campbell, *The Hero with a Thousand Faces,* Bollingen Series XVII (Princeton: Princeton University Press, 1973), pp. 3–4.

8. Joseph Campbell, *The Masks of God: Creative Mythology* (New York: The Viking Press, 1959), p. 4.

9. Ibid., pp. 4–6 *passim.*

CHAPTER 10

1. Hillman, James. "Betrayal" in *Loose Ends* (Zurich: Spring Publications, 1975).

2. Ibid.

CHAPTER 11

1. St. John of the Cross, *The Dark Night of the Soul,* translated by E. Allison Peers (Garden City, N.Y.: Doubleday and Company, 1959), p. 33.

2. Laurens van der Post, *A Mantis Carol* (New York: William Morrow and Company, Inc., 1976), p. 114.

3. James Hillman, *Loose Ends,* p. 53.

4. Ibid., p. 53.

5. Ibid., p. 54.

6. Morton T. Kelsey, *Companions on the Inner Way: The Art of Spiritual Guidance* (New York: Crossroad, 1983).

7. M. Scott Peck, *The Road Less Traveled* (New York: Simon & Schuster, 1979).

8. Rabindranath Tagore, *Later Poems of Rabindranath Tagore,* translated from the Bengali by Aurobindo Bose (New York: Minerva Press, 1976), p. 62.

9. Joseph Campbell, *The Hero with a Thousand Faces,* Bollingen Series XVII (Princeton: Princeton University Press, 1968).

10. Homer, *The Odyssey,* translated by W. H. D. Rouse (New York: New American Library, 1937). pp. 154–155.

11. Kelsey, *Companions on the Inner Way: Art of Spiritual Guidance* (New York: Crossroads, 1983).

12. Kabir, *The Kabir Book: Forty-Four of the Ecstatic Poems of Kabir,* versions by Robert Bly (Boston: Beacon Press, 1977), p. 7.

PART FOUR: INTRODUCTION TO THE STORIES

1. I am also publishing a series of Journeys of Transformation similar in form and content to the stories that follow, available from Amity House, Inc., Warwick, N.Y. 10990. The series will soon include individual studies of Jesus, Odysseus, the Quest for the Grail, and Isis and Osiris.

CHAPTER 12

1. A very witty translation of *The Golden Ass of Apuleius* is by Robert Graves (New York: The Pocket Library, 1954).

2. Robert Johnson, *She* (New York: Harper & Row, 1976).

3. C. S. Lewis, *Till We Have Faces* (New York: Harper & Row, 1963).

4. Erich Neumann, *Amor and Psyche* (Princeton: Bollingen Press, 1973).

5. James Hillman, *The Myth of Analysis* (Evanston: Northwestern University Press, 1972).

6. Maria-Louise von Franz, *A Psychological Interpretation of The Golden Ass of Apuleius* (Zurich: Spring Publications, 1970).

7. P. D. Ouspensky, *In Search of the Miraculous: Fragments of an Unknwn Teaching* (New York: Harcourt, Brace, and World, Inc., 1949), p. 145.

8. James Hillman, "Abandonment," in *Loose Ends.*

9. Ibid.

10. Plato, *The Symposium,* translated by Benjamin Jowett (New York: The Liberal Arts Press, 1957).

CHAPTER 13

1. Rumi, in *Selected Lyric Poetry of Jalaluddin Rumi,* translated by Edmund Helminski (Putney, Vt.: Threshold Books, 1984), p. 17.

2. Quoted in *The Triumphal Sun: A Study of the Works of Jalaloddin Rumi* (London and the Hague: East-West Publications, 1980), p. 12.

3. There are a number of fine studies of the life and work of Rumi, but there is one unique masterpiece of Rumi scholarship that I cannot recommend too highly. It is the work of Annemarie Schimmel, *The Triumphal Sun: A Study of the Works of Jalaloddin Rumi.*

4. Rumi, *"Divan-e kabir,"* 227/2561, hereafter referred to as D. Quoted in Schimmel, p. 20.

5. D 2572/26754, ibid., p. 21.

6. D 1493/157 27 40, ibid.

7. Rumi, *Mathnavi,* translated by R. A. Nicholson (London: George Allen & Urwin, 1950), I 1741, hereafter referred to as M.

8. D 336/3644, ibid., p. 22.

9. D 2186/23190, ibid.

10. Ibid., p. 53.

11. D 1081/11369, ibid., p. 23.

12. Ibid.

13. A. Golpmarh, *Mevlana Celaleddin Rumi,* (Istanbul, 1952, p. 54), quoted in Schimmel, p. 24.

14. D 1768/18521, ibid., p. 24.

15. Ibid., p. 26.

16. D 1499/15800, ibid., p. 42.

17. D2329/24655, ibid., p. 44.

18. D 2938/31183, ibid., p. 44.

19. Ibid., p. 43.

20. Ibid., p. 43.

21. Ibid., p. 20.

22. Rumi, *Open Secret: Versions of Rumi,* translated by John Moyne and Coleman Barks (Putney, Vermont: Threshold Books, 1984), p. 13.

23. Ibid., p. 46.

24. Ibid., p. 64.

25. D 683/7102 11, quoted in Schimmel, p. 36.

26. The chick-pea story is found in M III 4158 ff, quoted in Schimmel, pp. 140, 320–322, 327, 331–332.

27. Jalaloddin Rumi, *The Ruins of the Heart,* translated by Edmund Helminski (Putney, Vt.: Threshold Books, 1981) p. 34.

28. Rumi, *Diwan-i Shams-i Tabriz* 35486-7, hereafter referred to as DS. Quoted in William C. Chittick, *The Sufi Path of Love: The Spiritual Teachings of Rumi* (Albany: State University of New York Press, 1983), p. 238.

29. DS 3952, ibid., p. 238.

30. Rumi, *Fihi ma Fihi* 233/240, ibid., pp. 238–239.

31. DS 1277-79, ibid., p. 239.

32. DS 17584-5, ibid.

33. M II, 1255, 1257-8, ibid., p. 240.

34. Quoted, ibid., p. 149, from many sources in Rumi.

35. Rumi, *The Ruins of the Heart,* p. 3.

36. In several of our books, principally *Mind Games* and *The Possible Human,* we offer specific training techniques to develop the varieties of inner imagery.

37. DS 19817; DS 19466; DS 35279, quoted in Chittick, pp. 263–264.

38. DS 8077, ibid., p. 265.

39. M III 3901, quoted in Schimmel, p. 328.

40. Ibid., p. 332.

41. M III 4098 ff, ibid., p. 334.

42. M V 3853 ff, ibid.

Glossary

Alam al-mithal. The inner world of the Sufis, with as many different realities as all the outer worlds of the universe.

Aphrodite. The Greek goddess of beauty and love. In the myth of Psyche and Eros she represents the old order in which there was a great divide between the gods and the humans.

Archetypal shape-shifting. The process of moving from one archetypal identity (such as the Wise Old King, the Trickster, or the Great Snake) to another by using the skills gained from working with the imaginal body.

Asclepian. A complex of healing centers where art, mystery, and science met in ways that have yet to be matched in the modern world.

Asclepios. A Thessalonian god-man born before the Trojan War. He watched over the lives of the Greeks in a benevolent, caring, healing fashion and could cure any ill of mind or body.

Beloved of the soul. One's double in the extended realm of the soul; the exotype of the archetype, that one for whom one yearns, after whom one wanders, in search of potential reunion. For many people, the *Beloved* refers to the Divine Beloved within.

Betrayal. A wounding of the soul that acts as an agent of the sacred, marking an end of unconscious trust and providing the impetus for growth.

Enantiadromia. A big turnaround.

Entelechy. The dynamic purposiveness of the patterns of possibility encoded in each of us. For example, it is the entelechy of an acorn to be an oak tree.

Eros. The principle concerned with the interrelationship of psyche and nature, with symbiosis and connections between things.

Friend in Court. The archetype that helps us out of our stuck places and illumines our transitions.

Godseed. The divine essence inherent in the humanity of each human being.

I AM realm. The realm of the unitive or source level of being, of love and organicity, the realm we know as God.

Imago Amore. The image of the Beloved. For St. Francis, the *Imago Amore* was Christ.

Imaginal body. A nonphysical or "subtle" body, the development of which leads to higher faculties of perception and knowing. Unlike the kinesthetic body, it is a separate, externalized image.

Khidir. The legendary guide in Sufism, who comes to help one to reach the Beloved.

Kinesthetic body. The body image encoded in the motor cortex of the brain, experienced as the *felt* body of muscular imagination.

Logos. The principle of ordering and mastery essential to the creation and sustenance of civilization. Also, the energy, coding, and incarnation of the creative spirit of God.

Long Story. The tale told by Native Americans about the creation of the world and its creatures.

Mundus imaginalis. The imaginal world, the culture of the depths, the place where the forms and creations of existential life are conceived.

Namasté. A Hindu greeting meaning "The god within me greets the god within you."

Nootherapeia. Mind-healing, in which one is purified and rewoven into a new harmony of mind, body, and spirit.

Polyphrenia. The orchestration and integration of our many inner selves.

Pothos. A Greek word meaning "yearning," a state of soul in which the barriers between ourselves and the archetypal world are broken. *Pothos* refers to the spiritual component of love or the erotic component of spirit.

Prana. The energy of the life force, of creation itself.

Prigogine, Ilya. The Nobel Prize–winning physicist who has offered a theory of how a higher order emerges from the fluctuations created through new stimulation or information.

Prolepsis. A process in which one's own cosmic and earthly evolution, as well as one's personal historical evolution, is explored. At the same time, the process will help one build internally the imaginal ladder of archetypal and spiritual evolution in the imaginal body.

Proprioceptors. The antennae that form the inner sensing system—visual, auditory, olfactory, gustatory, tactile.

Psyche and Eros. An age-old myth that tells the story of the awakening of the immortal soul into time, giving us clues about our own metamorphoses.

Rumi, Jalaloddin. A great Sufi master and poet of the thirteenth century whose life epitomized the path of illumination through love.

Sacred psychology. The process and practice of soulmaking, requiring that we die to one story to be born to a larger story.

Sacred wound. A breaching of the soul or psyche by the larger story so that the world may be seeded with the psyche's newly released powers.

Shams-i Tabriz. A dervish and wanderer who became the Beloved of the soul for Rumi. In each other's presence, Shams and Rumi experienced the unity of Love and became for each other the reflection of God.

Story. The dynamic stuff of existence, the basic vibrational coding that calls being into form and connects one form with another. Story exists at three levels—the local, mythic, and universal.

Sufi. A Muslim mystic.

Sunset effect. A phenomenon in which old traditions or institutions that are in the process of fading out, cut loose with a blazing rush of activity.

Therapeia. "Doing the work of the whole" or "service to the gods." The model for developing the practice and process of sacred psychology.

THIS IS ME realm. The realm of the historical and factual, limited by geographical space and calendrical time; the persona of everyday existence.

Via negativa. A way of living the spiritual life in which attention is focused on a single point or a special mantra until consciousness is totally without an object and enters into union with Being.

Via positiva. A way of living the spiritual life in which growth and transformation are gained through the ability to orchestrate and integrate different states of consciousness, to use the senses and the body with greater awareness, and to tap the enormous richness of the imaginal realm.

WE ARE realm. The realm of the mythic, the symbolic, the archetypal. Durative and nonhistorical, it is the contact point for sacred time and sacred space.

Zikr. A spiritual practice of remembrance.

Musical Compositions

The following listings are suggestions and are drawn from music that we have used successfully in the teaching and practice of sacred psychology. The reader should feel free to use his or her own favorites, trying to keep them within the mood of the applicable area. Some of the selections from one area can be used in the two other areas at the guide's discretion.

Area One represents music that has been found to be particularly powerful as background music. It is also effective for guided imagery and meditation and during the evocation of altered states of consciousness.

Area Two is evocative music and is meant to stimulate and enhance the process itself.

Area Three represents music that has a celebratory character and is often used to accompany the conclusion of exercises and processes.

AREA 1: Background/Meditative Music

Seapeace Georgia Kelly. Heru Records, P.O. Box 954, Topanga, CA 90290.

Ancient Echoes Georgia Kelly/Steve Halpern. (See address above.)

Song of the Golden Lotus: The Mantric Music of Swami Kriya Ramananda Satsang Fellowship, Box 6156, Chicago, IL 60680.

Invocation to Isis Melissa Morgan/Diane Clarke. P.O. Box 4024, San Diego, CA 92104.

Music for Zen Meditation Tony Scott. Verve V6-8634.

Mysterious Mountain Alan Hovhaness. RCA AGL1-4215.

Journeys: Native American Flute Music R. Carlos Nakai. Canyon Records, 4143 N. 16th St., Phoenix, AZ 85016.

Crystal Meditations Don G. Campbell. Sound of Light, Box 835704, Richardson, TX 75083.

A Feather on the Breath of God: Sequences and Hymns by Abbess Hildegard of Bingen Hyperion Records Ltd., London, England.

A Wonderful Day Sweet People. Polydor 3100619.

Tibetan Bells II Henry Wolff and Nancy Hemings. Celestial Harmonies 006.

Planetary Unfolding Michael Stearns. Continuum Montage, 3640½ Watseka Ave., Los Angeles, CA 90034.

Ancient Leaves Michael Stearns. (See address above.)

Morning/Jewel Michael Stearns. (See address above.)

Perelandra Kevin Braheny. Hearts of Space Records, Box 31321, San Francisco, CA 94131.

A Rainbow Path Kay Gardner. Lady Slipper, Inc., P.O. Box 3124, Durham, NC 27705.

Dream Passage Daniel Kobialka. LiSem Enterprises, 1775 Old Country Road #9, Belmont, CA 94002.

Miracles Rob Whitesides-Woo, 427 Linnie Canal, Venice, CA 90291.

The Sky of Mind Ray Lynch. The Dawn Horse Book Depot, P.O. Box 3680, Clearlake, CA 95422.

The Fairy Ring Mike Rowland. Sona Gaia Productions, 1845 N. Farwell Ave., Milwaukee, WI 53202.

Ancient Dances and Airs Respighi. Mercury 75009.

Silk Road Kitaro. Canyon 051-052.

AREA II: Powerful and Potent Music to Evoke a Process

Heaven and Hell Vangelis Papathanassiou. RCA LPLI-5110.

Ignacio Vangelis Papathanassiou. Belaphon BLPS-19242.

Odes Vangelis Papathanassiou and Irene Pappas. Polydor 2473 109.

Opera Sauvage Vangelis Papathanassiou. Polydor 2473 105.

Oxygene Jean Michel Jarre. Polydor 2933-207.

Equinoxe Jean Michel Jarre. Polydor PD-16175.

The Sufi Dance and Song Album (Especially side two, selection one; recommended for the spinning exercise.) Sufi Publications, 65 Norwich St., San Francisco, CA 94110.

Tom Bozigian Presents Songs and Dances of the Armenian People, Volume III (Especially side two, selections five and six; recommended for the spinning exercise.) Special order from Derek Lawley (see Mail-Order Sources for Music).

Vision Calling Deborah Koff-Chapin. The Greater Spiral, P.O. Box 12515, Portland, OR 97212-0515.

The Tibetan Book of the Dead TMT Music Production, D-8000 Munich 40, West Germany.

Renaissance of the Celtic Harp Alan Stivell. Polydor 2424069.

Samuel Barber: Adagio for Strings RCA AGL1-3790.

Carmina Burana Carl Orff. Columbia 33172.

Finlandia Sibelius. Philips 9500140.

My Country Smetana. DGG 2707054.

Inside the Great Pyramid Paul Horn. Mushroom Records MRS-5507.

Koyanisquaatsi (soundtrack) Phillip Glass. Antilles-Island ZCASTA-1.

Concerto for Organ, Timpani and Strings Poulenc. Angel S-35953.

Symphony No. 3 Saint-Saens. RCA ATL1-4039.

Ecstasy Chaltanya Hari Deuter. Kuckuck 044.

Drums of Passion Olatunji. Columbia CS 8210.

Taizé: Wait for the Lord (Especially side one, selection three: "Confitemini Domino.") Special order from Derek Lawley (see Mail-Order Sources for Music).

AREA III: Celebratory Music

Chariots of Fire (soundtrack; especially side one, selection four: "Eric's Theme.") Vangelis Papathanassiou. Polygram Records, 810 Seventh Ave., New York, NY 10019.

Kosmos Tomita. RCA ARL 1-2616.

Pachelbel/Fasch: Canon in D Musical Heritage 1060Z.

Timeless Motion (Especially extended version of Pachelbel Canon in D.) Daniel Kobialka. LiSem Enterprises, 1775 Old Country Road #9, Belmont, CA 94002.

Caucasian Sketches: Procession of the Sardar Ippolitov Ivanov. Angel SR 40119.

The Moldau Smetana. Columbia, NY 30049.

Perles du Baroque (Especially side one, selection one: "La Sonnerie" by Marin Marais.) Arion Records. Cassette ARN 436342.

Snowflakes Are Dancing Tomita. RCA ARL 10488.

Hooked on Classics RCA AYKI 5022.

Missa Gaia Paul Winter and the Paul Winter Consort. Living Music LC 0002.

The Great Gate of Kiev, from Pictures at an Exhibition Mussorgsky. Quintessence 7059.

Sinfonietta Janacek. Angel S-36045.

Violin Concerto No. 1 in G Minor Bruch. Angel S-37210.

Violin Concerto in D, first movement Tchaikovsky. Angel-EMI 4XSS-32807.

Love at the Greek Neil Diamond. Columbia X1198.

You Are More Jean Houston and Howard Jerome. Special order from Derek Lawley (see Mail-Order Sources for Music).

Mail-Order Sources for Music

Spacemusic Catalog, Hearts of Space, P.O. Box 31321, San Francisco, CA 94131, (415) 495-0537.

Sound Choices, 2510 San Pablo Ave., Berkeley, CA 94702, (415) 845-2216.

Sound of Light, Box 835704, Richardson, TX 75803.

Selected Bibliography

Bateson, Gregory. *Mind and Nature.* New York: E. P. Dutton, 1979.

Berry, Thomas. "The New Story." *Dromenon* I (1978): 11.

Campbell, Joseph. *The Hero with a Thousand Faces.* Bollingen Series XVII. Princeton, N.J.: Princeton University Press, 1973.

———. *The Masks of God: Creative Mythology.* New York: The Viking Press, 1959.

Chittick, William C. *The Sufi Path of Love: The Spiritual Teachings of Rumi.* Albany: State University of New York Press, 1983.

Edelstein, E. J., and Edelstein, L. *Asclepius,* 2 vols. Baltimore: Johns Hopkins University Press, 1945.

Goddard, Harold. *The Meaning of Shakespeare,* vol. 2. Chicago: University of Chicago Press, 1965.

Gooch, Stan. *The Neanderthal Question.* London: Wildwood House, 1977.

Graves, Robert. *The Golden Ass of Apuleius.* New York: The Pocket Library, 1954.

Hillman, James. *Loose Ends.* Zurich: Spring Publications, 1975.

———. *The Myth of Analysis.* Evanston, Ill.: Northwestern University Press, 1972.

Homer. *The Odyssey.* Translated by W. H. D. Rouse. New York: New American Library, 1937.

Houston, Jean. *Life Force: The Psycho-Historical Recovery of the Self.* New York: Delacorte, 1980.

———. *The Possible Human.* Los Angeles: J. P. Tarcher, Inc., 1982.

James, William. *The Varieties of Religious Experience.* New York: Modern Library, 1936.

Johnson, Robert. *She.* New York: Harper & Row, 1976.

Jung, Carl. *Archetypes of the Collective Unconscious.* Bollingen Series XX. New York: Pantheon Books, 1959.

Kabir. *The Kabir Book: Forty-four of the Ecstatic Poems of Kabir.* Translated by Robert Bly. Boston: Beacon Press, 1977.

Kelsey, Morton T. *Companions on the Inner Way: The Art of Spiritual Guidance.* New York: Crossroad, 1983.

Lewis, C. S. *Till We Have Faces.* New York: Harper & Row, 1963.

Lovelock, James. *Gaia: A New Look at Life on Earth.* London and New York: Oxford University Press, 1979.

Luke, Helen. *The Inner Story.* New York: Crossroad, 1982.

Masters, Robert, and Houston, Jean. *Listening to the Body.* New York: Dell Publishing Co., 1978.

———. *Mind Games.* New York: Viking, 1972.

———. *The Varieties of Psychedelic Experience.* New York: Holt, Rinehart and Winston, 1966.

Meir, C. A. *Ancient Incubation and Modern Psychotherapy.* Translated by Monica Curtis. Evanston, Ill.: Northwestern University Press, 1967.

Miller, David. "Fairy Tale or Myth." *Spring,* 1976.

Miller, James Grier. *Living Systems.* New York: McGraw-Hill, 1978.

Neumann, Erich. *Amor and Psyche.* Princeton, N.J.: Bollingen Press, 1973.

Nietzsche, Friedrich. *The Joyful Wisdom.* New York: Frederick Ungar Publishing Company, 1960.

Ouspensky, P. D. *In Search of the Miraculous: Fragments of an Unknown Teaching.* New York: Harcourt, Brace, and World, Inc., 1949.

Papadakis, Theodore. *Epidauros: The Sanctuary of Asclepios.* Athens: Meletziz & Papadakis, 1978.

Peck, M. Scott. *The Road Less Traveled.* New York: Simon & Schuster, 1979.

Plato. *The Symposium.* Translated by Benjamin Jowett. New York: The Liberal Arts Press, 1957.

Prigogine, Ilya. *From Being to Becoming.* San Francisco: Freeman, 1980.

Renault, Mary. *The Bull from the Sea.* New York: Pantheon, 1970.

Rumi, Jalaloddin. *Open Secrets: Versions of Rumi.* Translated by John Moyne and Coleman Barks. Putney, Vt.: Threshold Books, 1984.

———. *The Ruins of the Heart.* Translated by Edmund Helminski. Putney, Vt.: Threshold Books, 1981.

———. *Selected Lyric Poetry of Jalaloddin Rumi.* Translated by Edmund Helminski. Putney, Vt.: Threshold Books. 1984.

Russell, Peter. *The Global Brain.* Los Angeles: J. P. Tarcher, Inc., 1983.

Schimmel, Annemarie. *The Triumphal Sun: A Study of the Works of Jalaloddin Rumi.* London and the Hague: East-West Publications, 1980.

St. John of the Cross. *The Dark Night of the Soul.* Translated by E. Allison Peers. Garden City, N.Y.: Doubleday & Co., 1959.

Tagore, Rabindranath. *Later Poems of Rabindranath Tagore.* Translated by Aurobindo Bose. New York: Minerva Press, 1976.

Thompson, William Irwin. *Darkness and Scattered Light.* Garden City, N.Y.: Anchor Books, 1978.

van der Post, Laurens. *A Mantis Carol.* New York: William Morrow & Company, Inc., 1976.

von Franz, Maria-Louise. *A Psychological Interpretation of The Golden Ass of Apuleius.* Zurich: Spring Publications, 1970.

Whitmont, Edward C. *The Return of the Goddess.* New York: Crossroad, 1982.

Index

Also by Jean Houston

Life Force: The Psycho-Historical Recovery of the Self
Godseed: The Journey of Christ
Manual for the Peacemaker: An Iroquois Legend to Heal Self and Society (with Margaret Rubin)
Public Like a Frog: Entering the Lives of Three Great Americans
The Passion of Isis and Osiris: A Union of Two Souls
A Mythic Life: Learning to Live Our Greater Story

Videocassettes

A videocassette of Jean Houston's television program, *A Passion for the Possible,* is now available through:

Mystic Fire Video
P.O. Box 422
Prince Street Station
New York, NY 10012-0008

Tel. Orders: 1-800-292-9001
Fax: 1-800-621-1699
E-mail: mysticfire@echonyc.com
Web orders: www.mysticfire.com

The selections are as follows:

A Passion for the Possible	$19.95
Companion Process Tape	$19.95
Two-tape set	$34.95

Discover more of yourself with Inner Work Books.

The following Inner Work Books are part of a series that explores psyche and spirit through writing, visualization, ritual, and imagination.

The Artist's Way: A Spiritual Path to Higher Creativity BY JULIA CAMERON

The Artist's Way Morning Pages Journal: A Companion Volume to The Artist's Way BY JULIA CAMERON

At a Journal Workshop (revised edition)*: Writing to Access the Power of the Unconscious and Evoke Creative Ability* BY IRA PROGOFF, PH.D.

Ending the Struggle Against Yourself: A Workbook for Developing Deep Confidence and Self-Acceptance BY STAN TAUBMAN, D.S.W.

Fearless Creating: A Step-by-Step Guide to Starting and Completing Your Work of Art BY ERIC MAISEL, PH.D.

Finding What You Didn't Lose: Expressing Your Truth and Creativity Through Poem-Making BY JOHN FOX

Following Your Path: Using Myths, Symbols, and Images to Explore Your Inner Life BY ALEXANDRA COLLINS DICKERMAN

The Inner Child Workbook: What to Do with Your Past When It Just Won't Go Away BY CATHRYN L. TAYLOR, M.A.M.F.C.C.

A Journey Through Your Childhood: A Write-in Guide for Reliving Your Past, Clarifying Your Present, and Charting Your Future BY CHRISTOPHER BIFFLE

A Life in the Arts: Practical Guidance and Inspiration for Creative and Performing Artists BY ERIC MAISEL, PH.D.

The Life We Are Given: A Long-Term Program for Realizing the Potential of Body, Mind, Heart, and Soul BY GEORGE LEONARD AND MICHAEL MURPHY

The Mythic Path: Discovering the Guiding Stories of Your Past—Creating a Vision for Your Future BY DAVID FEINSTEIN, PH.D., AND STANLEY KRIPPNER, PH.D.

Pain and Possibility: Writing Your Way Through Personal Crisis BY GABRIELE LUSSER RICO

The Path of the Everyday Hero: Drawing on the Power of Myth to Meet Life's Most Important Challenges BY LORNA CATFORD, PH.D., AND MICHAEL RAY, PH.D.

The Possible Human: A Course in Enhancing Your Physical, Mental, and Creative Abilities BY JEAN HOUSTON, PH.D.

The Search for the Beloved: Journeys in Mythology and Sacred Psychology BY JEAN HOUSTON, PH.D.

Smart Love: A Codependence Recovery Program Based on Relationship Addiction Support Groups BY JODY HAYES

Spiritual Passages: Embracing Life's Sacred Journeys BY DREW LEDER, M.D., PH.D.

A Time to Heal Workbook: Stepping-stones to Recovery for Adult Children of Alcoholics BY TIMMEN I. CERMAK, M.D., AND JACQUES RUTZKY, M.F.C.C.

True Partners: A Workbook for Building a Lasting Intimate Relationship BY TINA B. TESSINA, PH.D., AND RILEY K. SMITH, M.A.

The Vein of Gold: A Journey to Your Creative Heart BY JULIA CAMERON

Writing from Life: Telling Your Soul's Story BY SUSAN WITTIG ALBERT, PH.D.

Your Mythic Journey: Finding Meaning in Your Life Through Writing and Storytelling BY SAM KEEN AND ANNE VALLEY-FOX